BLOOD
& INK

BLOOD & INK

THE SCANDALOUS JAZZ AGE
DOUBLE MURDER THAT HOOKED
AMERICA ON TRUE CRIME

JOE POMPEO

WILLIAM MORROW
An Imprint of HarperCollins*Publishers*

Insert photographs are in the public domain except:
Pages two, top; three; four; five, top; and thirteen:
courtesy of the New Brunswick Free Public Library
Pages five, bottom, and seven, top: courtesy
of Kim Raymond Kowalczyk
Page eleven, top: New York *Daily News*
Page fifteen: Brian Smith
Page sixteen: Joe Pompeo

HarperCollins books may be purchased for educational, business,
or sales promotional use. For information, please email the
Special Markets Department at SPsales@harpercollins.com.

FIRST EDITION

Designed by Nancy Singer

Frames on pp i, iii, ix: @pvl0707/stock.adobe.com
All other ornaments: @PollyW/stock.adobe.com

Library of Congress Cataloging-in-Publication Data has been applied for.

ISBN 978-0-06-300173-2

22 23 24 25 26 LSC 10 9 8 7 6 5 4 3 2 1

For Jessanne, Ada, and Austin

CONTENTS

◈◈◈

CONTENTS

INTRODUCTION

◈

On the first day of February 2019, I stood in a small room on the third floor of the Somerset County prosecutor's headquarters in Somerville, New Jersey, a quaint borough nestled in a pocket of the state where the suburbs blend into countryside. The evidence unit supervisor, Ken Pryor, had allowed me to spend the morning in his office as part of my research into this book, which chronicles a bedeviling double homicide from a century ago. The media circus of its day, set in the nearby town of New Brunswick, this hoary old mystery had long since faded from the popular imagination. Pryor was now the steward of its vestiges, the tangible ones at least.

Before I arrived, he'd retrieved a stack of boxes and totes from the evidence vault. The first one I perused included autopsy reports, witness lists, fingerprints, and brooding photographs of a dusty rural road next to an abandoned farm. That's where the victims were killed late one night, their bodies carefully arrayed beneath a crabapple tree. The dead man was a prominent local minister, married to a proud matron from an illustrious New Jersey family. Beside him lay a working-class housewife from the church choir. Their murders, shrouded in scandal and intrigue, set off a tempest of sensational newspaper coverage, fueling a circulation war between the infant tabloids of Jazz Age New York.

I spoke to Pryor about these age-old publications while riffling through files on a table. He stood up from his desk and left the room, returning minutes later with a clear plastic packet. It contained several rare editions of a bygone tabloid newspaper that led a crusade against the main suspects. The papers had been locked away in the evidence unit all these years, slowly decomposing. Bits of brittle newsprint crumbled off the edges as I carefully laid out the front pages: GRAND JURY HEARS OF CLERGYMAN'S TRYST! GHASTLY STORY TOLD BY FINGERPRINTS! MRS. MILLS' GHOST!

After an hour or so, one of Pryor's colleagues, an evidence custodian named Mike Wilder, took me to an adjoining office. Here I found the real bounty, a trove of lonely forensic antiquities neatly packed into a half dozen or so storage bins. I'd become a voracious student of this crime and I suddenly held pieces of it in my hands: Handkerchiefs found at the murder scene. The star witness's day calendar. Ancient skeleton keys. The reverend's wire-rim glasses, snapped in two. I picked up a piece of shriveled sheer black fabric—a pair of stockings. Wilder told me the choir singer had been wearing them when someone put three bullets in her head and opened her neck from one ear to the other. Now, here they sat in a generic suburban office building, tucked away inside a blue plastic flip-top tote that looked like it came from Home Depot.

The minister and the choir singer have been dead for a hundred years, but the themes of their sordid tale still resonate. It's a story about dark secrets upending a community. About the media and the public's interaction with scandal and crime. About class, privilege, morality, love, betrayal, power, and the collision of these forces. It's also a story about ambition—triumphant at its best, but sometimes deadly. The beginning of the story is simple: four gunshots and two corpses. The way it ends is anything but.

THE CRABAPPLE TREE

It was midmorning on Saturday, September 16, 1922, a warm but partly cloudy end-of-summer day, described in local forecasts as "unsettled," when Pearl Bahmer and Ray Schneider found the bodies. They'd rendezvoused a little before 9:00 A.M. in the city center of New Brunswick, a then-192-year-old municipality along the railway corridor between Manhattan and Philadelphia. Once a rugged patch of swampland and cedar forest, situated on a winding river that empties into the Atlantic Ocean, New Brunswick had evolved into a bustling hub of industry, home to makers of wallpaper and fruit jars, ironworks and rubber shoes, musical strings and cigars and hosiery. As Pearl and Ray walked west, away from the city's shops, restaurants, and several nouveau theaters where locals took in the latest musical revues and D. W. Griffith films, they passed the imposing headquarters of Johnson & Johnson, founded in 1886, and the courtly brick buildings of Rutgers, the State University of New Jersey, chartered by King George III a full decade before the American Revolution. After a mile or so they reached Buccleuch Park, a bucolic seventy-eight acres with a colonial mansion that once hosted George Washington. This was the brink of the country-side, farmland all around. The British had tempted Washington into battle on these plains, but his men resisted the cry of war until their rivals withdrew, destroying several farms along the way. Two centuries later, the landscape was under threat once again, soon to be replaced by paved roads and suburban sprawl. The nearest farm, known as the Phillips farm, with a barn and an unoccupied two-story house, had fallen into disuse. Pearl and Ray crossed a small brook and turned onto the adjacent road, De Russey's Lane, a barren strip of dirt between two busier arteries leading to the center of New Brunswick. De Russey's Lane happened to be a popular destination for romantic escapades, which accounted for Pearl and Ray's excursion.

Pearl was a brown-eyed girl of fifteen, thin and pretty, with a coy smile and a short blond bob. Ray, twenty-three, had a chiseled face and neatly coiffed hair. He looked sharp in the photographs that would end up in the newspapers, handsome and smartly dressed in a white button-up and necktie. Ray and his wife had been separated for months; he and Pearl had been fooling around longer than that. Fooling around was very much on the agenda that morning, never mind the couple's age difference.

They followed a smaller trail off De Russey's Lane, lined by strawberry patches and masses of goldenrod. Amid the thickets and tall grass, as they came upon a clearing and a crabapple tree, something caught Pearl's attention.

"There is a man and woman there," she said.

Ray looked over. The two people lay next to one another on their backs, silent and motionless.

"Pearl, don't make any noise," Ray chided.

They snuck past and drifted into a field on the opposite side of the trail where, after they picked a secluded spot away from the snoozing couple, one thing led to another.

A short time later, reemerging on the lovers' lane, Pearl felt uneasy when they passed the crabapple tree once again.

"The people are still lying there," she said, lingering nervously in the brush, her pulse quickening. "Goodness, they are lying the same way as when I first seen them. Go over and look at them!"

Ray crept closer, with Pearl trailing behind. He circled around the pair until he stood at their feet. Pearl retreated to a nearby cedar tree as Ray studied them. Their chests didn't rise or fall. He saw blood and markings on the woman's head, bullet wounds, perhaps, all but confirming Pearl's suspicion: these were corpses.

RAY KNEW OF A HOUSE on the far edge of Buccleuch Park where they might be able to use the phone, but first they needed to get their stories straight. What were they supposed to tell the cops? Certainly not that they had gone to De Russey's Lane for the unseemly reason two red-blooded young people would have gone to De Russey's Lane. Ray came up with what he thought sounded like a better answer. If anyone asked, Pearl was to say, "We had gone out for mushrooms. I stopped in one field and he in another."

Pearl and Ray hurried back to the main road and rang the bell of a house where a young woman named Grace Edwards answered the door. Ray caught his breath and explained what they'd seen—a pair of bodies across the way, a man and a woman who looked like they'd been shot. Ray appeared shaken up, "like anyone that would come across two dead people," Grace thought. She gave Ray the phone.

"New Brunswick twenty-seven," he told the switchboard, specifying the exchange for police headquarters. As the operator patched the call through, Ray's nerves got the best of him. He tried to speak, but the words wouldn't come out. Grace took the receiver and did the talking for him.

Half an hour later, shortly before eleven o'clock, officers Edward Garrigan and James Curran arrived. Patrolmen didn't always have cars in those days, so they'd hitched a ride with a local motorist. They picked up Ray and drove down the lane, parking near the edge of the path that led to the crabapple tree. From there, they continued on foot. Ray stuck to the script when the officers asked what he and Pearl had been doing: *Looking for mushrooms.*

Ray stood back as Garrigan and Curran approached the crime scene. The bodies had been carefully laid out on their backs, side by side, about a foot apart, their feet closest to the tree trunk. The man's outstretched arm cushioned the woman's head, and her left hand rested atop his right thigh. Her legs were crossed at the ankles, right over left. The man wore black shoes and a dark gray suit with a white button-up and a long white necktie, secured by a gold clasp that matched the ring on his little finger. The woman's clothing was of a markedly different quality, with a blue-and-red polka-dot dress revealing coarse black stockings rolled down below the knee, disappearing into weathered brown shoes.

The bodies had been laid out quite perfectly, almost as if it had been the work of a mortician, Garrigan thought. He noticed that the grass near the corpses had been trampled down, whereas the rest of the brush in the vicinity was thick and high, but he didn't see any signs of a struggle.

Garrigan observed a brown scarf wrapped around the woman's neck and head, and a panama hat placed over her companion's face, just above his eyes, as if it had been put there to shield them from the sun. The woman's blue velvet hat sat on the ground beyond their heads. Pieces of handwritten paper lay scattered around the bodies, as well as two handkerchiefs and a dark leather billfold containing a driver's license.

It occurred to the officers that they faced a jurisdictional discrepancy. The bodies lay just over the border in the town of Franklin, part of Somerset County, whereas New Brunswick was in Middlesex County. "This is no case of ours," Curran said.

He walked back to the residence where Pearl and Ray had summoned the police and phoned one of his superiors, who then placed a call to the Somerset County authorities. Within minutes, a detective was on the way.

In the meantime, a reporter arrived from New Brunswick's *Daily Home News*, the local publication of record. Even for a small newspaper in central New Jersey, crime was familiar terrain, as befit the times. The *Home News* had covered raids on local gambling dens and the seizure of moonshine imported from a gang in Brooklyn. In a neighboring town, a man had confessed to choking his wife to death and beating her with the blunt edge of an ax, blaming the massacre on bootleg hooch. In another nearby town, the *Home News* reported on the discovery of a dead New Yorker who the police believed "was engaged in some hazardous occupation, such as a gambler or a bootlegger, or possibly that he was a victim of the Italian mafia." Still, the *Home News* had never covered a story like the one now unfolding at the crabapple tree.

The reporter, Albert Cardinal, stood in front of the bodies as flies buzzed all around. Cardinal made a more thorough inspection than the officers had. He peered down at a bullet wound near the woman's hairline, almost in the middle of her forehead. The small ring of black powder around the hole gave him the impression she had been shot from close range. What really got him was the woman's "ghastly stare," as he would later describe it, "as though she died in horrified fright."

Cardinal looked at the woman's companion, whose eyes were closed, a single gaping bullet wound just above his right ear. He walked around the bodies and made a mental note of every detail that stood out: three or four empty bullet shells that looked like they came from a .32. The woman's wedding ring. The way her dress tightly hugged her body. The angle of the man's head, which looked to Cardinal like it had been tilted. He marveled at how perfectly composed their clothing was. It was as though they were "peacefully at rest," he thought.

Cardinal knelt to get a closer look at several items placed between the bodies. Near the victims' knees he saw a handful of papers arranged in a stack, except for a few pieces that the breeze must have carried a couple of feet away. Garrigan warned him not to sift through the papers, so he examined the top two sheets without disturbing the pile. They looked like letters, scrawled in pencil on cheap paper. He transcribed a bit of text: "Please do not laugh at this. I know I am a crazy cat, but I cannot be different."

The real bombshell lay near the man's left foot, where Cardinal set his eyes on a professional card lying in the grass. According to Garrigan, it had initially been propped against the man's left heel, like a curator's label in a museum exhibit. Whoever killed the man wanted whoever found him to know exactly who he was. Cardinal turned the card over. He read the name, printed in bold gothic letters, and jotted it down on a slip of paper: "Rev. Edward W. Hall."

Edward Hall was a prominent Episcopal minister whose congregation at New Brunswick's St. John the Evangelist included some of the city's most affluent residents. His wife, Frances Noel Stevens Hall, was a daughter of old money with illustrious ancestors and ties to the Johnson & Johnson dynasty. Cardinal could tell this was an even bigger scoop than he thought, with all the makings of a major scandal. He rushed out of De Russey's Lane and made it back to the newsroom before the first edition went to press.

THE CALLING CARD WAS AN unambiguous clue as to the dead man's identity, but the officers needed confirmation. They got it when another bystander showed up, Elton Loblein, who had pulled over to talk to Curran while the officer stood guard on the nearby main road, Easton Avenue. Loblein, as it happened, knew Edward Hall personally. Garrigan instructed him, "Just lift the hat off the man's head and see if you know him." The recognition was immediate and unequivocal: Edward Hall.

Loblein, a veterinary surgeon, noticed what the others hadn't.

Blood speckled Hall's gold-wire-rimmed glasses. Powder marks tinged the hole in his head. The hair around the edge of the wound had been burned off. The letters and the woman's scarf were stained with blood. Loblein lifted the scarf to see her face, though he hadn't the slightest idea who she was. Then again, as Loblein would later recall, "Her face was in such a condition it would be very hard to recognize her even if you had known her." Loblein did, however, spot three bullet holes in the woman's face. When Loblein inspected the woman's neck, he discovered the source of the vermin that were marching into her mouth, up her nose, all over her cheeks and jaw. There was a deep gash from ear to ear, filled with maggots, which decorated Hall's face as well.

Daniel Wray, city editor of the *Daily Home News*, came upon the group. He had known Reverend Hall for years, and he was stunned when he saw the body. Hall had married into a wealthy and prominent family. Now he lay dead in a lovers' lane next to a woman who was clearly not his wife. Wray picked up the letters, about ten of them in all. Garrigan looked on without protest.

The unsigned missives were scrawled in a feminine, almost juvenile hand. Wray scribbled down a few excerpts. "You are a true priest," one of the notes read. "You see in me merely your physical inspiration."

Who was the mystery woman, and what was her connection to Hall? The questions raced through Wray's mind as he sped back to the *Daily Home News* to rush the first edition to press.

THE HEIRESS

Around seven thirty on the evening of Thursday, September 14, two nights before Edward Hall's body was found, the phone rang at 23 Nichol Avenue, a Victorian mansion where Hall had lived with his wife, Frances, for a little more than a decade. One of the couple's maids, twenty-year-old Louise Geist, paused her work in a bedroom on the second floor and scurried across the hallway to answer the call. A woman on the other end of the line asked for the reverend.

"Is that for me?" Edward called out from the bathroom.

"Yes," Louise replied.

"I'll be out in a minute."

Louise went back to work, though she couldn't help but over-hear Reverend Hall's side of the conversation.

"Yes . . . Yes . . . Yes . . . That's too bad . . . Yes . . . Couldn't we make arrangements for about eight fifteen? . . . Goodbye." *Click*.

Before long, Edward came down and put on his coat. Frances entered from the porch. "I am going to make a call, dear, and will be home soon," Louise heard the reverend say. She passed through the kitchen and went out onto the back stoop, where Reverend Hall appeared moments later.

"Isn't this a lovely evening?" he said.

Hall bade Louise good night. She watched as he walked down the street, disappearing into the dusk. She would not see him alive again.

The next morning, Friday, Louise awoke to the sound of shutters being drawn on the first floor, a telltale sign that Reverend Hall had gotten up early to catch a train to New York. Louise hopped out of bed and hurried downstairs to prepare breakfast. When she walked into the dining room a little after seven, however, she was greeted not by the reverend, but by his brother-in-law Willie Stevens, usually the last one to the table for breakfast. Seeing him at that hour was rather odd, but then again, Willie was nothing if not a little odd.

A lumbering five foot ten, Willie had a singular appearance, with an ice cream scoop of bushy black hair, thick eyebrows, a doughy face framed by petite spectacles, and a mustache befitting a walrus. In Willie's fifty years, he'd barely worked, save for a few years when he was employed by a local contractor. He'd spent most of his adult life at 23 Nichol Avenue, where his second-floor bedroom overflowed with scholarly reading material. He devoured the newspapers and smoked a pipe, but he could also come across as something of a dimwit. He was, one might say, an eccentric.

"What are you doing up so early?" Louise asked.

"I would rather have Mrs. Hall tell you," Willie cryptically replied, suggesting something amiss.

As Louise passed the coatrack in the hallway, she put two and two together: the reverend's hat was not hanging in its usual spot. He hadn't come home.

Louise didn't think much of it. The reverend always seemed to have a good excuse on those nights when he returned home late. His car had broken down. He'd missed the train back from New York. Someone needed a ride somewhere. On the other hand, Louise had never known him to stay out all night. She figured that after his appointment the previous evening, he must have been summoned back out on a sick call. Edward Hall would have stayed at the bedside of an ill friend or parishioner no matter the hour, or so Louise told herself. She set the table for three and acted none the wiser when Frances came down for breakfast about twenty minutes later.

Frances was neither beautiful nor glamorous, despite her considerable wealth and aristocratic blood. She had a stocky build, which went well with her old-fashioned wardrobe. A reporter uncharitably described her as having "a face to look twice at—a long, narrow face" with a "firm, tight-lipped mouth, a suggestion of hair on the upper lip, a broad chin." A crescent-shaped scar accentuated her right temple, and she had "unusually prominent" black eyebrows. Another journalist dispensed with the euphemisms altogether, stating that Frances had "the head and features of a man." Her pince-nez glasses suggested, quite accurately, a woman of a different era. A new century ripe with opportunity had dawned and women's roles in society were changing, but Frances wanted nothing to do with any of that. She wore her conservatism with pride.

While Frances never had children of her own, she was devoted to her family and its legacy, as well as to charity and her church, St. John the Evangelist, where she had taught Sunday school before meeting Edward, seven years her junior, when he ascended the pulpit there in 1909. She was everything you'd expect of a well-bred woman from the late-Victorian age: proper, imperious, and, of course, private. To a servant like Louise, Frances had a haughty air about her, but something seemed different when Louise greeted her employer that Friday morning in the dining room.

Frances sat down and picked at her food, hardly eating. Louise hadn't set out the small silver water pitcher used by Reverend Hall to mix up his instant coffee substitute. Normally, Frances would have reminded Louise to retrieve it, but not today. There was an unspoken tension, and Louise finally piped up to break the awkward silence.

"Is Mr. Hall going to have breakfast in bed?" she asked, playing dumb.

"Louise," Frances replied, "Mr. Hall has not been home all night. I do not know where he is."

"Maybe he had an accident. Have you called the police?"

"I did. There hasn't been any accident." Frances had phoned the station around 7:00 A.M., but to avoid any unpleasant notoriety, she didn't specify that Edward was missing.

Louise couldn't help but notice an incessant jingling as she cleared the table. Frances held a set of car keys and rustled them nervously. That went on for most of the day as she paced the floor, rushing over to the window whenever she heard a car slow down outside the house. This antsy behavior did not suit Frances Hall, ordinarily a picture of calm and composure. As Louise would later say, "She had never acted this way before."

That afternoon, Frances summoned her two sisters-in-law. She also consulted with the family attorney, Edwin Florance, a former mayor of New Brunswick and New Jersey state senator. Beyond that, Frances had no other visitors, no telegrams, and certainly no hints as to Edward's whereabouts. However, Louise eavesdropped on an intriguing phone call around 11:00 P.M. Her ears perked up when she heard Frances say, "No, there was nobody else. He was friendly with her. She's in the choir."

Before Frances went to bed that night, the other maid, thirty-eight-year-old Barbara Tough (pronounced *too*), brought her a glass of water. Barbara saw no tears on Mrs. Hall's cheeks, but she thought her face looked puffy, as if she'd been crying. "Oh, Barbara, where is Mr. Hall?" Frances moaned. "Oh, I hope I will get strength to bear it."

FRANCES NOEL STEVENS HALL CAME from New Jersey royalty on both sides: the Stevenses and the Carpenders. She took immense pride in her noble ancestry, which stretched back to the founding of the republic. Frances's great-grandfather Ebenezer Stevens was the stuff of grade-school history books. He hurled tea into Boston Harbor and joined the Continental Army after the Battle of Lexington, later corresponding with founding fathers such as Thomas Jefferson and James Madison. Another of Ebenezer's many great-grandchildren, descended from his first and second wives, was a prominent New York woman who became a famous author. Her name was Edith Wharton.

Frances's grandfather on her maternal side, Jacob Stout Carpender, was an early member of the New York Stock Exchange, whose wife descended from a man who gave the third public reading of the Declaration of Independence. Frances's uncle Charles J. Carpender accumulated his wealth from a wallpaper company that later leased its headquarters to the founders of Johnson & Johnson. One of her cousins married Louise Johnson, the daughter of James Wood Johnson.

In New Brunswick, Frances's family was akin to the Boston Brahmins. Their tony neighborhood, also home to the newly established women's college of Rutgers University, was a menagerie of Carpender domiciles, including a twenty-one-acre retreat with a Tudor-style manor surrounded by immaculate landscaping and walking trails, a slice of English countryside in the middle of New Jersey. Frances's residence, a three-story Victorian filled with dark wood paneling and heavy mahogany furniture, occupied a leafy plot that took up a full city block. She practically couldn't throw a stone without hitting an aunt, uncle, or cousin. One cousin, a stockbroker named Henry de la Bruyere Carpender, resided with his wife,

Mary, in an adjacent lot on Nichol Avenue. Another cousin, Edwin Carpender, lived around the block with his wife, Elovine.

Frances had lived in New Brunswick since she was an infant, but she was born in Aiken, South Carolina. The region was said to be favorable for treating tuberculosis, and her father, a Civil War veteran named Francis Kerby Stevens, had moved the family there in hopes of recovering his health. He succumbed to the disease in February 1874, six weeks after Frances's birth, leaving behind his thirty-four-year-old bride, Mary Noel Carpender Stevens, and three fatherless children: Frances, William, and the oldest of the bunch, four-year-old Henry. After her husband died, Mary took the children north and settled in New Brunswick with the rest of the Carpender clan.

Frances presumably had the same rearing as any member of America's Gilded Age gentry. She attended Miss Anable's School, a private academy where New Brunswick's finer young ladies practiced their reading, writing, arithmetic, and etiquette. Then came the cadence of society life: dinner receptions, weddings, afternoon teas, and, of course, Sunday church.

As a young woman, Frances took up charitable work. During the Spanish-American War, she formed a Red Cross auxiliary, which collected aid items and sundries for wounded soldiers. She was active in her local YMCA, where she helped organize recitals, stage performances, and benefits. She was a devoted fundraiser for New Brunswick's city hospital, which would later become Robert Wood Johnson University Hospital, and she organized card games to raise money for ailing infants.

In addition to her philanthropic pursuits, Frances was a lady of leisure. There were sojourns in Europe, jaunts to Atlantic City, summer vacations in Maine, and afternoons at the New Brunswick Country Club. The one thing that seemed to have eluded her was a suitable match. Frances was an outlier in an era when marriage had immense bearing on an upper-class woman's identity, and a bride's average age was twenty-one. She'd been a bridesmaid numerous times, as well as a maid of honor. But by the time she turned thirty-five, in 1909, she'd heard no wedding bells of her own. She remained closest to her mother, and they spent their days reading, dining, and playing cards. For a while, it seemed all but certain that Frances would end up a spinster. Fate had other plans.

ON THE MORNING OF SATURDAY, September 16, some thirty-six hours after Edward had gone missing, Frances awoke from another restless night and, after breakfast, phoned her cousin Edwin Carpender. "I knew something terrible had happened," she later told a prosecutor, "and he seemed the only one I could get hold of." When Edwin arrived, Frances explained everything that had transpired: Edward leaving the house Thursday night, his absence through the following day, her sinking fear that he must be dead, or else why wouldn't he have come home or called by now? "I am almost crazy," Frances said.

Edwin, who had been out of town the previous day, was taken aback. This was the first he'd heard of Edward's disappearance, and he could see the situation had rattled his ordinarily steely cousin. It did all sound strange and foreboding, but the best thing to do was to remain calm. No use jumping to conclusions. Surely there had to be a logical explanation. In the meantime, Edwin and his wife, Elovine, one of Frances's closest friends, tried to distract her. After they drove Frances downtown to run errands, including a ten-dollar check deposit, Elovine kept Frances company into the early afternoon, when the phone rang. Albert Cardinal, the *Daily Home News* reporter, had returned from the crime scene and was trying to establish, discreetly, whether Frances was yet aware of Edward's death.

"Is this Mrs. Hall speaking?"

"Yes."

"Is Mr. Hall home?"

"No."

"When will he be home?"

"Why do you ask me these questions? Has anything happened to him?"

"I would rather let somebody else tell you."

Frances hung up and immediately dialed the family attorney, Edwin Florance. She told him to get down to the newspaper offices right away and figure out what on earth was going on.

THE TABLOID EDITOR

Phil Payne's eyes lit up when he heard about what was going on down in New Brunswick. It had only been a matter of hours since Ray Schneider and Pearl Bahmer first stumbled upon the bodies. But word about the dead minister was already ricocheting through the whiskey-drenched, smoke-filled newsrooms of New York City's major newspapers, from Adolph Ochs's *New York Times*, to William Randolph Hearst's *New York American*, to the late Joseph Pulitzer's *New York World*. Payne worked for a much younger newspaper, one particularly well suited to lurid melodrama: the New York *Daily News*, America's first true tabloid.

Founded in 1919 by Joseph Medill Patterson, scion of the illustrious Medill dynasty that controlled the *Chicago Tribune*, the *News* was a runaway success, and Payne had recently been promoted from city editor to acting managing editor. It was the biggest job in the newsroom, a sardine-can-like bullpen of dark wooden desks strewn with candlestick telephones and teetering stacks of paper. If and when Payne dropped the "acting" part from his title, he would become, at twenty-nine, the youngest managing editor of a metropolitan daily in the United States. Exactly one week after his promotion, the story of the New Brunswick murders broke.

Handsome and youthful, Payne had a warm smile and unruly brown hair that he sometimes tamed into a pompadour. His friendly round face was framed by spherical tortoiseshell glasses, which magnified his gray eyes. Payne was an astute disciple of the budding tabloid genre. The idea was to deliver news to the masses in a manner that was not only informative but utterly thrilling. With gigantic photos, screaming headlines, and a compact layout that wouldn't have looked out of place next to a pulp magazine, a tabloid newspaper thrived on prurient subject matter and larger-than-life characters. When Payne learned about the murders on lovers' lane, he knew this one had it all: blood, scandal, money, people with money behaving badly. He also knew exactly which reporter to unleash on the wilds of New Jersey.

At the *Daily News*, a group of fearless young newswomen were making names for themselves thanks to the heavy play that Payne gave their work. The leader of the pack was Julia Harpman. Newly wed and recently recovered from a near-fatal car crash, the beautiful twenty-seven-year-old had begun her career straight out of high school in her hometown of Memphis, where she helped her mother edit the local women's page for ten dollars a week. Before long, she was covering general assignment stories, gaining enough experience to land a job at Knoxville's *Journal and Tribune* for forty dollars a week. By early 1920, Harpman had bigger plans. She arrived in New York with little more than a borrowed squirrel-fur coat, sixty-three dollars in cash, and a stack of clips. The first few city editors she approached didn't have any work. But they saw the determination in Harpman's deep brown eyes. One of them suggested she try the *Daily News*.

When Harpman showed up in Phil Payne's office, he agreed to give her a trial, assigning her to cover a controversial vestry conclave at Church of the Ascension on Fifth Avenue. While there, Harpman stumbled upon a political forum that happened to be taking place on a different floor of the parish house. She slid into the meeting room and observed the former New York governor William Sulzer in the middle of a rant about curbing the Supreme Court and abolishing the Senate.

"Did you get the story?" Payne asked, referring to the vestry conclave, when Harpman returned to the newsroom.

"I did," Harpman told him, "and also another."

Payne hired her on the spot.

Like many reporters at the *News*, Harpman immediately took a liking to Payne. He was kind and jovial with a good sense of humor, as well as the requisite quick temper of a hard-boiled editor. After Harpman proved her mettle for a few months on general news— "that is, any story of any nature [that] was given to me"—Payne moved her to more alluring assignments: "crime stories, stories of murder, robberies, kidnappings, disappearances and anything of that kind." A year after her hiring, Harpman's salary rose from thirty-five dollars a week to sixty dollars, the highest of any woman on staff. (Though non-management salaries topped out at $125 for the male theater editor.) It was a demanding and fast-paced gig that involved jumping on a train at a moment's notice, whenever a big crime broke within two hundred miles of New York. Harpman thrived on the rush. "I never got tired," she recalled. "I loved my work."

Her tenacity paid off. "She had become recognized as the star reporter," Payne said. "She had shown a flair for criminal work, had a mind that had marvelous deductive capacity, so I had begun to use her almost exclusively on that line of work." The double murder in New Brunswick had Harpman's name written all over it. As one of her colleagues recalled, Payne put her on the case "the moment it broke."

AT THE TIME OF THE murders, the world had emerged from the throes of war, flu, death, and sacrifice. Those who survived were eager to let loose. Thus began an enchanting era of opulence and consumption, as well as dizzying innovation, from radio and the cinema to automobiles, transatlantic flight, and penicillin. The official posture of the times was temperance. America's Volstead Act went into effect in January 1920, banning alcohol across the United States. But it ended up having the opposite effect. Prohibition sparked a bacchanalian revolt against moderation and prudence, chipping away at the last vestiges of the Victorian moral code, and making way for all the modern pleasures that would come to define the Roaring Twenties. Skirts rose to the knee. Lovers went joyriding after dark. Planes soared across the ocean. Actors and athletes became idols. Beauty pageants drew scantily clad ingenues to the seaside. Speakeasies filled up with flappers dancing the Charleston. And American tabloid newspapers, yet another garish flamboyance of the postwar boom, chronicled it all, with an emphasis on crime, celebrity, and trivial obsessions that provided a refreshing chaser to years of distressing world news. As one 1920s tabloid editor put it, "Tabloids were just as inevitable as jazz. They are as truly expressive of modern America as World Series baseball, skyscrapers, radio, the movies, Trudy Ederle, Billy Sunday, taxicabs, and beauty contests. They are feared because they are jolting the pillars of conservatism."

The *Daily News* and its soon-to-follow tabloid competitors were poised to capture the excess of the age, and to chart its dark underbelly. With the election of Warren G. Harding, the decade began with a poker-obsessed womanizer in the White House. Crooked political bosses ran rampant, especially in New Jersey, where Frank Hague ruled Hudson County and Nucky Johnson established a "boardwalk empire" in Atlantic City. Organized crime flourished, thanks to the advent of bootlegging. "Rum rows" lingered off the coasts of Long Island and the Jersey shore. Prohibition inadvertently fueled a significant increase in burglaries, assaults, and homicides. By 1926, more than twelve thousand murders were being committed annually, as the country's murder rate ticked up to a high of nearly ten per one hundred thousand people.

The media became obsessed with homicide during the 1920s. Gangster shootouts made for good copy, but newspapers were more enthusiastic about killings of a domestic variety, especially when sex was involved or, better still, rich and famous people. When Joe Patterson founded the *Daily News* in 1919, after stepping back from his family's *Chicago Tribune*, stories like these found a natural home. As a friend observed, Patterson ranked the subjects that most interested readers as follows: "(1) Love or Sex, (2) Money, (3) Murder." He believed that readers were "especially interested in any situation which involved all three."

Patterson had first encountered the tabloid form several years earlier. While traveling through Europe, he became a fan of London's *Daily Mirror*, a tabloid newspaper founded at the dawn of the century by the landmark British publisher Alfred Charles William Harmsworth, First Viscount of Northcliffe. Lord Northcliffe was a powerful newspaper magnate and society fixture whose publishing empire wielded great political influence. He owned the *Evening News*, the *Daily Mail*, and the *Times*, but the *Mirror* put him on the vanguard of so-called popular journalism. The *Mirror*'s size was compact, larger than a magazine, but much easier to handle than a clumsy broadsheet. (The word "tabloid" came from the compressed tablets that a London-based pharmaceutical company began marketing in the late 1880s.) It was an easily digestible news product with an eye for sensational topics like scandal and crime, and it appealed to the middle and working classes, who could handily consume its contents on a subway car or, should they be so inclined, inside a crowded pub. As Northcliffe proclaimed with the paper's maiden issue on November 2, 1903, the idea was "to be entertaining without being frivolous, and serious without being dull."

For Patterson, who dabbled in socialism and became something of a renegade in his wealthy conservative family, the *Mirror*'s everyman sensibility held considerable appeal. But the photographs impressed him most of all. There were lots of them, especially on the front page, which typically consisted of three or four large images as opposed to an endless sea of text. On big news days, such as when a German U-boat torpedoed the *Lusitania*, a single photograph might occupy the entire cover. Newsmen initially resisted the idea of pictures being just as important as text, if not more important. But it slowly caught on, especially with advances in printing technology that made it possible to reproduce photos quickly and on the cheap. As the legendary editor Arthur Brisbane is said to have famously remarked in 1911, "Use a picture. It's worth a thousand words."

Patterson visited Northcliffe to pick his brain about the newspaper business. "New York's got to have a picture tabloid," Northcliffe implored during one of Patterson's trips to England. "I don't care who starts it. If the rest of you don't see the light soon, I'll start one myself!" In the UK, the *Mirror* sold nearly a million copies per issue, packed with advertising every single day. Surely New York City, a booming cultural and commercial capital with a population of more than five million, was the perfect landscape for an American tabloid to flourish. Patterson and his cousin cum business partner, Robert McCormick, had already flirted with the idea of expanding from Chicago to New York. A tabloid venture would give Patterson a pet project while McCormick consolidated his grip on the *Chicago Tribune*. Win-win.

They formalized the plan at the tail end of the war, on a pleasant summer evening in 1918, in the undulating Champagne region of France. Patterson, then thirty-nine and an infantry division captain, had returned to field headquarters from a three-day engagement in which the Allied forces pushed back a major German offensive. McCormick, thirty-eight and recently convalesced from a near-death experience on the front, had stopped by for a visit before returning stateside. They sat on a straw pile outside an old farmhouse along the River Ourcq and passed a bottle of Scotch back and forth, gunfire thundering in the distance, enemy shells illuminating the night sky. Patterson pitched his tabloid as follows: Half the content would be photos, the other half news and features. It would be humorous, plainspoken, and streetwise. The industry was now competing for people's attention with movies and, before long, it would have radio to contend with as well. What Patterson knew, and others would soon realize, was that newspapers needed to be just as irresistible as these newfangled technologies.

It didn't take much convincing. As McCormick later recalled, "I said we would get started on it right away."

Eleven months later, after Patterson and McCormick each returned from war in one piece, the *Daily News* came alive. The cousins had secured a loan and set up the *News* in lower Manhattan, where a few dozen journalists and business employees crammed themselves into a small office rented from the *Evening Mail*. Patterson bombarded the brass with letters and telegrams from Chicago. They were elbowing in on the most crowded and competitive field in the country. New York had seven other morning newspapers and ten afternoon papers, the largest of which, Hearst's *Evening Journal*, sold nearly 700,000 copies a day, dwarfing the number with which the *News* debuted—between 150,000 and 200,000 copies, according to historical records. Patterson relished the gamble.

On June 26, 1919, after several months of preparations and planning, the inaugural sixteen-page issue of the *Daily News* hit stands for two cents. On page 5, an editorial spelled out the tabloid's mission:

> With the pictures we shall give you short, concise news stories. . . .
> No story will be continued to another page—that is to save you the
> trouble. The print will be large and clear. You can read it without

eye strain. The paper is, as you see, of convenient size. You can turn the pages in the subway without having it whisked from your hand by the draft.

Compared to other papers that same day, Patterson's tabloid—initially called the *Illustrated Daily News* before they truncated the name—looked as if it beamed down from outer space. The front pages of the broadsheets were filled with dense stories about the peace treaty process and congressional bills. The *News* led with a juicy morsel of society gossip: the Prince of Wales, shown atop his steed in a towering front-page photograph, was expected to visit the Goelets and Vanderbilts at their Rhode Island summer mansions. Inside the paper, readers found shorter and snappier versions of the same foreign, domestic, and local news that everyone else was reporting, but also provocative photo spreads, copious cartoons, and a detective series by E. Phillips Oppenheim. On the back page, a quintet of femme fatales advertised a ten-thousand-dollar contest seeking "the most beautiful girl in Greater New York."

After the initial novelty wore off, circulation plummeted from the low six figures to the low five figures. But in the fall of 1919, it began to climb back up. First to sixty thousand a day. Then one hundred thousand in December, and three hundred thousand the following September. By the time Phil Payne worked his way up to managing editor in the fall of 1922, the *News* was selling six hundred thousand copies a day, making it the country's third-largest newspaper.

PAYNE WAS AN IDEAL RECRUIT for Patterson's rowdy pirate ship. His mischievous nature, cocksure demeanor, and fiercely competitive spirit fit well with the loud and irreverent tabloid ethos. In the words of one of his reporters, he was "a whale of a newspaper editor. He smells a story ahead of the others." That sense of smell made up for

Payne's poor vision and partial deafness, physical deficiencies that were no match for his frenetic mind, its gears always turning with story ideas that would shock and dazzle the town. "He had a quirky imagination, the naivete of a child coupled with considerable ingenuity, all of which made him a good editor," one of his colleagues recalled, and he "did not believe in doing anything conventionally if a spectacular method could be found."

Born in 1892 in San Francisco, to an English father and German mother who had emigrated from the United Kingdom, Payne spent his early life in the Muskoka region of Ontario, Canada, where his mother was treated for tuberculosis. Growing up in a quaint lakeside village called Gravenhurst, he landed his first newspaper job at the *Gravenhurst Banner*, which hired him to set type, collect bills, and deliver papers. The Paynes then moved to Perth Amboy, New Jersey, about twenty minutes from New Brunswick. Payne was a zealous athlete, competing in swim meets and boxing matches, and handling publicity for his local baseball and basketball teams. He studied chemistry in school and then worked for a chemical company, but when a reporter's job opened up at his hometown newspaper, the *Perth Amboy Chronicle*, he answered his calling. Payne's career soon took him to a bigger paper across from Manhattan, the *Hudson Dispatch*, which covered Jersey City, Hoboken, Union City, and West New York, where Payne relocated in 1913. Life was good and Payne was in love. Her name was Helena Bechtold, just a few years younger, dark-haired and pretty. They married and settled into a house on the Palisades, where they could stroll to a cliff top overlooking Manhattan's Upper West Side. They spent their honeymoon at a cottage in Gravenhurst and made the trip an annual summer tradition.

In 1917, after the United States entered World War 1, Payne enthusiastically signed his draft card. As a married man with a nonworking dependent spouse, he could have avoided conscription altogether. But Payne waived his exemption. There was something of a heroic streak in him. Early one Sunday evening while putting the paper to bed as editor of the *Dispatch*, Payne had discovered flames shooting out from the basement. When the firefighters arrived, they found Payne battling the conflagration with buckets of water. Now, he was determined to serve his country.

Before enlisting, Payne was discharged from a voluntary training camp in Plattsburgh because of his impaired vision. Undeterred, he later persuaded the local draft board to send him to Fort Dix, where he trained for two months only to once again flunk his physical exam. When the Knights of Columbus sought volunteers for war relief work, Payne threw up his hand, finally making it to France in the summer of 1918 as a field secretary. His official duties were with the Knights of Columbus War News Service, chronicling battles such as Saint-Mihiel and the Argonne. When not reporting and writing, though, Payne eagerly lent a hand however he could. One day, he hopped in a rickety Ford with a leaky radiator and transported a hundred thousand cigarettes from Paris to the Lorraine front.

Payne's Knights of Columbus service was not without danger. He witnessed a captive German pull out a concealed revolver and shoot dead a Jersey City boy who had been assigned as the prisoner's escort. He slept in tents out in the open listening to aerial torpedoes plummeting to earth, German planes sometimes flying so low that their machine guns sprayed bullets into the woods. "To stand or lie helpless in the darkness listening to the whining drone of the enemy planes and wondering where the next bomb was going to drop," Payne recalled, "was enough to fray the nerves of the bravest." When Payne returned home in November 1918, after six months on the battlefields, he skewered the war censors who had bowdlerized his copy, feverishly hammered out on a typewriter with French letters. "The greatest copy butchers ever gathered in the editorial rooms of any newspaper were rank amateurs in comparison," he wrote. But Payne also reflected proudly on the work of his fellow war correspondents. "I felt, and I think the others did too, that we were lucky to have a chance to work on the biggest story that has broken since the creation of the world."

AFTER THE WAR, PAYNE TOOK a job with Hearst's *Chicago Herald-Examiner*. He worked as a staff correspondent first in Chicago and then in New York, writing features about troops returning from overseas. In November 1919, Payne caught the break that would change his life forever: a gig at the *Daily News*. Within six months, as the *News* signed a lease for bigger headquarters, in a five-story loft building at 25 Park Place, Payne was promoted to city editor. "He was quick to spot a good story," wrote one of his contemporaries, "and he whipped his reporters into pursuing every clue to a dead end."

Payne understood the qualities that made a tabloid tick: drama, scandal, spectacle, celebrity, and crime. He shared Patterson's enthusiasm for pictures, and he helped pioneer news photography. In the fall of 1920, Payne put one of his photographers on a stakeout of the city's restive Sinn Fein sympathizers. The instinct paid off when a bloody Thanksgiving riot erupted outside St. Patrick's Cathedral, giving the *News* an array of action shots for the following day's front page. Weeks later, Payne sent a *Daily News* correspondent and a photographer to the Canadian wilderness to meet a trio of navy balloonists, who had found their way to safety after disappearing earlier in the month. "Close your eyes and try to picture a dazzling waste of snow," he wrote in a curtain-raiser about the expedition. "It was through such country that the balloonists fought their way. How they managed to live, nobody has been able to find out yet. Perhaps they were able to kill a few rabbits or a porcupine."

Payne's rise at the *News* coincided with the dawn of an era that brought a smorgasbord of sordid sagas. The sex-fueled manslaughter scandal of Hollywood star Fatty Arbuckle, to name just one, graced the front pages for weeks on end in the fall of 1921. For assignments like these, Julia Harpman was Payne's secret weapon. She didn't have to go very far to find a high-profile murder—the one that put her on the map happened a block from her apartment on Manhattan's Upper West Side. The victim was Joseph Bowne Elwell, a socialite bridge player and playboy found slumped in a chair in the drawing room of his four-story granite town house, barefoot and pajama clad, blood streaking from the hole where a bullet had pierced the center of his forehead. "For weeks," wrote Ishbel Ross, another lady-reporter luminary of the day, "Miss Harpman wrung the last bit of drama from this story."

Harpman's performance on the Elwell case was a testament to Payne's instincts in hiring her. He believed strongly in her work. He also drove her hard, pushing her to follow every lead, no matter how small. The Elwell killing was never solved, but it wouldn't be long before Payne and Harpman were chasing yet another impenetrable murder mystery.

THE REVEREND

On a dreary evening in June 1909, 150 parishioners filed into St. John the Evangelist to meet and mingle with the Reverend Edward Wheeler Hall, their newly appointed rector. As raindrops pelted the roof of the modest red-brick church covered in ivy, Hall looked upon his flock and thanked them for the generous reception. "It is a great pleasure to take charge of a church in as good a condition as St. John's," he gushed, his inveterate charm immediately evident.

At twenty-eight, Hall had a youthful glow offset by thinning hair, and brown eyes that beamed at his congregation under arched brows. While he was entirely average in height and build, and neither exceedingly handsome nor particularly hard on the eyes, Hall's personality was intoxicating. He exuded a gregarious charisma that instantly warmed the parishioners crowded around him. "That he made a decided impression on them is no doubt," one attendee noted. "He has a personality that soon makes friends, and before the reception was over, he and the members were as if they had long been associated together." For his first sermon, Hall explored the theme of the Resurrection, quoting from St. Paul's Letter to the Philippians.

"If we could only count the consequences of our acts," he preached, "there would be very little sin."

Hall's penchant for oratory was apparent from a young age. At Polytechnic Preparatory School in Brooklyn, he served as vice president of the Literary and Debating Society, and president of the Interscholastic Debating League. Prior to that, Hall attended the highly competitive choir school at Manhattan's Grace Church, a genteel institution for boys typically no younger than eight. He made such an impression that a rector of Grace Church was said to have endowed Hall's higher education at Hobart College in Geneva, New York, where he was rumored to have been a "rather wild youth," though a studious one. Hall pledged himself to the Sigma Phi fraternity and continued to excel academically, winning prizes for rhetoric, philosophy, essay-writing, and English. He graduated cum laude in 1902.

Hall then attended the General Theological Seminary of the Episcopal Church and was ordained in one of the largest classes in the history of the Episcopal Diocese of New York. In 1909, Hall was serving as curate at St. Mark's Episcopal Church in Basking Ridge, New Jersey, when a position opened at St. John the Evangelist. The new role meant Hall would now have his own congregation, one that included a number of prominent families. His fifteen-hundred-dollar salary afforded him a modest apartment near the church, where his widowed mother and sisters joined him. Once Hall settled in, there were parishioners to meet, sermons to write, weddings and funerals to officiate, and charity events to attend, like a Thanksgiving dinner for needy children. For the youth of St. John's, Hall was the life of the party. He entertained them with endless rounds of Prisoner's Base and Blind Man's Buff, or games he would simply make up. With the Boy Scout troop that Hall established, he set up a basketball court, planned trips to the Jersey shore, and bicycled with the Scouts up and down George Street. Hall was a meticulous bookkeeper, and he endeavored to improve the tidiness of church records. He formed a council to manage the multiple organizations that had sprouted within St. John's, and he undertook physical improvements, such as a parish house on an adjacent plot of land.

For the first annual Christmas fair of Hall's rectorship, he hired the Midget Athletic Club, which dazzled the audience with acrobatics and clown acts. He brought in students from Rutgers to compete in fencing bouts, and he corralled the men of the church for a talent show. Among the women of St. John's who staffed an array of booths were two bachelorettes: a young beauty named Mattie Long and Frances Stevens.

Frances had grown up in New Brunswick's larger Episcopal congregation, Christ Church, but she had begun teaching Sunday school at St. John's and occasionally attended services there. As Hall put his stamp on St. John's, Frances became more involved. Perhaps she was smitten with this fine young rector breathing new life into the parish. Hall was smitten, too—just not with the thirty-five-year-old Frances.

At twenty-seven, Mattie Long was roughly the same age as Hall, whose twenty-ninth birthday approached. She worked as a schoolteacher and took care of a widowed mother, something Edward could relate to. They seemed, in many ways, a perfect fit, and it was no surprise that a romance blossomed. Mattie hoped Edward would ask her to marry him. She was mistaken: Edward proposed to Frances instead

What did Edward see in Frances? It's not inconceivable that her wealth had something to do with it. (In 1922, the newspapers reported that she was worth $1.7 million, the equivalent of nearly $30 million today, though she later disputed this.) As for Frances, becoming the wife of an esteemed local cleric may have been a way to further enhance her social position. (It also may have been preferable to becoming an old maid.)

On the afternoon of July 20, 1911, New Brunswick's upper crust filled the pews of Christ Church, transformed into a wilderness of palms, ferns, and gladiolas. As the organist commenced the nuptial music, the guests turned their heads toward the entrance, where Frances appeared in a princess gown of rich white silk and Mechlin lace. It was the same one worn forty-three years earlier by Frances's mother, who gave the bride away.

Clutching a bouquet of roses and lilies of the valley, her tulle veil done up in coronet fashion with orange blossoms, Frances proceeded down the aisle and took her spot at the altar beside the maid of honor, her longtime friend Sally Peters. She locked eyes with her groom-to-be, whose best man had traveled from Vermont. Following the officiant's sermon, Frances and Edward recited their vows and exchanged rings. They hosted a reception at 23 Nichol Avenue, where guests showered the newlyweds with silver, furniture, china, paintings, and checks. Edward made plans to move into the mansion after their European honeymoon. It may have been a curious match, it may have been a marriage of convenience, but whatever the truth of their relationship, Edward and Frances had promised themselves to one another, in sickness and in health, 'til death do them part.

For Edward, he had another eleven years, one month, and twenty-five days to go.

BACK AT THE PHILLIPS FARM, as the maggots worked their way up Edward's nostrils and under his eyelids, George Totten surveyed the crime scene through circular eyeglasses that looked too small for his face. He'd arrived at the crabapple tree with several other county officials more than an hour after the bodies were found. With twenty-eight years of police work to his name, Totten had played an active role in every major murder investigation that unfolded during his tenure as Somerset County's chief detective. His homburg hat kept the sun out of his eyes as he noted subtler clues that may or may not have had any significance, such as the *G* inscribed on Hall's tie clip. County physician William Long made his own inspection, determining that unless Hall had been sleeping at the very moment he was shot, someone had to have closed his eyes and repositioned his glasses postmortem. (The physician also noted that Hall's fly was zipped up.) County Sheriff Bogart Conkling began packaging up evidence: the love letters, the handkerchiefs, a set of keys, a .32-caliber cartridge—it was unclear what happened to the other three—and Hall's calling card, now propped up by some tufts of grass near the reverend's foot. Totten wasn't sure if the victims had died where their bodies were found, or if they'd been taken to De Russey's Lane after perishing elsewhere. But in the absence of a gun, Totten knew this was no suicide pact. "Everything points to murder," he said.

By early afternoon, the Phillips farm had come to look more like a country jamboree than a homicide investigation. In a chaotic scene that would have horrified any student of the burgeoning forensic sciences, curiosity seekers arrived in droves, to the point where the patrolmen either couldn't hold them back or didn't bother trying. They parked their cars along adjacent roadways and trudged through fields to the awaiting circus. The mob freely roamed and gawked, some stomping about the corpses, picking up the reverend's hat and the woman's scarf. Pieces of bark were stripped from the crabapple tree, morbid souvenirs. An onlooker later remarked, "You could not believe it possible, in a place as isolated as that, that people could come in such numbers in ten minutes."

Totten was inside the farmhouse when a second reporter from the *Daily Home News*, Frank Deiner, showed up and said, "I think I can identify the woman."

Denier, who lived around the block from the Hall home, knew something the others did not. There were rumors Hall had been "friendly," as Deiner put it, with a woman named Eleanor Mills, a choir singer at Hall's church. Totten immediately escorted Deiner through the crowds to the blood-soaked patch of earth where the bodies lay. Deiner leaned in, drew down the woman's scarf, and squinted past the maggots. There was no doubt in his mind—this was Eleanor Mills, wife, mother, and devoted congregant of St. John the Evangelist.

Before long, Frances's family attorney, Edwin Florance, and her cousin Edwin Carpender arrived on the scene. They'd received word about the murders, and they needed to see the truth with their own eyes. Standing over the bodies, they could hardly believe it was real. Before the county undertaker pulled up to retrieve the bodies, Carpender leaned down and took Hall's cold dead hand in his own.

Shortly after one o'clock, Elovine Carpender returned with trepidation to 23 Nichol Avenue. She had learned of Edward's death and now had to inform Frances of the grim news. She climbed the stairs to the second floor, where Frances awaited her. "What you feared has happened," Elovine said. "He is dead."

Hearing these words, Frances abandoned her reserve. As Elovine put it, "She broke down completely." Elovine hugged her friend as the emotions poured out. Frances regained her composure, and after she caught her breath and dried her eyes, she went downstairs to the parlor, where visitors were arriving to pay their respects. Her ordeal had only just begun.

THE CHOIR SINGER

Eleanor Mills had been missing for a day and a half when her husband, James Mills, dropped by the home of one of her sisters. James, better known as Jimmy, or Jim, was anxious about Eleanor's disappearance, but not at all hysterical. He certainly wasn't concerned enough to summon the police. If there had been a honeymoon phase during Jim and Eleanor's seventeen-year marriage, it was a distant memory. Their frequent bickering and quarrels often rose to a volume loud enough for the neighbors to hear. Sometimes Eleanor would drown Jim out by singing loudly, or she would cover her ears and wail, "BLAH BLAH BLAH BLAH BLAH." It was by no means a violent marriage, but neither was it a happy one. Sex was out of the question. The thought of it, Eleanor told Jim, was abhorrent to her.

Jim had last seen his wife on the evening of Thursday, September 14, around the same time Frances last saw her husband. Jim had worked all day as a janitor at the Lord Stirling Elementary School. He then tended to chores at St. John's, where he worked a side job as the parish sexton, maintaining the boiler and mowing the grass, tending to the hearth in the winter and closing up after

Sunday services. By seven thirty, Jim was back home again at 49 Carman Street, where the Mills family lived on the second floor. He sat on the porch in the rear of the house, working on some window-box planters that Frances had commissioned. Eleanor, in her blue-and-red polka-dot dress, came up from the front stoop, where she'd been chatting with their sixteen-year-old daughter, Charlotte. She breezed past her husband, went inside, and emerged again moments later, now in a blue hat with gray trim and a brown shawl with deep pockets. Jim looked up from his handiwork and asked Eleanor where she was going.

"Follow me and find out," she snarled, scurrying down the steps and disappearing into the night. Jim brushed off Eleanor's cold and sarcastic reply. As he later told a grand jury, "I didn't pay any notice to it."

Now, on Saturday afternoon, as Eleanor's absence stretched into its second day, Jim grew more concerned. That's what brought him to the home of Augusta Tennyson, one of Eleanor's ten siblings, who hadn't seen or heard from her sister. Augusta agreed it was strange, but there was nothing she could offer in terms of an explanation. Jim bade her good day and started back home, about a fifteen-minute walk up the road. He hadn't gotten very far when a young girl caught up to him. Mrs. Tennyson, the girl explained, needed him to come back. He turned around at once.

Minutes later, Jim found Augusta at the house of a neighbor with a telephone. She alerted Jim to the news that had just come across the switchboard: the bodies of Reverend Hall and an un-identified woman had been found on an abandoned farm outside of town. Jim's mind raced as he rushed back home, where a neighbor consoled Charlotte. The girl had just been told what her father al-ready suspected: Charlotte's mother was dead.

JIM MILLS AND ELEANOR REINHARDT tied the knot rather abruptly in December 1905, taking their families by surprise. A year prior,

Eleanor had been a carefree seventeen-year-old enjoying a Christ-mastime sleigh ride with a few dozen classmates from New Bruns-wick High School, belting out "Jingle Bells" under an early-winter's moon. Now, midway through her senior year, barely above the age of consent, Eleanor abandoned her studies. She had first met Jim on a rainy night when she was fifteen. That evening, Eleanor was visiting one of her girlfriends, who insisted on an escort as Eleanor got ready to leave. "Here's my brother Jim," the friend said. "He'll see you home. It's too late for you to go alone in this rain."

That innocent walk marked the beginning of a relationship that led Jim and Eleanor to the home of a local clergyman at the end of 1905. "As the young lady appeared of age and they were accompa-nied by her prospective sister-in-law . . . the minister performed the ceremony as desired," the *Daily Home News* reported. "The bride, who is a pleasant, attractive little lady, is well known in this city, and has a large circle of friends who are much disappointed at being cheated out of a chance to throw rice." The euphemistic wedding an-nouncement continued, "The parents of Mrs. Mills appear to have been as much in the dark as everyone else in regard to the marriage, and the youthful husband, who does not appear to be much over 21 years of age"—Jim was in fact one month shy of his twenty-eighth birthday—"seems to have considered it best that his wife's people should learn of the happy event after it had been consummated rather than before."

There was, of course, a very practical reason for the shotgun wedding, though Eleanor's belly did not yet betray any obvious sign of it. Charlotte Mills arrived just seven months later. Instead of a high school diploma, Eleanor had been given a daughter, her life's trajectory now etched in stone. In another four years, a son named Daniel followed.

The family of four squeezed themselves into the second-floor apartment and attic of 49 Carman Street, a two-story wood-frame house just a few blocks from the opulent Hall mansion. It was a claustrophobic four-room dwelling, with no plumbing and a leaky roof. Eleanor, whose father was a low-paid factory watchman responsible for a traditional German family of twelve, was no stranger to a cramped working-class household. But she dreamed of more, and she might have even attained it had the circumstances of her life been different.

With hazel eyes and an unblemished complexion, Eleanor could have looked glamorous if only she had money to afford the bedazzled evening gowns, glittering headbands, and long pearl necklaces that were de rigueur at furtive cocktail parties in New York. Eleanor eschewed jewelry, insisting that it "didn't suit her." Instead, she fashioned her hair into a voluminous brown bob that complemented her Mona Lisa smile. Her wardrobe was simple—tailored suits that hugged her 118 pounds, plain velour hats atop her five-foot-three-inch frame, low-heel oxfords with broad ribbons on her small feet. Even her summer dresses were straightforward and unassuming, though tasteful. She was an expert at crochet and made her own clothes, underwear and all, as well as outfits for Charlotte and Daniel—anything to save a dollar here or there. Eleanor also had a knack for cooking, especially German dishes—pot roast and sausage roll; apple cakes bursting with raisins, cinnamon, and powdered sugar. She was perfectly happy "puttering in the kitchen," as Charlotte put it, and she worked hard tending to the home, rising at seven each day to tidy up, polish the woodwork, and make sure every last tassel on the rugs and drapes was laid neat. Eleanor did her best to improve upon their simple apartment, an effort that didn't always sit well with her parsimonious husband. One time, after setting aside some money from her meager housekeeping budget, Eleanor put down an installment on a wicker chair that she and Charlotte had spotted in a shop window. When they brought it home, in Charlotte's recollection, "the heavens pretty near fell."

What Eleanor lacked in wealth she made up for in personality and talent. Vivacious and voluble, she'd been blessed with a shining soprano voice that distinguished her in the choir at St. John's, prompting an observation that she "could sing like a nightingale." Eleanor had joined the choir as an adolescent. By the time she reached adulthood, settling into the monotony of her marriage and the challenges of raising children on a bare-bones budget, the choir provided not only spiritual solace but a respite from the tedium of working-class domesticity. Eleanor also found an escape in books. "They make me dream," she once mused. "I hate to come back to realities." If ever she came across a word whose meaning evaded her, she would look it up. Jim was impressed by his wife's good vocabulary and knack for oratory, once bragging that Eleanor could get up on a chair and "make a speech or a sermon better than a lot of the men and women and preachers you ever heard. She'd take a text from the Bible, and in no time, she'd have a pretty clever sermon framed out of it, and would be preaching away." In fact, Charlotte said her mother sometimes wrote sermons for Reverend Hall and left them on the desk in his study.

Though Eleanor hadn't finished high school, Jim boasted that she "had a better education than a lot of women who have gone to college." Eleanor could speak, read, and write in her family's native tongue. She had a worldly mind, often daydreaming of Europe or China or Japan, imagining their sights and sounds and smells. She would sometimes regale her daughter with tales of these faraway lands, only to confess, "Oh, I'm just making it up. I like to think about it."

Jim, on the other hand, was neither the brightest nor the most handsome. Born in 1878 to parents who had emigrated from Ireland, he was a stick figure of a man, though not particularly tall, with a long sloping nose and sunken cheeks. Once upon a time, Eleanor must have seen something when she gazed into his blue eyes, or ran her fingers through his thin, dark brown hair. But after nearly two decades of marriage, her husband's dirty khaki overalls, faded cloth cap, and cheek full of tobacco left much to be desired. People described Jim Mills as meek, mild, and dim. An even less charitable characterization suggested that he was "as colorless as a catfish." In the words of his own brother, "We called him Simple Jim when we were boys."

Jim wasn't enthusiastic about learning, having entered the workforce rather than go through secondary school. His own daughter couldn't help but look down on his lack of education. Even without formal schooling, Charlotte argued, "You could always study and read and find out things if you worked at it. Mother did." Jim wasn't entirely without interests. In his younger years, he had been a catcher and first baseman for the New Brunswick Independents. He'd broken three fingers, and the injuries were his trophies. "Those were the days when we didn't use gloves, masks, or chest protectors, but we was ball players," he bragged. Jim was a cobbler by trade and had worked at a shoe factory for a time. He also enjoyed carpentry, as evidenced by a variety of woodwork that adorned the Mills home. Still, Jim's career prospects were limited. Between his positions as school custodian and church sexton, he supported his family of four on an average of thirty-five dollars a week.

The Millses' financial situation, as with many couples, was a marital stressor. Jim seemed resigned to his station, content with a simple existence of hard work and struggle. Eleanor believed there was more to life, that people had been put on earth to make something of themselves, to have dreams and ambitions and ideals. She loved her children, and she took pride in her home, but if she could go back in time, she might have chosen a different path. "Be something, kid," she would say to Charlotte, who thought of her mother more as a friend, or an older sister. They were extremely close, even sharing the attic after Eleanor grew weary of rooming with her husband. Young Dan, who had inherited the taciturn nature of the Mills men, shared a bedroom with Jim.

Charlotte took after her mother. She was smart, outgoing, well-spoken, confident, spunky, and driven. They shared secrets and confided in one another. Eleanor admitted to Charlotte that even in her early years with Jim, "she felt tied down and hemmed in and her marriage had been a terrible blunder." Mother and daughter stuck together when things grew difficult at home, even if Eleanor would sometimes admonish Charlotte for being insufficiently respectful. "He is your father," she would scold. Charlotte and Jim didn't have the strongest bond, nor did they see eye to eye. Jim didn't think Charlotte should bother with high school. He'd gone off to work when he was young, so why shouldn't his children do the same? Eleanor made Charlotte promise to graduate, a promise she hadn't been able to keep for herself. She thought Charlotte would make a good musician and told her she wanted her to have "some kind of a future." She begged her not to marry until she was sure she'd found the right man, until she was certain she was in love. "Have some kind of life," Eleanor would implore her daughter. "Don't live as I've had to. Do you understand me?"

Eleanor sometimes found ways to make a little extra cash. For a brief time during the Great War, she found work with a local rubber plant inspecting gas masks. Eleanor's home life was such that buying a new bed or upgrading some of the apartment's rickety furniture would inevitably lead to an argument. Amid the contretemps that erupted when she came home with that new wicker chair one night, she and Charlotte stormed out and walked over to St. John's. There was a pair of reasonably comfortable chairs in Reverend Hall's study, and that is where they slept.

THE HALL AND MILLS FAMILIES lived a few blocks apart, but inhabited different worlds, one of wealth and privilege, the other of want and hardship; one conveying status and property, the other a lack thereof. They mingled and spent time in one another's company, but as church colleagues, not social equals. Still, they were close enough that when Eleanor needed to have a kidney removed in January 1922, the Halls arranged for a three-hundred-dollar loan from the church, which Jim agreed to pay back at the rate of ten dollars a month. That August, when the Halls vacationed in Maine and Willie Stevens visited the Jersey shore, they paid Jim to house-sit at their mansion, where he slept every night for three weeks. Similarly, it was Edward who arranged Jim's position as church sexton. A couple of weeks before the murders, when Eleanor needed a tooth extraction and couldn't find anyone to perform the procedure, the Halls referred her to a dentist in Newark. Edward, instead of Jim, accompanied her to the appointment.

Eleanor found ways to repay the Halls' generosity. She would often make embroidered pieces for Frances as birthday or holiday gifts. Frances, knowing that Eleanor loved flowers, would invite her to take in the lush gardens and fern-filled greenhouses on the mansion grounds, often sending her home with a bounty of vegetables. Frances sometimes gave the Millses other little presents as well—fine fabrics out of which Eleanor could make blouses, or a set of towels with the letter M emblazoned in a blue cross-stitch. On the day before Eleanor disappeared, the Halls took Eleanor and another devoted churchwoman, Minnie Clark, on a picnic to Lake Hopatcong, in northwestern New Jersey. The trip had become an annual tradition, a gesture to thank Eleanor and Minnie for their hard work at St. John's. (Only five people had keys to the church; Eleanor and Minnie were two of them.) The group took a boat ride on the lake, and Frances later joined the women in the water.

St. John's gave Eleanor not only a social milieu, but the existential purpose she so desperately craved. She immersed herself in church work, from sewing, clerical tasks, and tidying the chancel to charity events, choir practice, and meetings of the Ladies' Auxiliary. As with other women of the congregation, her devotion grew when Reverend Hall came along. Apart from her domestic responsibilities and her children, the church was an incredibly important aspect of

Eleanor's life, and nothing or no one could take that away from her. When the shoe factory where Jim worked relocated to Brooklyn, Eleanor told him he was welcome to move there and come back to visit at his leisure. New Brunswick was where all her friends and family were, she insisted. Charlotte knew better: "Most of all, she didn't want to leave the church. . . . She had nothing else but drudgery and disappointment, not a thing."

Outside of activities related to St. John's, Frances did not socialize with Eleanor. Edward, on the other hand, frequently visited 49 Carman Street. His presence wasn't necessarily a cause for suspicion. House calls came with the job, and Eleanor was heavily involved in matters related to the church, where Frances had been Charlotte's Sunday school teacher. Sometimes Edward would pop by in the evenings and join the family around an old banged-up piano, lending his seasoned tenor to classics like "Love's Old Sweet Song" and "In the Gloaming." Charlotte cherished a big red book he had given her, filled with sheet music to marches and ballads. Edward gifted books to Eleanor as well, including a Bible written in German, which she counted among her most treasured possessions.

Edward also sent letters from his travels. "I hope some day you will visit Boston and see for yourself some of these beautiful buildings and statues—and other places too," Hall wrote in one. "My regards to all the family." Jim liked the Halls just fine, but he never let Eleanor forget that they were cut from a different cloth. "They're high monkey-monks," he would say, in Charlotte's recollection (although surely she meant "muckety mucks"). "You're not in their class and never will be."

THE EXACT PROVENANCE OF EDWARD and Eleanor's love affair is a mystery. In one telling, the flames began when Eleanor accepted work as a part-time housekeeper for Edward's elderly mother. In another, the seeds were planted when Reverend Hall was summoned to act as a peacemaker in a quarrel between Eleanor and her mother-in-law. Others suggested a lovestruck encounter when Edward ministered to Eleanor during an illness. Perhaps the sparks began to fly after one of the Friday choir rehearsals Edward regularly attended, or as they locked eyes during Sunday mass, Eleanor crooning from the choir stall, Edward gazing at her from the pulpit. In some ways they seemed like kindred spirits: two talented singers, well-read, upwardly ambitious, yearning to better themselves in life, each mired in an unsatisfying union with a considerably older spouse.

Whatever the case, in the several years leading up to the murders, it was clear that a strong bond had formed. They were frequent companions, and Eleanor came to be seen as an influential member of Hall's inner circle, a development that aroused jealousy and resentment among members of the congregation. Their intimate rapport was evident by at least 1917, when Eleanor entered the hospital with appendicitis and Hall kept a bedside vigil. As Eleanor later told Charlotte, the reverend pleaded, "You must get well, Eleanor, you must, for my sake."

In the year or two before Eleanor died, Charlotte began to sense a change in her mother. Eleanor seemed happier than she'd ever been. She smiled more, laughed more, sang more, and, as Charlotte noticed, she always seemed to be at her best upon returning from a visit with Reverend Hall. She spent more and more time at St. John's, whether to help with errands, replenish the flowers in Hall's study, or bring him one of her fresh-baked apple cakes. Eventually, the amount of time and attention Eleanor lavished on St. John's became a flash point in her quarrels with Jim. "There isn't another married woman that runs up there like you," he barked during one such feud. "This has got to be stopped." In another caustic exchange, Jim snapped, "You would do more for the church than you would do for me." To which Eleanor replied, "Yes, why wouldn't I? I care more for Mr. Hall's little finger than I do for your whole body."

As far as outward appearances went, Edward and Eleanor

passed off their relationship as that of a close friendship and spiritual bond—a doting minister and one of his most loyal parishioners.
But gossip simmered within the congregation. The reverend and
Mrs. Mills were a little too close. She had too much of a spell over
him. She stepped out of bounds—too forward, too sure of herself.
How did she always know about certain church affairs before they
were announced? Who did she think she was rearranging the list of
hymns after they had been agreed upon, knowing she could count
on the reverend's approval? As one choir member put it, "Mrs. Mills
was of a very antagonistic disposition. She usually got her way because Mr. Hall usually backed her up on what she wanted."

After Edward and Eleanor were found dead on the Phillips
farm, the gossip spilled into public view. But in the weeks leading
up to the murders, they relished their secret love affair and dreamed
of a new life together, one without the baggage of their marriages,
the prying eyes of their church mates, and the cruel opprobrium of
polite society.

In the summer of 1922, as Edward and Frances prepared to em-
bark on their annual vacation to Islesford, Maine, an island hamlet
south of Bar Harbor, Edward and Eleanor hatched a plan to keep
diaries for one another during their three weeks apart. They met
furtively on the morning of his departure, sharing a few "sweet"
but "all so short" moments, in Edward's recollection, before the time
came for him to set off on the journey north. His eyes lingered on
Eleanor as she turned and walked away down the street, only a half
mile from the spot where their mutilated bodies would be found a
month and a half later.

The Halls' boat from New York set sail late that afternoon.
"Every moment I have been with you dear dear heart," Edward
journaled while on board, headed for a stopover in Boston. "Every
moment you are with me."

He filled his foggy New England holiday with hikes and boat

rides, books and socials, solitary reverie and theological contemplation. Sometimes he played the organ in the guild room of the inn where he and Frances stayed. Every night, he scribbled away in his small brown book for Eleanor. "I want to fondle and caress you oh so much. I want to hold you close to my arms and know you are safe and happy and warm. Dearest we were made for each other's arms—that is our heaven. Our home and every moment away from there is a moment away from home. Good night dear, dearly beloved. All the universe of love crushed into my love for you."

The highlights of Edward's vacation were his trips to a larger adjacent island, where there was a post office. Letters from Eleanor sometimes awaited him. "I want letters every five minutes now—I am a Pig pig pig," he gushed in his diary after receiving one on August 5. "Oh how I devoured every letter of the card and the envelope." Edward wrote to Eleanor by post as well. He usually kept the messages discreet, lest Jim should stumble upon them, but sometimes he simply couldn't help himself. He signed his letters "D.T.L.," short for the German words *dein treue liebe*, "your faithful love." The letters alluded to a rendezvous on the Friday of his return to New Brunswick, August 25. The two lovers often met at a secluded bench in Buccleuch Park, a short walk from De Russey's Lane and the old Phillips farm. In one particularly steamy missive, Edward wrote:

My own true dear loyal and wonderful gypsy Queen. . . . Perhaps it would be better to meet at our Road on Friday afternoon than at 49 what do you think? But to see you anyway and to hold you, crush you and pour my burning kisses on your dear body and to look deep deep into those wonderful eyes of love! and just drink of the most wonderful things in life—Our love. Wholly-completely yours—dear heart—storing up health and strength to be your Gypsy King—strong in that love which has the strength and calm and peace of those quaint hills and the depth and wonder and mystery of these refreshing glittering seas about me. Rejoice. Dearest—dream, dream, dream . . . Life is infinitely sweet and blessed, to have known such love as we have known is to know God, to know eternal life, to know bliss in its greatest ecstasy. Please, dear heart, and blessing, for I love you more than words can tell and my every prayer is for the Divinest blessings for you. And to know that even this love is growing, ever growing.

D.T.L.

Edward and Eleanor surreptitiously exchanged love letters in New Brunswick as well, sometimes using Eleanor's hymnal as a vessel. The letters found between their bodies revealed Eleanor's all-consuming passions for her "true priest," her "dearest darling boy," her "babykins"—a mix of saccharine musings and pent-up sexual energy, overlaid with bursts of religious fervor. "Do I love you too much?" she wrote in one. "I know that now I could leave you, yes, Even your physical presence, and go into a convent. You are always in my mind and heart but there I wouldn't see anyone else touch you, call you 'dear,' rub your tired body."

In other letters, Eleanor dissected the plot of *The Mother of All Living* by Robert Keable, a former Episcopalian minister whose earlier novel, *Simon Called Peter*, tells the story of a priest's affair with a nurse. *The Mother of All Living* also centers around adultery. "This man Keable certainly knows people's hearts," Eleanor wrote. "I love Chris and Cecil's few hours together, how he vows he will kiss her before leaving Mallory's. Oh, it is sweet darling—but nothing compared to our love."

Above all, the letters betrayed Eleanor's thirst for something bigger and better than the life she knew:

Oh darling if I had an income of my own, I would be very selfish I guess. I'd build a waiting love nest where I could dream unmolested and not care if I ever saw people to talk to. Books and music, pictures, oh what treasures I would have. The birds, butterflies, wild squirrels and all I could see in the woods and fields and sky is my dream. People would

*mean nothing. I'd rather watch the bugs and ants as they crawl along—
don't you love to watch an ant as it creeps along? Honey there isn't a
house large enough for me. My dreams are as big as the earth. I need
the great outdoors to breathe, live in. Nature, as God created it, is what
I feel a part of and I am a part of it—it calls me just as I yearn for the
truest things. And darling sweetheart, that is why I long for our love to
be the truest—ideal—as pure as we can make it, for then it is truest to
nature and things of God's creating.*

Eleanor had more to say, but she had to cut the letter short.
"Darling, I could rave for hours, but I must stop as there are peepers
around."

BACK AT 49 CARMAN STREET on the afternoon of September 16, Jim
processed the shock of his wife's death as Charlotte dried her eyes.
A neighbor informed Jim that he was wanted down at Hubbard's
Morgue, where the bodies had been taken. Jim arrived in a daze
and was greeted by Detective George Totten, who held up a pack
of letters scrawled in what appeared to be a woman's hand. Some
of the penmanship was borderline undecipherable, but Jim knew it
well. "That's my wife's handwriting," Jim said. Totten then officially
delivered the news already flying all over town: Jim's wife had been
found dead with Reverend Hall.

Totten had some questions for the widower. He drove them to
Jim's workplace, the Lord Stirling School, to sit down for a preliminary interrogation.

Later that day, as newspaper reporters descended on New
Brunswick to cover a story that would dominate front pages in the
months to come, Jim gave his first interview to the press. "Dr. Hall
was my best friend," he declared, embellishing their relationship.
"When I was down and out this summer he came and took me to
the hospital. He took care of me like a father. He was the kindest
man I ever knew and his heart was tender for anybody in trouble.

He wouldn't have hurt a hair on anyone's head, and I can't explain why he was killed. Nobody had threatened either him or my wife as far as I know."

Jim's soliloquy continued, "I can't explain why he or my wife were together there or wherever else they might have been, unless it was to talk over some church matters. They worked together a great deal. I can't imagine Dr. Hall and his wife ever having words about my wife. The Halls were such a loving couple, he was so devoted to her. They were not the kind of people to have words about anything. They were so gentle and kind."

With these remarks, Jim painted a wholesome and sanitized picture of two marriages that had, in reality, broken down. Despite his obfuscation, the truth was about to come out.

6

"HARK! HARK, MY SOUL!"

Frances Hall was first questioned on the morning of Sunday, September 17. In deference to the wealthy widow, the authorities left her alone on Saturday to grieve, even as they grilled Eleanor's less privileged husband, Jim Mills. Now that Frances had taken time to collect herself, she had no choice but to open her door to Detective George Totten and his boss, Somerset County Prosecutor Azariah Beekman. They arrived at her mansion, where the family attorney, Edwin Florance, waited beside her.

The hour-long interrogation was predictably tame, apart from a moment when Beekman euphemistically gauged Frances's awareness of the "intimate friendship" between her husband and Mrs. Mills. "I would not call it an intimate friendship," Frances replied. She responded promptly and confidently, albeit a bit anxiously, to each question. A few matters in particular needed clearing up.

The first matter concerned two witnesses who'd reported a curious sighting in the early hours of Friday morning. Allan Bennett, a neighbor of the Halls', and William Phillips, night watchman for the New Jersey State Women's College across the street, had been roused by the barking of Bennett's dog between 2:30 and 3:00 A.M.

They went outside to determine what had provoked the canine out-burst and saw a woman dressed in a polo coat. She slipped through the gate of 23 Nichol Avenue and entered the house. The woman, as it turned out, was Frances Hall. She confirmed this to Totten and Beekman while nervously describing her movements on the night of Edward's disappearance.

Frances explained that, after Edward's telephone call, he told Frances he was heading to the church. Eleanor had summoned him with questions regarding the hospital bill from her kidney operation. Frances didn't expect Edward to be out very long, but the minutes of his absence turned into hours. Concerned and anxious, she asked her brother Willie to accompany her to St. John's. Maybe Edward had fallen asleep in his study? Around 2:00 A.M., they walked to the church and, finding the doors locked and the lights off, returned home. They entered through the rear door, Frances said, failing to account for why only she, and not Willie, had been seen doing so. She couldn't explain why or how Edward ended up in that field with Eleanor. As Beekman recalled, "Mrs. Hall said that she knew of nobody who had a grievance against him."

Frances and Willie weren't the only ones who paid a visit to St. John's in the middle of the night. Jim Mills must have just missed them, or vice versa. After waking up around 2:00 A.M. and realizing Eleanor hadn't returned, he threw on a pair of overalls and walked over.

"I thought that my wife had been taken sick in the church," Jim told Beekman in a separate interrogation on September 17. "She was not a strong woman, and I knew of no other place to look for her. . . . I looked all over the church for her but there was nothing to indicate that she had been there."

Jim and Frances crossed paths several times the next day, first encountering one another at St. John's around 7:00 A.M.

"My husband hasn't been home since last night," Frances said.

"My wife hasn't been home since last night either," Jim replied.

Later that morning, Frances twice visited 49 Carman Street to speak with Jim. During one of their conversations, Jim said, "What do you think? Is it an elopement?"

"It must be foul play, or they would be home," Frances replied.

Frances later denied hearing Jim say this, and Jim claimed the elopement remark was "just something that came into my mind." His explanation strained credulity, but then again, whenever someone prodded Jim about his wife's cheating, he pleaded ignorance. "I take no stock in any of the malicious stories that are now going around," he told a reporter. Jim even had an explanation for the love letters. "She was fond of reading books of romance. She very often copied passages from these books that struck her fancy. She used to carry them in her brown scarf, and one day I demanded that she show them to me. They were harmless things, so I forgot about them."

Later in the afternoon on the day the bodies were discovered, Frances sat on the front porch preparing funeral notices. Jim walked up the driveway of the Hall mansion, climbed the front steps, and collapsed into a chair, regaining his composure after Frances fetched aromatic spirits of ammonia. When he asked Frances what she thought of the whole situation, Frances wept, declaring of her husband, "I would trust him more than I would trust myself."

A WEEK LATER, ON SUNDAY, September 23, Frances stepped out of a detective's car in front of the Middlesex County Courthouse, accompanied by one of her maids, Louise Geist, and her best friend, Sally Clarkson Peters. A fervent suffragist and member of the League of Women Voters, Peters was the same age as Frances, with the same privileged Episcopal upbringing. At forty-eight, they were as close as two people could be outside the bonds of marriage. With Edward's death, Sally became an even more intimate companion, rushing down from New York as soon as she caught wind of the tragedy, and never straying far from Frances's side.

To avoid detection by the growing number of journalists stalking about town, Frances entered the courthouse through the basement, sneaking in by way of a door intended for coal delivery. Once inside, she lowered herself into a chair in the offices of Middlesex County Prosecutor Joseph Stricker, where she was questioned for two hours. A stenographer took notes as the assembled officials pressured Frances to concede her husband's infidelity, each inquiry a bit more impertinent than the last.

"You suspect Mr. Hall and Mrs. Mills might have gone away together?"

"No. Absolutely no."

"They had always been extremely friendly?"

"Friendly, yes."

"No one else in Dr. Hall's company as much as Mrs. Mills?"

"I should say he saw others as much as he did her."

"Did not Dr. Hall receive a great many telephone calls from Mrs. Mills?"

"I should say only occasionally."

"Didn't it seem that Mr. Hall and Mrs. Mills were extremely friendly?"

"No."

"No suggestion of improper relations between them?"

"Absolutely none."

Toward the end, it was suggested that the widow's "anxiety to preserve [Edward's] reputation in the community, and to keep intact [her] belief in him," outweighed her desire to see his killer apprehended.

"I am so sure of his guiltlessness," Frances shot back, "that no matter what came to light—"

She paused.

"You must certainly want the guilty party brought to justice?" one of the interrogators continued. "If that had to be done at the expense of disclosing some things that would not reflect well on the character of your husband, would you want that done?"

"His friends know he can do no wrong," Frances countered, "whatever you have found."

When Frances emerged from the courthouse nearly two and a half hours later, the press awaited. She held up her handbag to block the cameras, her face obscured by a heavy mourning veil that Julia Harpman, of the *Daily News*, described as being "as black as the night which clothed in secrecy the movements of the slayer." Amid the frenzy, Frances stumbled and had to practically be lifted into a waiting car. Sally Peters announced to reporters that Frances would dictate a prepared statement back at 23 Nichol Avenue.

When the reporters arrived, Frances invited one of them inside to represent all the newspapers in a brief interview. She entered the drawing room on Peters's arm, in a black crepe de chine dress, no jewelry, her gray hair brushed back from her broad forehead. She began with the prepared statement, detailing her movements from the Wednesday before Edward's disappearance to the Saturday morning when he was found. Then she entertained questions.

"Did you have any feeling of enmity or jealousy toward Mrs. Mills, or did you ever quarrel with her?"

"Absolutely not."

"Or anyone else?"

"No."

"You have stated that you do not know the perpetrators of the crime. Do you know anybody who might have done this, or have you any ideas to the motive?"

"Not the slightest," Frances replied, tears welling behind her pince-nez glasses. "I have the utmost trust and confidence in my husband, and I know of nothing wrong that he has ever done."

THE NOTION THAT JIM AND Frances were ignorant of the affair defied reason. Rumors had circulated for some time, and their virulence was now laid bare. "People are coming forward," the *New York Times* reported, "to tell of having seen Dr. Hall and Mrs. Mills together on lonely roads outside New Brunswick in the past." There was the pharmacist on Easton Avenue who served them ice cream sodas. There was the boy at school who asked Charlotte Mills, "What are your mother and Dr. Hall doing so often together up in the sixth ward?" There was the man who'd bumped into Edward and Eleanor on a train back from Manhattan one evening. "It was not any of my business if they ran around on expeditions," he said.

St. John's teemed with gossip. Members of the choir, as one of them told the local newspaper, had been "acutely conscious" of Edward and Eleanor's "intimacy" for two years—the way they danced together at church socials, the sight of Eleanor accompanying the reverend to his study at the conclusion of every rehearsal. Investigators learned that Eleanor was known to leave notes for Edward in the church kitchen, between the pages of a hymnal or prayer book, in a large book on a low shelf in Edward's study. There were whispers she had left one for him the day of the murders. A shed behind the church was said to be their secret love nest. One day, in the summer of 1921, a man from the choir spotted Edward and Eleanor in Manhattan, walking together "like bride and bridegroom" in front of the Rivoli Theatre at Broadway and Forty-eighth Street. "Mrs. Mills was hanging on Mr. Hall's arm with both hands," he told the authorities. "She was looking up at his face, smiling."

Other parishioners said Edward and Eleanor had spent several days together at the Haddon Hall Hotel in Atlantic City, where they were seen splashing around in the ocean. A vestryman named Ralph Gorsline, who would later become a key figure in the case, admitted that one of his colleagues "had gone to Rev. Mr. Hall, and in a friendly spirit, spoken to him about the gossip and suggested to him that measures of some sort be taken to put an end to the unpleasant situation." One of the most well-traveled tales involved a summer retreat at Point Pleasant for the women of the congregation. On the first day, Frances had accompanied the group down the shore to help them settle in. When Edward and Eleanor went for a spin in the reverend's sedan, "Mrs. Hall raised ructions," according to someone familiar with the incident, who noted that "Mr. Hall and Mrs. Mills were the talk of all Point Pleasant." Another day, when Edward left to drive one of the women home, Eleanor threw herself down on a cot and burst into tears. "When he goes away, one half of me goes with him," she wailed.

The most tantalizing revelations came from Eleanor's friends and family. Her next-door neighbor Millie Opie told reporters that the reverend would visit three or four times a week, usually in the afternoons when Jim was at work. Eleanor once confided to Millie that she was so unhappy in her marriage, she considered fleeing for an Episcopalian retreat. "I have got to get away," she said.

There was talk that Edward and Eleanor were planning to run away to Japan or China. One of Eleanor's sisters, Elsie Barnhardt, told an investigator that Edward was prepared to leave Frances whenever Eleanor "said the word." These rumors gained credence with the discovery in Edward's safe deposit box of roughly forty thousand dollars in securities, mostly Liberty bonds. He had acquired ten thousand dollars of that sum in 1921, when Frances's mother died and her estate was settled. It was unclear how he had come to possess the remainder of it, or for what purpose he had squirreled it away.

EDWARD HALL WAS LAID TO rest on Monday, September 18, two days after the discovery of his body. Although Jim Mills did not attend, parishioners filled the pews of St. John's for his funeral, and it was noted that the majority were women. A hush came over the congregation as Frances Hall walked slowly into the church, escorted by her brothers, Henry and Willie Stevens. Purple asters, pink carnations, and multicolor orchids adorned her husband's casket. She settled into a pew and lowered her head, keeping it bowed even as she rose to the chords of the opening hymn, "Hark! Hark, My Soul!"

After a brief and simple service, the funeral party pushed past a crowd of some two hundred onlookers, including a small army of photographers who furiously snapped away as Henry shielded his sister from the cameras. Three limousines and a hearse soon departed for Brooklyn, where Edward was interred in the Stevens family vault at Green-Wood Cemetery. As his body was sealed away for all eternity, Frances steeled herself. She didn't shed a tear.

Eleanor's funeral the following morning at Hubbard's Morgue was humble by comparison, although Charlotte did manage to send her mother to the grave in a six-hundred-dollar solid mahogany coffin, bearing a wreath of dahlias sent by Frances Hall. (Some speculated that Frances paid for the coffin as well.) Of the twenty attendees, none of Eleanor's fellow choir members came to pay their respects. Jim buried his face in his hands and Charlotte's sobs rose above a clergyman's eulogy. As the mourners sang "Jesus, Lover of My Soul," an undertaker tiptoed around swatting flies.

After the service, the funeral cortege drove to Van Liew Cemetery in North Brunswick for Eleanor's burial. Both victims had now been sanctified and returned to the earth. But for their loved ones, closure remained elusive.

"BILLY GOAT! BILLY GOAT!"

One of the first tasks for the authorities was to stitch together a timeline of Edward and Eleanor's movements. They established that, sometime between seven and seven thirty on the night of the murders, Eleanor ran into her neighbor Millie Opie. She asked Millie's opinion of the new polka-dot dress she was wearing. She'd made it herself, trimmed with the same ribbon Edward had used to tie Christmas gifts for Eleanor. Millie, who owned a phone that Eleanor sometimes used, told Eleanor that Edward had called earlier that afternoon and left a message. Eleanor went home, where she saw Charlotte, preparing to leave for a visit with her aunt. Eleanor found a nickel to call Edward from a pay phone at the grocery store around the block, telling Charlotte to wait for her. The grocer overheard Eleanor planning to meet someone. Minutes later, back at the house, Charlotte was already gone, never to see her mother again. Eleanor then caught a trolley a few blocks away.

Meanwhile, Edward was seen walking along George Street, away from the Hall mansion. "It's a fine day, isn't it?" he remarked to a married couple who sat on their porch across from St. John's. Eleanor was next seen getting off a trolley at the end of the line on

Easton Avenue, near Buccleuch Park. Witnesses placed Hall in this vicinity around the same time. One woman swore she'd passed both separately, within minutes of each other, around 8:00 P.M. Each was walking in the direction of the Phillips farm, Eleanor "in a dreadful hurry," Edward with his hands in his pockets.

Numerous people who lived near the farm described hearing shrieks and gunshots a short while later, although there was little agreement on the exact time. Nine o'clock? Eleven thirty? One resident, Norman Tingle, who had been stargazing with his wife, recalled hearing three or four shots between a quarter after ten and ten forty-five. "They were fired within a half minute of one another," he told Beekman and Totten. Norman's wife, Nettie, thought she heard a woman screaming right before the shots rang out. The incident transpired shortly after they'd seen a shooting star, which Nettie believed was a harbinger of death. "Somebody has gone west," she had said.

As the days turned into weeks, officials still had no idea what happened in those dark fields, or why. The absence of a weapon, as well as the nature of the wounds, ruled out the possibility of a suicide pact or a murder-suicide. Frances and her handlers insisted it must have been a robbery gone awry. Edward's gold pocket watch was missing, and no cash was found on his body, even though he was known to carry money.

The authorities entertained a different theory, which took shape as the investigation progressed into the fall. They posited that the unoccupied but still furnished farmhouse on the Phillips property, about seventy-five feet from the crabapple tree, had served as a trysting spot. Someone, or some people, followed Edward and Eleanor to the farm. A confrontation ensued. It turned physical, accounting for scratches that the coroner had noticed on Eleanor's face and Edward's hands. Amid the scuffle, a pistol was drawn. Screams. Shots. Silence. Afterward, Eleanor's throat was cut, and the bodies were staged. It was a crime of anger and vengeance, but also of intimacy.

Evidence emerged to suggest the killings had taken place where the bodies were discovered. The prosecution had ordered a soil analysis from the laboratory of E. R. Squibb & Sons, known today as Bristol Myers Squibb. "If the carotid arteries of a person weighing 129 lbs were severed after the heart had stopped beating," the Squibb report found, "the volume of blood shed under these conditions might be as little as one pint. . . . The fact that only 0.8 of a pint of blood was found in the soil on which the bodies of Rev. Hall and Mrs. Mills were found is very good evidence that Mrs. Mills was shot before her throat was cut. . . . Nor is it likely that we would have found 0.8 of a pint of blood in the soil if the bodies had been transported to the spot after the murder."

What catalyst had set the grisly chain of events in motion? Investigators focused on one of the love letters discovered with the bodies, which they believed Eleanor had left for Edward the morning of the murders. Had someone found the note and read it before Edward did? Was this the final indignity for one of their spouses? Perhaps. But there were no witnesses or evidence linking Frances or Jim to the crime scene. Willie Stevens vouched for his sister's statement. The Halls' gardener and handyman, Peter Tumulty, a sturdy guy with white hair, confirmed that neither of the Halls' cars had been used on the night of the murders. Frances came under suspicion for sending the coat she'd worn that night to a cleaner in Philadelphia. But it turned out she'd had the coat dyed black as part of her mourning wardrobe, and the employee who received it didn't see any bloodstains. As for Jim, he'd conversed with his downstairs neighbor at 9:00 P.M. and was seen purchasing a bottle of soda water at the corner store near his house around eleven. Charlotte confirmed Jim was home when she went to bed around ten fifteen, after she and Daniel had returned from visiting their aunt. She said there was "nothing unusual" about her father's behavior.

Frances's brothers did not escape suspicion. It just so happened that Henry, now nearing his fifty-third birthday, was an expert marksman. A graduate of Rutgers College, Henry had gone into the arms and ammunition trade after working as an engineer for a bridge company. His job involved going out on the road for Remington Arms and demonstrating shotguns. Later in his career, he operated a shooting school at Atlantic City's Million Dollar Pier. Henry had retired from the arms business in 1920, but his home in Lavallette, a toothpick of a town separating the Atlantic Ocean from Barnegat Bay, boasted a gun room.

Henry was a consummate outdoorsman, five foot eight with a ruddy face, thick graying hair, and a black mustache not quite as robust as his younger brother's. Henry and his New England–bred wife, Ethel, enjoyed their quiet life at the beach with Henry's eighteen-foot boat. They'd recently given up a Manhattan apartment in order to live year-round in their twelve-room oceanfront colonial. It was the largest house in Lavallette, filled with brass lamps and expensive paintings and the smell of burning driftwood, as well as books on astronomy, birding, and hunting. Henry was fond of trap-shooting, but he said it had been nearly twenty years since he'd fired an ordinary revolver, and he swore he'd never fired an automatic, the weapon believed to have killed his brother-in-law.

Henry's alibi placed him about fifty miles southeast of the murder scene, on the beach in Lavallette. He was fishing there until half past ten with several other locals who could vouch for his whereabouts. Two days later, on Saturday afternoon, he'd barely gotten a line out when a station agent from town approached him on the boardwalk and placed a telegram in his hand. It was from Henry's cousin Edwin Carpender: "Edward has been killed."

Henry ran back to the house, got dressed, and caught the first train to New Brunswick. At a transfer station, newsboys were hawking that afternoon's edition of the *Daily Home News*, hot off the presses. The murders were all over the front page.

"That was the first I knew of it," Henry told prosecutors, referring to the fact that Edward's death was a homicide.

Willie, fifty years old and an inveterate bachelor, also owned a firearm, which he kept "under lock and key" inside 23 Nichol Avenue. There were conflicting reports as to whether it was a .38 or a .32, the latter being the type of gun that fired the fatal shots. In either case, it didn't matter: Willie's revolver was corroded, and the firing pin had been filed off, rendering it useless.

Willie aroused the authorities' interest nonetheless, if only because of his oddball nature. For starters, there was Willie's decidedly juvenile fascination with firefighters. He visited them daily at the headquarters of Hook & Ladder Co. No. 3, to play cards or run errands or shoot the breeze. With a modest allowance that Willie received from the family trust, he treated the firemen to steaks and helped them cook dinner. He was considered an honorary member, permitted to ride in a fire truck on occasion, to try on their uniforms, and to march in their parades, proudly carrying an American flag that he'd bought them. When a major fire broke out at a grocery store, Willie was seen running down the steps of the Hall mansion to battle the conflagration, only to be summoned back inside like a child. Allegedly, he once started a small fire in his own backyard, donned a helmet, and valiantly extinguished the blaze.

In addition to hanging around with firefighters, who found him to be as harmless as he was amusing, Willie enjoyed wintering in Florida and summering down the shore. He also frequented New Brunswick's downtrodden Hungarian quarter, loafing on front stoops and chatting with the locals, sometimes writing letters for them to earn a little extra money. He was warm with the neighborhood children, but not inappropriately so—he sent one little girl a box of fruit from Florida. The Hungarians found Willie to be good-hearted and kind, and they earned his friendship because they didn't laugh at him, apart from certain youngsters who would tease, "Billy goat! Billy goat!" Willie was sensitive to taunts. Sometimes he would storm out of the fire station yelling, "I am not coming in here anymore!"—only to come crawling back the following day. He cut a duncelike figure in the newspapers, which evoked such phrases as "the subnormal individuality of 'Fireman Willie' Stevens." Prosecutors similarly described Willie as having "the mind of a child."

Willie may have been childlike, but he wasn't stupid. The books in his bedroom included tomes on engineering, botany, entomology, metallurgy, and other esoteric subjects, which Willie studied while puffing his pipe. He had an impressive memory, whether reciting the history of an old Spanish chapel or rattling off the Latin names of flowers. His was a fascinating mind, but in 1922, the study of the mind was inchoate. A widespread clinical interest in developmental psychology didn't begin to take hold until the end of the decade. A new term, "autism," first emerged in the early 1900s, referring to a subset of schizophrenia. It wasn't until the 1940s that the disorder and its close cousin, Asperger's syndrome, were first explained as we know them today. Willie, in retrospect, may well have fallen somewhere on this spectrum. But without a nuanced vocabulary to describe his intellectual capacity, people generally regarded him as a wackadoo. He'd had enough of that.

On the afternoon of September 29, following a ninety-minute interview with investigators, Willie emerged from the courthouse in downtown New Brunswick escorted by two detectives. He stopped to address the assembled journalists.

"I want you fellows to understand that I don't want to be referred to as 'Willie' anymore," he said. "You must address me either as William or Mr. Stevens. I'm not a half-wit, as you have been saying, and I'm not a sissy."

Willie pulled from his pocket what one newspaperman described as "as manly looking and evil smelling a briar pipe as one would want to see." He thrusted it in front of the reporters' noses. "Smell that!"

Pipe or no pipe, there was no denying that Willie was coddled by his younger sister and unable to control his own finances. The $150,000 he was said to have inherited from his mother had been put into a trust at Henry's suggestion. Detectives were told that Edward Hall controlled Willie's meager weekly stipend, and that he and Willie had quarreled over it. They also heard talk of suspicious comments Willie had made. Days after the bodies were found, he popped into a cigar store and said to the owner, "I want you to deny any rumor you hear regarding . . . our family." In another instance, the day *before* the bodies were found, Willie was gabbing with Captain Michael Regan at Hook & Ladder Co. No. 3. Regan remarked that things were slow around town. Willie replied something to the effect of "Maybe they are now, but something big is going to pop soon." Willie later told reporters, "I did say something like that, but I meant nothing by it. I was only joking." The family attorney, Edwin Florance, said, "If you knew Willie as I did, you wouldn't be surprised at anything he said. Willie is not to be taken seriously."

Despite the voluminous scuttlebutt, officials weren't any closer to figuring out who had killed Edward Hall and Eleanor Mills. Asked about the state of the investigation toward the end of September, John Toolan, the assistant prosecutor for Middlesex County, said, "We haven't eliminated anybody."

There was, however, at least one person with a strong hunch about the murders.

8

THE FLAPPER

The day before her mother's funeral, Charlotte Mills received an unexpected visitor. Peter Tumulty, the Halls' gardener, came with a special delivery for the bereaved sixteen-year-old. Frances and her entourage were on their way to Brooklyn, where Edward was to be interred at Green-Wood Cemetery. Before the limos pulled away, Frances had written a message for Charlotte on a piece of heavy parchment stationery, embossed with a large gold *H* at the top and bold script below:

> *Dear Charlotte,*
> *Do not worry. Everything will be alright. You will be looked out for.*
> *Sincerely,*
> *Mrs. Hall*

Later, Charlotte showed the note to reporters. Her eyes welled with tears as she lamented, "I don't think they'll ever get the person who did it. Mrs. Hall knows less than anyone else, I think."

Within the week, Charlotte's opinion of her former Sunday school teacher turned to ice. "Although Mom liked Mrs. Hall very much, I never did like her," she said, speaking to reporters at the home of her aunt Augusta Tennyson. "We never got along together, either when I was in Sunday school or personally." According to Julia Harpman of the *Daily News*, Charlotte "bitterly assailed the widow of the rector, declaring that she hated Mrs. Hall." Harpman pointed out that Charlotte had spoken warmly of Frances just a few days earlier, but Charlotte wouldn't elaborate on her volte-face. She would only say, "I have changed my opinion about that." Speculating about the killer, Charlotte said, "A woman did it, and it was a woman who was jealous of my mother and wanted revenge." She described an incident that she'd shared with detectives: Eleanor once fell ill after drinking a cup of coffee prepared by Frances. Eleanor later joked that if the coffee hadn't come from Frances, she would have thought "somebody was trying to poison me." Maybe somebody *was* trying to poison her, Charlotte implied. She didn't accuse Frances directly, but she tiptoed tantalizingly close. "I think more than one person killed my mother," she said. "A woman directly connected with the immediate families concerned, I am sure, can solve the mystery."

In Charlotte Mills, the newspapers found an alluring subject, pert and vivacious, with good looks, confidence, charisma, and a requisite dash of theatrics. "She speaks her mind freely, and she looks older than she is," the *New York Herald* observed, noting that despite Charlotte's tender age of sixteen, "she appears sometimes to have the wisdom of 30."

Bursting with ambition and dressed in the latest cuts, her dark hair cropped into a stylish ear-length bob, furs around her neck and skin showing below the knee, Charlotte was a symbol of modern femininity. Her generation was coming of age with the right to vote, a desire to work, a loss of inhibition, and visions of a life beyond dutiful homemaking. She could hardly lay claim to the cosmopolitan glamour of Manhattan's flapper set—the Zelda Fitzgeralds and Josephine Bakers of the world. But Charlotte nonetheless personified the spirit of the movement, described in a 1922 article titled "A Flapper's Appeal to Parents": "We are the Younger Generation. The war tore away our spiritual foundations and challenged our faith. We are struggling to regain our equilibrium. The times have made us older and more experienced than you were at our age." If Frances Hall represented the last gasps of a dying worldview, Charlotte Mills embodied the inexorable currents of change. Speaking to reporters at her aunt's house, she declared, "Mrs. Hall does not like flappers, and I'm a flapper."

CHARLOTTE'S INSINUATIONS WERE RED MEAT for the newspapers, which oozed speculation in the absence of any real progress in the case. The investigation was, by all accounts, a bumbling one, compounded by the reality that modern forensics was still in its infancy. The first police crime laboratory wasn't established until 1910 in Lyon, France, by the renowned criminologist Edmond Locard. By the early 1920s, American pioneers such as August Vollmer and Oscar Heinrich had broken new ground in ballistics, fingerprint pattern matching, and handwriting and bloodstain pattern analysis. But the meticulous application of science hadn't penetrated the broader American police complex, especially not a relative backwater like central New Jersey.

The earliest stages of the Hall-Mills investigation were at best insufficient, and at worst comically ham-handed. The crime scene had been treated with utter carelessness. Reporters and civilians stomped about the bodies and handled the evidence. Not a single police photograph was taken. The initial autopsies, if you could even call them that, were cursory and vague. Somerset County physician William Long miscounted the bullet wounds and paid little regard to Eleanor's near decapitation: "Anterior surface of neck badly decomposed, probably due to some external violence." Long did, however, see fit to open Eleanor's abdomen, confirming she was not with child. He later claimed he had performed only a "superficial examination" because Beekman, the county prosecutor, did not order a full autopsy. Beekman, in turn, claimed he was under the impression that Totten had "[taken] the matter up" with Long.

To rectify these errors, a posse of detectives and gravediggers set out under cover of darkness on Friday, September 29, toward Van Liew Cemetery in North Brunswick. Beekman, in the face of mounting pressure not only from the press, but from the governor of New Jersey, had ordered the bodies to be exhumed. Carrying pickaxes and lanterns, and taking care to avoid the detection of reporters, the group trudged to the low mound of earth where Eleanor Mills had been buried ten days earlier. They worked swiftly by the light of their flames and spoke in hushed tones, managing to lift the coffin well before daybreak. Edward's exhumation followed a week later, when his body was removed from the Stevens family vault at Green-Wood Cemetery and taken to the nearby Kings County Morgue.

This time, not a nick or blemish went unnoticed. Edward's autopsy determined he had been killed by a single bullet, which entered his head above the right temple and popped out the back of his neck near his right ear. His assailant was fewer than three feet away when the trigger was pulled. The small, blood-clotted abrasions on Edward's hands and fingers suggested he may have put up a fight.

Eleanor had been shot three times—in the middle of the forehead, in her right temple, and through her right cheek. Each bullet had cracked her skull and any one of them would have been enough to cause death. There was a fourth wound in the middle of her upper lip, which may have been caused by a stray bullet. "An 8 inch necklace incision," the autopsy report stated, "was found at the root of the neck, penetrating to the anterior vertebrae. . . . The windpipe was severed and retracted. The carotid arteries and interior jugular veins were severed on both sides. The esophagus was severed, also the soft parts to the vertebrae. . . . In the back of the neck there remains but 4 inches of unsevered skin and tissue."

The belated autopsies weren't the only blunder to attract public scrutiny. Newspapers highlighted jurisdictional tensions that stymied the investigation. The bodies were found in Somerset County, but the victims and their families resided in Middlesex. Officials from both counties, with assistance from the New Jersey State Police, projected a spirit of cooperation. But conflicts spilled into view. The authorities in Middlesex would say an arrest was imminent; the Somerset authorities would say the opposite. Middlesex County Prosecutor Joseph Stricker would suggest they were getting closer and closer; Somerset County Prosecutor Azariah Beekman would concede they weren't really getting anywhere. Moreover, residents of rural Somerset County resented their tax dollars being spent on an investigation involving a bunch of fancy people from New Brunswick.

Perhaps no one felt more frustrated than Charlotte Mills, whose inference that Frances might have been involved blossomed into a full-throated indictment.

"I think the Hall family know almost everything that has happened," Charlotte told Beekman when he interviewed her on October 2.

"Charlotte," the prosecutor replied, "do you realize that people do not kill other people unless they have a motive for doing so? Why do you think that the Halls took the life of your mother?"

"Nothing but jealousy."

IN LATE SEPTEMBER, A LETTER arrived for Edward I. Edwards, the governor of New Jersey.

> *Dear Governor,*
>   *I am Charlotte Mills, of New Brunswick. My mother, as you know, was murdered two weeks ago and it seems to me that the investigation is not bringing results. I have received letters from strangers saying that*

the political gang is running things. Can that be true? As we have no means whatever to get legal help is there not some way, dear Governor, to help me find the murderer of my mother?

Anxiously,

Charlotte Mills

The letter appeared in newspapers on Thursday, September 28. Charlotte told the *Daily News* she wrote it on her own initiative, but investigators suspected she'd been encouraged by newspapermen. The day after her desperate plea appeared on the front pages, Charlotte turned up at Edwards's personal office in Jersey City, the power center of New Jersey's Democratic Party machine. The governor's secretary informed Charlotte that Edwards was out, and she waited around for an hour before heading back to New Brunswick. When Edwards learned of Charlotte's visit, he dictated a reply to her, which the *New York Times* printed in full. "My dear Miss Mills," the letter began. "I have read your pathetic appeal to me with profound regret and heartfelt sympathy for you in your extremely bereaved state of mind. I can assure you that even previous to receiving your communication, I had become actively engaged in endeavoring to assist, in every way possible, the authorities of Somerset and Middlesex Counties." Edwards said he had ordered the state troopers to take on a bigger role in the investigation, and he assured Charlotte that justice would be served. "There is no need for you to spend a single penny of your limited means to carry forward the investigation. . . . The shocked conscience of the State of New Jersey will never be satisfied until the murderer or murderers of your mother are apprehended."

Edwards summoned prosecutors Beekman and Stricker for a long meeting in Trenton. The media attention surrounding the case, much of it critical, had swelled to epic proportions, and the governor, now campaigning for a United States Senate seat, demanded

progress, as did local officials. The county freeholders of Middlesex and Somerset each offered a one-thousand-dollar reward for
information leading to an arrest and conviction. New Brunswick's
Daily Home News published scorching editorials, amplified by the
New York papers, calling for the murders to be solved. As the
leaves on the trees turned from green to red, the drumbeat of neg-
ative publicity reached a crescendo. The New York *Evening World*
summed it up nicely in a blistering takedown splashed across the
front page: BLUNDERS AND OMISSIONS IN HALL-MILLS MURDER CASE
SHOW STUPIDITY OR WORSE. It was time for the prosecutors to make
a move.

ON THE EVENING OF SATURDAY, October 7, detectives surprised Willie at home and hauled him down to the Somerset County Courthouse, without Frances or anyone else noticing. When Willie arrived
in a small, isolated room, Azariah Beekman and several other officials awaited him. For several hours, they went at Willie hard, each
interrogator holding a typewritten memorandum with transcripts
of everything Willie had said during their previous interviews over
the past three weeks. They made him go over the story again and
again, trying to catch him in any subtle deviation. They took out the
victims' bloodstained clothes and thrust them into Willie's hands.
They raised their voices and cursed and insisted Willie was hiding
something. For the most part, Willie took the inquisition calmly, but
at crucial moments, his temper flared. "Don't you call me a liar!" he
snapped. "You can't call me a liar!"

Back at the Hall mansion, Frances eventually realized Willie
was missing. Sally Peters went out to look for him around the neighborhood, but he was nowhere to be found. With no sign of Willie by
midnight, Sally got into one of Frances's cars and sped over to the
New Brunswick police station. Unaware that Willie was detained
in Somerville, the New Brunswick cops fanned out in pursuit while
Sally and others kept vigil with Frances. Around 2:00 A.M., they sat

in the drawing room as the Somerset County detectives pulled up to the rear of the house and dropped Willie off. Frances became enraged when Willie told her what had happened. She'd recently hired a new lawyer, Timothy N. Pfeiffer, a former New York prosecutor better equipped than her family attorney to handle a high-profile murder case. In a statement to reporters, Pfeiffer likened the midnight interrogation to a kidnapping. "The action of the prosecutors is like that of a bunch of Turks," he said. "Everything else having failed, they are going out with battle axes."

It was true that the prosecutors failed to extract anything incriminating. Their reputations were now on the line, and possibly, so were their careers. "This murder must be cleared up," Governor Edwards declared. "There has been too much time lost already. . . . I want the murderer arrested, whoever he is. I expected an arrest yesterday and was surprised when there was none. . . . The people of this state are anxious to have this mystery solved."

Thanks to Charlotte, Edwards's patience with Beekman was wearing thin. Luckily for Beekman, he already had a new suspect.

THE SIDESHOW

The night after Willie's interrogation, reporters stood around waiting for a newsbreak, on their twenty-third day chasing a mystery that had become a front-page sensation from New Brunswick to California. Four persons of interest were cloistered away inside the Middlesex County Courthouse, a hunk of Greek Revival architecture crawling with curious spectators. They had arrived throughout the evening, gathering around the building's six Doric pillars of California redwood. The *Daily Home News* put printing-press operators on standby in case an extra edition needed to be rushed out. "An arrest is certain tonight," the whispers went.

In an unexpected twist, authorities had circled back to the same people with whom their investigation began: Ray Schneider and Pearl Bahmer, the young man and his teenage companion who first alerted police to the bodies. Schneider had been inside the courthouse since midafternoon, Pearl since 7:00 P.M. Two of Schneider's pals were sweating under the interrogation lamps as well: Clifford Hayes, twenty-one, and Leon Kaufman, fifteen.

Authorities initially became interested in Ray and Pearl in connection with Edward Hall's missing gold watch, one of the most bedeviling details of the case. The timepiece was unaccounted for by the time Officers Edward Garrigan and James Curran arrived at the crime scene, before the crowds descended. It hadn't turned up in any pawnshops, all but negating the possibility of a robbery gone awry. Pearl had made conflicting statements about whether she'd seen the watch when she and Ray first laid eyes on the corpses, before summoning the police. She initially told detectives she had seen it, but later insisted she'd been mistaken. Separately, in an odd coincidence, newspapers alternately reported that Reverend Hall had baptized or confirmed Pearl the previous year, after she joined St. John's from a Roman Catholic parish. All of this warranted a closer look.

Prosecutors first questioned Ray and Pearl in late September. During the interrogation, Ray explained that they'd seen a movie at the Strand Theatre on the night of the murders, before going their separate ways around nine thirty. Ray then met up with Clifford Hayes and Leon Kaufman. He said they spent the rest of the evening knocking around aimlessly in Buccleuch Park, across from the Phillips farm. "Yes, we were out there late," Ray admitted. "Not very near the Phillips farm, but as far out as the Parker home. I didn't hear any shot or shouts or scream."

Two weeks later, the prosecution hauled in Ray, Pearl, Hayes, and Kaufman for further questioning, which is what brought those curious crowds to the courthouse on the evening of Sunday, October 8. Inside, a new picture of the night in question began to emerge. Kaufman said he bumped into Schneider and Hayes around ten thirty in front of the Rivoli Theatre. They saw Pearl with an older man who appeared to be drunk. Pearl and the man walked northwest, away from New Brunswick's downtown, in the direction of Johnson & Johnson and Rutgers. Ray insisted on trailing them. "Schneider took off his coat and said that he was going to fight the man," Kaufmann recalled. The trio pursued Pearl and her companion down an embankment toward the Raritan River, where

Pearl appeared to be crying. Schneider told his friends the man with Pearl was her no-good father, Nick Bahmer, the owner of a poolroom and speakeasy downtown, who vigorously objected to his adolescent daughter's association with Schneider. Hayes lifted his sweater and Kaufman saw that he had a pistol. "We're protected with this," Hayes said.

Pearl and Nick continued to walk along the river, their destination unclear. Schneider's group lingered behind, but by the time they came upon the entrance of Buccleuch Park, Pearl and Nick were nowhere to be seen. The three friends looked around, circling the perimeter, but there was no trace, so they walked to Schneider's house on the eastern lip of the park. The hour grew late, and Kaufman went home.

While Kaufman relayed this information to officials, reporters milled about the courthouse. He was released around 11:00 P.M. Pearl walked out shortly thereafter. Schneider and Hayes remained inside. Just before two o'clock in the morning, Middlesex County Prosecutor John Toolan appeared with an update: "We are working on a definite lead, but do not wish to divulge the nature of same at this time. When the matter is fully worked out we will give out the news."

It wasn't until noon the next day that Azariah Beekman gave the press its much-awaited scoop: "Upon information in the prosecutor's office, obtained from Schneider and other witnesses, we felt obliged under the situation to prefer a charge of murder against one Clifford Hayes."

THE INFORMATION LEADING TO HAYES'S arrest had been extracted after nearly twenty-four hours of intense questioning, the third degree. Hayes and Schneider were kept awake all night in separate rooms until Schneider finally cracked. He said that after splitting up with Kaufmann, he and Hayes wandered down Easton Avenue and

onto De Russey's Lane, looking for Pearl and Nick. Ray was prepared to give Nick a piece of his mind, or something worse. Around
midnight, they spotted two people beneath a crabapple tree, about
seventy-five feet from the Phillips farmhouse. They crept closer
in the darkness, coming within a yard of the unsuspecting pair.
Unprompted, Hayes whipped out his pistol and fired four shots.
Schneider was taken aback. He lit a match and leaned down toward
the lifeless bodies. "My God," he cried out, as they turned and fled
the scene. "You have made an awful mistake!" It wasn't Nick and
Pearl that Hayes had killed, but Edward Hall and Eleanor Mills.

Schneider signed a three-hundred-word statement affirming his
story. Police then transported him to the Somerset County Jail to
be held as a material witness. When Hayes exited the Middlesex
County Courthouse for his own ride to the jail, bystanders saw not
a cold-blooded killer, but a mild Irish boy with a small frame, wavy
hair, and sharp blue eyes. He had a loving family and a good reputation, including an honorable discharge from the U.S. Navy. As far
as respectability went, he possessed more of it than Ray Schneider.
Reporters yelled out questions as detectives escorted Hayes to an
automobile. His lawyer dictated a statement from the accused: "Do
you think I'd be fool enough to stay around here for three weeks if
I had committed this crime? I am innocent, and they know it, and
so does everyone else in New Brunswick."

As Hayes made the fourteen-mile drive to Somerville, John
Toolan, the assistant prosecutor of Middlesex County, came out to
speak with the press.

"Well, you'll all be away from here in a day or so," he said. "This
spoils a perfect story, doesn't it?"

Skepticism rained down.

"How do you account for Mrs. Mills's throat being cut?" one
reporter asked.

"Now, don't cross-examine me!" Toolan snapped.

The reporters scurried over to Beekman, who officially took over the case now that Schneider's statement had placed the murders in Somerset County.

"Have the authorities the gun and knife with which Mr. Hall and Mrs. Mills were slain?"

"I refuse to answer."

"Has Hayes made a confession?"

"Please don't ask that question. You will have to guess at that."

"Was the shooting, in your opinion, due to mistaken identity?"

"I cannot answer that question."

"Can't you tell what you believe was the motive for the murder?"

"I refuse to state at the present time."

The newspapers didn't buy it, and neither did the people of New Brunswick. Hundreds of them gathered in front of the courthouse to air their indignation. "Someone had to be made a goat," it was said. The arrest was met with derision by Jim and Charlotte Mills, who didn't believe Clifford Hayes *or* Ray Schneider had anything to do with the murders. One of Edward Hall's sisters said, "We are all mystified by the arrest of this boy Hayes. I simply cannot understand it, none of us can. We think it is just a fishing expedition." The only person to publicly embrace Ray's story was Frances Hall's closest confidante, Sally Peters. "Isn't it wonderful?" she gushed. "I hope the prosecutor is satisfied now."

THE ALLEGATIONS AGAINST HAYES FOUND no support from Pearl, who suggested that if anyone could fly into a murderous rage, it was Ray. "He was very jealous of me and accused me of going with other fellows and threatened to shoot me," she told Beekman. "Once Raymond threatened to cut me with a knife and placed it against my stomach, although afterwards he pretended he was fooling about this. . . . He told me once that he shot a man in the arm." Pearl struck a similar chord in media interviews, suggestively telling reporters that while she and Ray had gone on many walks, they'd never ventured onto De Russey's Lane until the morning the bodies were discovered. "Ray seemed to take me right to the spot," she said. "I want to see Clifford get off."

Pearl was, by all accounts, a wayward adolescent, frail and wan, with a fifth-grade education and a record of delinquency. Her mother was dead, her father was a criminal and a drunk, and her nine siblings were scattered between different households. It was perhaps no wonder that Pearl, lacking the bedrock of domestic stability or positive role models, cavorted with a troublesome lothario eight years her senior. With her ash-blond bob, light blue eyes, and dimpled cheeks, Pearl had caught Ray's attention when he was working as a motion picture operator at the Strand in downtown New Brunswick. It was one in a long list of jobs that Ray, whose wife had left him a year after their wedding, couldn't hold down. He'd been fired from another local theater over complaints of offensive remarks to female patrons. He'd moved back in with his parents.

Pearl soon joined Ray as a material witness in the Somerset County Jail. Their saga took yet another dark turn when, in an interview with Beekman, Pearl lodged a shocking allegation. "About six months ago my father started to be nasty with me," she said. "The first time he did anything improper with me was when he bought me a new dress. After he bought me the dress he took me walking out by Johnson & Johnson's, and he kept putting his hands up my dress."

Nick Bahmer was no saint. He had an impressive criminal record, having served eight months for assault and battery and two years for highway robbery. Was he so depraved as to molest his own daughter? After police located Nick while he was out for a drive in a new Dodge he'd purchased with his second wife's inheritance, he vehemently denied the charge. Pearl was his own flesh and blood, Nick pleaded during his arraignment, flinging up his arms. Later, in jail, he put his head in his hands and proclaimed his innocence.

"This is a frame-up," he said. "They're trying to hold me in this case and I have nothing to do with it." Even Nick thought Schneider's story was ludicrous. "I could get down on my knees and swear that Hayes didn't kill them."

The *Daily News*, with Phil Payne's keen eye for tabloid photography, filled its pages with striking pictures of the characters in this dubious sideshow: Ray Schneider's parents posing solemnly on their front porch. Nick Bahmer on the front page in a dark blazer, clasping the bars of his cell, staring blankly at the world outside. Pearl walking toward the Somerset County Courthouse in her Mary Janes and looking melancholy inside the jail.

On October 10, Pearl received a visit from Julia Harpman, who described her subject as "a lamp in which the light has burned low." With her white-stockinged legs crossed beneath a skirt of the same color, Pearl told Harpman she'd attempted suicide two months earlier, "because of her father's treatment and because she had quarreled with Schneider." She expressed her desire to date "single fellows" before finding the right one to settle down with. She disputed Schneider's allegations. "Pearl declared yesterday that neither she nor her father had gone near the Phillips farm or Buccleuch Park that night," Harpman wrote in her article for the *News*, which Payne splashed across the front page of the following morning's edition: BAHMER GIRL'S FIRST STORY.

In the meantime, Beekman's case against Hayes began to unravel. Hayes revealed that the pistol he carried that night was a prop with blank cartridges, which he'd bought for the Fourth of July. A reporter asked Beekman if he believed Schneider had told the truth. "Truth?" Beekman replied, with an air of exasperation. "We are not trying to determine the truth of his statement. I don't have to do that. All I have to do is look for a reasonable basis for prosecution."

Hayes had popular opinion on his side. City officials voiced their support. Sympathetic callers swarmed his parents. Townspeople raised money for his legal fees. An angry mob set upon a county

detective mistakenly believed to be responsible for Schneider's confession. "To hell with informers!" the aggressors screamed. An editorial in the *Trenton Times* declared, "Whatever the motive behind
the strange antics of the prosecuting officials in the New Brunswick
murder case, they certainly are bringing the good name of New
Jersey into disrepute all over the country."

Desperate for a break in the case and anxious to bring the mystery to a close, the prosecution had made an epic miscalculation in
charging Clifford Hayes. Beekman's chief detective, George Totten,
managed to convince his boss that it was time to make Ray come
clean. On the evening of October 10, Totten walked into the Somerset County Jail in downtown Somerville. Ray had been withering
in his cell with a fever from an infected wound, his nerves jumping
from lack of sleep. Totten asked the warden to bring him up from
the holding pen. Ray sat down in a tiny interrogation room and Totten offered him a cigarette, peering into his hollow eyes. Wisps of
smoke floated up toward an electric lightbulb as the two men went
over Ray's statement again and again, to no avail. They'd been at it
for a few hours when Totten had an idea. Perhaps a more menacing
atmosphere would encourage Schneider's honesty? Totten stood up
and turned off the light.

"Now, Raymond," he said, "I'm going to let you sit in the dark
for a while. Think it over."

Ray fidgeted anxiously as Totten continued to chip away at his
account, detail by detail. After another thirty minutes, Schneider
suddenly sprung up.

"I'll tell you the truth," he stammered. "It wasn't Cliff who killed
them."

Totten turned the light back on and Ray collapsed into his chair.
He said he'd made up the story about Hayes because he'd been led
to believe that Hayes had turned on him. The lie weighed heavily
on his conscience. Earlier in the afternoon, Hayes's parents had visited the jail. Through the bars of Ray's nearby cell, he stared at the

loving family, tears streaming down their cheeks, sobs echoing as Mrs. Hayes handed her son a fresh-baked pie and a suitcase full of clean linen.

"When I saw Mrs. Hayes with that big pie," Schneider said, "I thought what a skunk I was in framing him up like that. And when I saw in the papers that my own mother had taken it as hard as Mrs. Hayes, I felt very badly."

Ray let out a sigh of relief. Before he was led back to his cell, he told Totten he expected to have his first good night's sleep in days.

THE FOLLOWING AFTERNOON, SCHNEIDER AND Hayes appeared before a judge for a brief hearing. Beekman handed the judge a copy of Schneider's new deposition and the judge read it over at a plain wooden table surrounded by lawyers. Then he looked up and made it official: Clifford Hayes was a free man.

Hayes approached the friend who had so grievously wronged him. Ray recoiled, as if expecting a punch, but Hayes extended his arm and the two shook hands. He walked out of the jail and entered a baby-blue roadster with his attorneys. When the car pulled up in front of the Hayes family's prim white cottage on the edge of Buccleuch Park, Cliff waved to the hundreds of neighbors and townspeople who had gathered to welcome him home. There were so many well-wishers it took Hayes several minutes to reach the porch where his parents waited with tears in their eyes. The family collie, Rex, barked joyously at the happy reunion, which the *Daily News* captured on its front page. As Julia Harpman observed, "No one has ever doubted Hayes's innocence and his arrest was taken seriously only because it brought grief to the young man's family. Probably never before has the arrest of an innocent person caused such indignation."

While Hayes celebrated, Ray went back to his cell. Two months later, he was convicted of perjury and sentenced to two years in a state reformatory. Nick Bahmer was released in late October, after

Pearl recanted her allegations against him. Two women and one man testified that Pearl admitted inventing the charges, and a judge committed her to Newark's House of the Good Shepherd, a reform facility for wayward girls. Whether or not there was any truth to Pearl's claims of sexual abuse mattered little—she was a powerless, troubled young girl, and in 1922, a jury probably wouldn't have believed her anyway.

As for Azariah Beekman, the Hayes fiasco was another embarrassment. "In baseball parlance," one newspaper chided, "Beekman's score would be one out, no runs." The humiliated prosecutor needed another lead, and fast.

10

"HOUSE OF MYSTERY"

The news appeared in the October 21 edition of the *Fourth Estate*, a trade publication: PAYNE MANAGING EDITOR OF NEW YORK DAILY NEWS. Six weeks earlier, Payne had assumed the role on a trial basis. Now, with the blessing of his boss, Joe Patterson, Payne's coronation was complete. Photographed in the *Fourth Estate*, his desk a jumbled mess of papers, Payne looked every bit the newshound, with a snug waistcoat, rolled-up shirtsleeves, and tousled brown hair poking through a green eyeshade visor. "Payne is 29 years old," the article noted, "and is believed to be the youngest managing editor of a metropolitan daily in the United States."

In the span of ten years, Payne had gone from writing amateur sports dispatches for his hometown newspaper to commanding the newsroom of America's third-largest newspaper. Having seduced the masses with its exuberant coverage, captivating photography, addictive reader contests, and brazen stunts ("What do you think of me sending a reporter out to buy pistols in New York and New Jersey," Payne asked Patterson, "to show how easy it is for a crook to get weapons?"), the *Daily News* now sold more than half a million copies a day. The response on Madison Avenue was similarly enthusiastic, as evidenced by the paper's advertising growth in the automotive, financial, and real estate sectors. In Chicago, Patterson's *Tribune* had surpassed William Randolph Hearst's *Examiner*. Now Patterson threatened Hearst's dominance in New York.

For the *News*, the Hall-Mills mystery was an embarrassment of riches, and Julia Harpman reaped its fruits. "As new evidence is gathered and theory after theory is advanced and then discarded," she wrote, "it seems certain that the two met death near where their bodies were found, beneath the scrubby crabapple tree, which is now denuded of its foliage and many of its branches, through the wantonness of souvenir seekers."

Visitors to the Phillips farm sometimes numbered in the thousands, their cars bearing licenses plates from near and far: New York, New Jersey, Massachusetts, Pennsylvania, Maryland, Illinois. Vendors hawked balloons, popcorn, peanuts, and soft drinks. Local merchants planted signs advertising their services and wares. The entire vicinity was shrouded in mystique, with dark rumors suggesting that bootleggers, gamblers, and other criminals fraternized there. The two-story farmhouse, nearly one hundred years old and aged by weather and neglect, became known as the "house of mystery." The Phillips family, who'd bought the home and its 148.5 acres in 1906 from the De Russeys, for whom the adjacent road was named, moved out in November 1921. In July 1922, an unidentified purchaser acquired the property, stipulating that it was to remain fully furnished, from the couches and beds all the way down to a working telephone and a water stand in the kitchen. As Harpman observed, "The huge square mahogany piano in the living room seems to wait anxiously for the touch of soft, white fingers. The grates in the wide fireplaces are freshly blackened and are swept spotlessly clean." In a notable twist, the anonymous buyer had arranged the sale through the same trust officer who managed Willie Stevens's estate, which was either an uncanny small-town coincidence, or a clue that someone in the Hall-Stevens orbit owned the property. (Could Edward have secretly acquired it as a clandestine lovers' abode?)

In either case, crime-scene tourists pillaged the farmhouse, carrying away anything they could get their hands on: rugs and chairs, candlesticks and lamps, small fragments of ivory from the piano keys. A lone "no trespassing" sign could hardly deter the hordes. Some were audacious enough to scale the roof, while others simply crowded around and peered through the windows. Those who couldn't get a view from the front elbowed their way onto a smaller side porch. It eventually collapsed under the weight.

By now, dozens of journalists were tramping around New Brunswick, enough to keep telegraph operators on their toes with a constant deluge of "news dope." Taxi drivers had no complaints, nor did the area's eateries and hotels, which sometimes turned people away for lack of available rooms. The *Daily Home News* marveled at the influx of writers and photographers from larger metropolitan dailies: "So keen has been the competition to unearth every clue and to solve all of the puzzling intricacies that attend the case, that many of the reporters have worked unceasingly, often going without sleep." The article mentioned several of the more prominent ones by name, including the mystery writer and *New York American* correspondent Arthur B. Reeve, *New York World* reporter Mazie Clemons, and a certain "Miss Hartman" [sic] of the New York *Daily News*. The demand for information was so great that Harpman, a tawdry tabloid reporter, found herself competing with the almighty *New York Times*, which spilled more ink on the case than anyone else. Asked about its Hall-Mills coverage, *Times* publisher Arthur Ochs said, "When the *Daily News* prints it, it is sex. When we print it, it is sociology."

The newspapers filled their pages with every tidbit that leaked out of the investigation. Suspicions emerged that phones had been tapped, both in the Hall household and the office of the Middlesex County prosecutor. It was revealed that pages containing Eleanor and Edward's favorite hymn, "Peace, Perfect Peace," had been torn out of several hymnals in the choir loft. A brief hubbub ensued over a tie clip, inscribed with the letter *G*, that Hall wore when he was killed. Frances claimed her husband had found the accessory at St. John's, keeping it for himself after the rightful owner failed to come forward. The local busybodies knew better—it was a gift from Eleanor, they whispered, and the *G* stood for the first letter of Hall's pet name for her: "Gypsy."

Frances's cousin Edwin Carpender came under scrutiny over reports that he'd taken a box of letters and documents from Edward's church office shortly after the bodies were discovered. Carpender swore the only items he'd retrieved that day were the reverend's vestments, in preparation for the funeral. Henry Stevens was back in the headlines as well, this time concerning his absence, eleven years earlier, from Frances and Edward's wedding. Henry reportedly declined an invitation after hearing "stories reflecting on the rector's habits," though he vehemently denied this. "I was traveling in New England at the time, demonstrating shotguns, and since I was scheduled to be in a certain place at the time, I did not ask for a vacation," he said. "The marriage took place at the busiest time of the year for me, but I sent my sister a congratulatory telegram and a present. Besides, another reason for not going to the wedding is that I am an outdoor man and dressing up for formal affairs is very objectionable to me."

Ralph Gorsline, the vestryman and choir member who had publicly acknowledged church gossip about Edward and Eleanor's relationship, now found himself under suspicion. A forty-two-year-old Spanish-American War veteran and married father of one, with an angular face and hollow cheeks not dissimilar from those of James Mills, Gorsline happened to work at a manufacturing company run by one of Frances Hall's cousins. He'd gone joyriding with Eleanor the previous year, and he now alleged, contrary to the evidence of Eleanor's long-held feelings for Edward, that Eleanor made an unwanted pass at him. Confronted at home by reporters, with his ten-year-old daughter on his lap, Gorsline claimed, "Once she said to me, 'You are my ideal man. I'm not happy with my husband.' I'm no saint, but I did not like that sort of an approach."

Gorsline could not escape murmurs alleging that "two eyewitnesses concealed their knowledge of the crime as long as possible, because they did not wish their presence at the Phillips farm at night to become generally known, because of the reputation of the neighborhood as a rendezvous." Gorsline admitted to officials that, on the night of the murders, he'd given a ride to a fellow choir member named Catherine Rastall, a blond bachelorette of twenty who worked as a stenographer for a local lumber company. But he and Rastall insisted they hadn't gone to De Russey's Lane or the Phillips farm. Rather, they explained, Gorsline had bumped into Rastall after a movie downtown, and he unburdened her of the walk back to her house near Buccleuch Park. "He took me directly to my home in Senior Street," she said. "We arrived there about ten thirty."

In another mysterious twist, Gorsline's green Apperson caught fire the day after he was questioned. If the vehicle had been privy to anything incriminating, it was of no consequence now: the car was burned beyond repair. "I seem to be the victim of unfortunate circumstances," Gorsline lamented.

ONE DAY, AN AMBITIOUS YOUNG attorney named Florence North arrived in New Brunswick and introduced herself to Charlotte Mills. North was twenty-five years old, originally from Bergen County, New Jersey, and said she had come to Charlotte's aid—pro bono—at the encouragement of "a group of charitably inclined women in New York." Smart, confident, and well-dressed, North had studied under the renowned prosecutor Grace Humiston, nicknamed "Mrs. Sherlock Holmes." "I am first a woman, with a tender sympathy for [Charlotte]," North told a reporter. "And I am a lawyer with the instinct of a detective. Not enough lawyers, especially in lines of criminology, understand that they should be detectives, too."

North's motivations weren't entirely clear. To an extent, she appeared to be emulating her mentor, who had solved a famous murder that shook Harlem in 1917. Whatever the case, North's most notable contribution involved a bundle of love letters, postcards, and diary entries from Edward to Eleanor. They'd practically been hiding in plain sight, tucked away in a handbag of Eleanor's that Charlotte had recently stumbled upon, hanging on the back of a door inside the Millses' apartment. Charlotte gave the letters to North, but North did not in turn provide them to Azariah Beckman. "The prosecutor refused to cooperate with me, so I didn't cooperate with him," she said. "I didn't want him to bungle the letters the same way officials have bungled the whole case." Instead, North sold the letters to William Randolph Hearst's *New York American*, insisting the proceeds were for Charlotte, whose father did in fact collect a five-hundred-dollar check. (North denied taking a commission.) From there, the letters ricocheted around the country, reprinted in newspapers from Delaware to Texas to Missouri and everywhere in between.

"Only four more days and I will be home again," Edward gushed in one. "Fling your arms now to the wide heavens, for the heavens of heavens cannot contain the vast infinite love that pours more and more out of my heart toward you—you most wonderful lover—WE most wonderful LOVERS."

The discovery of the letters was significant because the notes found at the crime scene had been written by Eleanor, which left open the possibility of an unrequited romantic obsession. Edward's letters confirmed the passion was mutual. "They certainly made a sucker out of me," Jim Mills finally admitted. When reporters told Jim that Frances disputed the letters' authenticity, he replied, "Mrs. Hall had better get a new pair of glasses."

On the afternoon the letters first appeared in the *New York American*, Tuesday, October 17, Frances Hall and her brothers were summoned for yet another interrogation. Accompanied by their attorney Timothy Pfeiffer and Sally Peters, whose arm Frances clung to as she approached the prosecutor's office, the group passed a large crowd of gawkers and journalists as they disappeared into the Middlesex County Courthouse. Two hours later, Frances emerged with her entourage, huffing out of the courthouse and into the maelstrom of reporters and flashbulbs. As they hurried over to an idling sedan, cameras clicking all around, Pfeiffer threw his raincoat over Frances's head, and Sally held up a purse to further obscure her companion. Frances wobbled into the car and slumped herself into a corner of the backseat, her head dropping to her shoulder as if she lacked the will to hold it up. A photograph of her dramatic exit appeared on the cover of the following morning's *Daily News*. Frances was not yet familiar with the tabloid's editor, Phil Payne, but he had become her tormentor. "Mrs. Frances S. Hall, rector's widow, tried to dodge our cameraman," a caption taunted, "but this picture proved she failed."

To Mrs. Hall's handlers, this latest round of questioning was yet another affront to the dignity of an innocent widow. What they didn't know was that the prosecution had discovered a new witness, and this witness was about to shatter Frances Hall's world.

THE PIG WOMAN

Julia Harpman couldn't have picked a better moment to resume work at the *Daily News*. She'd spent the better part of eighteen months recovering from a crippling automobile accident, in which a trolley car struck the taxi Harpman was riding in, leaving her partially paralyzed for a period of time—albeit $15,115.74 richer, thanks to a successful lawsuit against the Eighth Avenue Railroad Company, in which Phil Payne testified on her behalf. During Harpman's convalescence, there was an intensification in her relationship with Westbrook Pegler, a newsman she'd met in 1920 while covering the Joseph Bowne Elwell murder. Pegler was drawn to Harpman's beauty, sweetness, and wit, but also to her journalistic ferocity, which belied an inherent shyness. He respected Harpman's individuality and ambition, supporting her resolve not to trade a promising newspaper career for idle domesticity. If they were to become man and wife, Harpman was to remain a hardworking reporter. With that assurance in hand, Harpman accepted Pegler's marriage proposal, converting to Catholicism ahead of the nuptials. They wed on August 28, 1922, at Church of the Blessed Sacrament on the Upper West Side, and moved into an apartment on Walton

Avenue in the Bronx. In another few weeks, Harpman, known to her beloved as Julie, was back at the *News* full-time, covering the Hall-Mills story.

Toward the end of October, Harpman turned her attention to the emergence of a game-changing lead. "An eyewitness," she reported, "has made an affidavit in which is described the shooting of the couple on the Phillips farm on the night of Thursday, September 14. The affidavit, which is in the hands of Prosecutor Beekman, is the backbone of the State's case." Harpman worked her sources, pestering contacts in local law enforcement. "The identity of the mysterious woman," she reported, "is zealously and jealously guarded by officials."

Harpman made it her mission to identify and locate the witness. In the recollection of one of her colleagues, she "found a female hermit who ran a pig farm who said she saw the shooting and could identify who did it. She said she had been riding across the countryside on her donkey when the event took place." Harpman thought the woman's story was both intriguing and implausible. She mentioned it to some of her peers in the competitive but nonetheless collegial Hall-Mills press corps. According to Harpman's colleague, that's how she ended up getting scooped. "These gentlemen," he later recalled, "scoffed so loudly at the impossibility of the Pig Woman's story that the girl didn't file on it." Harpman's reluctance came back to bite her the following day, October 24, when she saw the front pages of the afternoon papers. EYE-WITNESS VERSION OF HALL TRAGEDY, the *Evening World* declared. "Jane Gibson, Farmer, Hunting Corn Thieves on Phillips Farm, Is Declared to Have Seen Two Couples Quarreling and Heard Shots and Man's Name."

The mystery witness was a mystery no more, and before long, you'd be hard-pressed to find anyone in America unacquainted with Jane Gibson. "She is a vigorous woman," reported the *New York Times*, "who speaks English and German and appears to be much better educated than the average woman in her circumstances. Her home is in an old barn converted into a dwelling, about 100 yards off Hamilton Avenue. Mrs. Gibson owns forty-eight pigs, five dogs, five mules and some chickens, and has a good crop of corn growing on her farm."

"With none of the characteristics of the modern woman," the *New York Herald* observed, "living in a shack the outside of which is covered with roofing paper, raising pigs and trading mules for a living apparently, but nevertheless tilling some sixty acres of land and raising a corn crop that must be worth a good deal of money, Mrs. Gibson is a living contradiction, as she is an intelligent, well bred woman."

"Her skin," as the *Tribune* described it, "is burned a coffee brown and is weather beaten from exposure. Her hair is a rich chestnut." Harpman called Gibson "a typical pioneer type of woman, strong and stolid," a "stocky . . . widow about fifty" who "has locked within her deep bosom the story of how the Rev. Edward Wheeler Hall and Mrs. Eleanor Mills . . . met their death beneath a crabapple tree."

Gibson had first shared this story with Detective George Totten earlier in the month, when Ray Schneider and Cliff Hayes sat in jail. She had known Totten for years, having once resided in Somerville, where Totten worked for the Somerset County prosecutor's office. She phoned him and implored him to pay her a visit, explaining she hadn't come forward sooner because she didn't want to get mixed up in the messy affair. But now that stories about the wrongly accused Hayes boy filled the papers, she couldn't stand by and watch an innocent young man go down for a crime that wasn't his. "He didn't do it," Gibson said, in Totten's recollection. "I was an eye-witness to the murders."

Days later, when Totten and his colleagues interviewed Gibson at the Middlesex County Courthouse, they asked her again why she decided to speak up. "The mule, the pigs, and I," Gibson replied, "could not get it out of my mind."

After the first articles about Gibson hit newsstands, journalists swarmed her farm, about a mile or so from the crabapple tree. Upon arrival, they encountered a hostile subject. Photographers said she tried to smash their cameras, and reporters couldn't coax her into talking. "I don't know anything about the case except what I read in the newspapers," Gibson snapped.

The following day, October 25, Gibson had a change of heart, granting an interview to a group of reporters milling about her barnyard. They listened raptly as Gibson provided a partial account of what she had seen and heard on the evening of Thursday, September 14.

It all began shortly before nine o'clock—ten o'clock, really, because Gibson did not observe daylight saving time—with the yelping of one of Gibson's dogs. Believing that someone had been stealing her corn, Gibson figured the pooch had caught the thief red-handed, scaring him away. She hurried outside to her mules in the barn, eschewing the fastest of the bunch, Buster, for her beloved Jenny.

"What I wanted was Jenny's sagacity," Gibson explained to the reporters, as she nuzzled the brown animal on its bed of straw. "Isn't she pretty?"

Gibson and Jenny set out in pursuit, heading northeast in the direction of the Phillips farm. After riding around for half an hour or so, there was still no sign of the thief. Something else caught Gibson's attention as she and Jenny cut across the adjacent Phillips property. She heard voices coming from the direction of the farmhouse. She crouched down on Jenny's neck and rode nearer, squinting into the distance, where she saw two men and two women arguing. The contretemps became heated. A physical quarrel ensued. Then, the fatal climax: four shots, a man and a woman falling to the ground, a woman screaming. Gibson swore she could identify the shooter, despite the darkness of the night.

Harpman, along with the other reporters, scribbled down the gory details. Then she wrote it all up and filed the copy to her editors in Manhattan. As it happened, Phil Payne had a separate scoop to accompany Harpman's Pig Woman story—an exclusive photograph of Edward Hall during a church outing to Asbury Park, on the beach in a tank top, surrounded by ten women from St. John's in their bathing suits and swim caps. (Eleanor was not among them.) Payne enlarged the photo and put it on the front page under a headline promoting Harpman's article: MRS. GIBSON'S MURDER STORY. On page two, Gibson's voice leapt off the page:

Those awful shrieks of Mrs. Mills are plainer in my ears tonight than they were at the moment of the murder. They haunt me. My mind is filled with those cries and I cannot sleep at night. . . . I am sorry I had to be mixed up in the affair, but it seems I was put there that night for a purpose. . . . If I had only called out I might have prevented the murder. Oh, I wish I had shrieked or made some sound, but it all came so suddenly, and I was stunned. I could do nothing. . . . Jenny was frightened and ran away. I was glad to get away and I did not want to think about it again. But I could not forget it. . . . The Bible says, "Thou shalt not kill," and when one takes vengeance into his own hand, justice must be done. No money could buy my silence, and no one could frighten me into saying what was not true. . . . The time will come soon when everything about the case will be told. Then I will have more to tell.

Gibson made good on her word. Over the next few days, as she continued blabbing to prosecutors and the press, different permutations of her story began to emerge. Some details became more vivid. Others conflicted with previous accounts. She signed different statements that said different things.

In one version, Gibson and Jenny approached the intersection of Easton Avenue and De Russey's Lane when Gibson saw a man and a woman walking toward the farm, their faces illuminated by a car that happened to be pulling into the lane at the same moment, before it stopped, backed up, and turned around. Gibson observed the woman's gray knee-length coat. The woman's stocky male companion had a dark mustache and bushy hair, a description that could have suggested either of the Stevens brothers. Gibson followed them to the crabapple tree, keeping enough distance to avoid detection. Then she watched the murders in horror.

In another subsequent telling, Gibson's story became more riveting still. Crouching low on Jenny behind a camouflage of sumac bushes, Gibson heard the woman in the gray coat demand, "How do you explain these notes?" Edward was shot first. Then Eleanor ran away and hid among shrubs between the crabapple tree and the farmhouse. The shooter found her with the assistance of a flashlight, dragging Eleanor back to the crabapple tree as she fought for her life. "Don't! Please, don't!" Eleanor screamed, before the killer shot her dead. Gibson returned to the scene of the crime around 1:00 A.M., partly out of curiosity, partly because she'd lost a moccasin and hoped to find it now that the moon had risen. When she got close to the tree, she saw the same woman in the gray coat, alone and sobbing over Edward's dead body.

One detail stood out in each of these tales, and it was the most damning of all. As the gun was pointed at Edward, Gibson heard the woman in the gray coat cry out, "Oh, Henry!"

GIBSON WAS CATNIP FOR THE newspapers, an eccentric raconteur who quickly became the star of their coverage. "She hints at a life of adventure, of culture, of old lineage," reported the *New York Tribune*. "Mayflower ancestors, travels with Barnum's circus, riding to hounds in Kentucky." As the *Evening World* put it, she was "one of the oddest characters in a tragedy presenting many queer types."

When Gibson answered the door of her rustic home on the night of October 26, she found yet another reporter clamoring for an interview, Marguerite Mooers Marshall, a romance novelist of some renown and columnist for the *Evening World*, whose warmth was rewarded with an invitation inside. Marshall sat down by the glow of a kerosene lamp and wooed Gibson with flattery until her life story flowed forth. She grew up in Kentucky, where her father raised horses and Gibson became an equestrian in her own right, before leaving home at age sixteen to join the circus as a bareback rider. "I always loved animals, and I could always manage 'em," she said. After traveling with the circus for several years, Gibson married a minister with a place in the country. They lived comfortably and had a child named William, now twenty-one, the same young man who had greeted Marshall when she stepped out of a cab a short while earlier. The minister died when William was still an infant, leaving mother and child to fend for themselves. "I had to work. I loved animals and knew how to handle them, so it just seemed the natural thing to keep a farm," Gibson continued. "First, I had one down in Pennsylvania. Then I sold to good advantage and came here to New Brunswick. My boy and I built this house in which you're sitting with our own hands." The original farmhouse had burned down twelve years earlier.

When Marshall asked Gibson if she attended church, Gibson rose from her chair and walked across the room. She stooped down to the lowest shelf of a shabby bookcase and pulled out a heavily bound family Bible. Marshall admired the beautiful pictures and clear, splendid print.

"This is my church," Gibson said. "Every night I read it. Before I told about *the terrible thing*"—emphasis hers—"I read in my Bible and I prayed."

Marshall left Gibson's farm with a notebook full of quotes and a sympathetic impression of the singular, but nonetheless "wholly sane, wholly normal, wholly straightforward" woman who had turned the Hall-Mills case on its head. The following afternoon, the *Evening World* hit newsstands with Marshall's glowing portrait of the Pig Woman.

BRAVE, BIBLE READING FARMER WOMAN, LIKE STURDY PIONEERS OF OLD, IS MRS. JANE GIBSON, HALL MURDER WITNESS

Her Honesty and Courage Startling Contrast in Murky Atmosphere of Scandal, Snobbery and Lies Pervading New Jersey Community

---

Despite Marshall's flattering portrayal, Gibson's credibility was beginning to come into question. The more that reporters dug into her past, the fuzzier the picture became, starting with the matter of Gibson's marriage. Gibson presented herself as the widow of a clergyman. But she was known to many in the area as the wife of William Easton, a fifty-six-year-old toolmaker very much still alive. Easton's car was sometimes seen in Gibson's barn. The city directory listed the same address for both. When reporters confronted Easton outside the factory where he worked, he refused to provide any details about his marital status, but said of Gibson, "She has a brilliant mind." Easton's boss showed reporters paperwork identifying his wife and next of kin as a Mrs. J. M. Easton. The 1910 Census, however, listed Easton's wife not as Jane Easton, but Jesse M. Easton, and the 1920 Census identified Jane Gibson as a "partner" in Easton's household.

"Easton is not my husband," Gibson insisted to a reporter. She then told authorities that William Easton was her second husband.

They'd had a son, William Jr., nicknamed Willie, and had lived together in Trenton, where Jane Gibson once ran a furniture store. Gibson confirmed this version for certain reporters, claiming she and Easton had divorced, while disputing it to others. "Willie is not my son," she said. "He is the son of my sister, Mrs. Jesse May Easton, and she is the wife of William H. Easton."

When reporters did actually track down a sister of Gibson's, Mrs. Madeline Williams of Bayonne, New Jersey, there was no mention in their conversation of any Jesse May Easton, or the circus, or Kentucky, where Gibson claimed her parents still lived— despite the fact that her mother, Salome Cerrenner, also resided in Bayonne. Madeline gave the newspapers a much different account of her sister's upbringing. She had been born Jane Eisleitner, fifty-two years before, in New York City, and ran away from home at the age of fourteen or fifteen. Years later, she turned up in Bayonne, where Madeline and their mother, now remarried, were living. Gibson took up sewing for a while, then opened a poultry shop and candy stand. She shared a house with two men, one of whom was known to Madeline as Mr. Easton, and two children. Eventually, Gibson moved thirty miles south to the New Brunswick area, where Madeline later visited the pig farm and "had a fine time." As Harpman suggested of the wildly conflicting accounts, "Ghosts of a hidden past are brought to the light of day to throw discredit on the amazing story of Mrs. Jane Gibson."

Gibson's convoluted history wasn't the only reason to question her reliability. While some neighbors described her as an honest and hardworking woman who generally minded her own business, others painted Gibson as a troublemaker whose tales of pilfered corn were greatly embellished. One nearby resident told reporters that Gibson "could not be telling the truth and that she simply had decided it would be profitable to appear in the spotlight." She was said to have charged a fee to pose for the newspapers, as well as selling photographs, statements, and her life story. A woman up the road named Anna Fraley suggested Gibson had invented her eyewitness account based on details she'd picked up from press coverage. "Mrs. Gibson has been reading the newspapers," Fraley sniffed. A pile of New York dailies visible through the screen of Gibson's window corroborated Fraley's assertion.

Timothy Pfeiffer, the attorney representing Frances Hall and her brothers, told reporters that the woman Gibson saw on the farm was most certainly not his client, who "was in her home the entire evening of September 14," he said. "Any other statement to the contrary is without foundation." Pfeiffer did, however, concede that Frances's alibi could not be corroborated. Neither of the maids had seen Frances after Edward walked out the door around 7:30 P.M. Nor had Willie Stevens, who was cloistered away in his room until Frances summoned him hours later. The only other person known to be in the house that night was Frances's ten-year-old niece, Frances Voorhees, who'd come for a visit. Young Frances last saw her aunt around 9:00 P.M., when the elder Frances watched the girl say her prayers before turning off the light.

Pfeiffer asked a reporter if it was true Gibson had claimed she heard the woman in the gray coat utter, "Oh, Henry!" When the reporter replied in the affirmative, Pfeiffer said, "Well if she did make that statement, it would be of great benefit to Mrs. Hall's side of the case." Henry Stevens, after all, had provided the names of ten people who could testify he was in Lavallette, sixty miles from New Brunswick, on the night of the murders. Henry also produced a fishing diary documenting the evening. "Just about sundown, I had caught my third bluefish," he said.

Jane Gibson's entrance into the case only further overwhelmed Azariah Beekman. Public pressure continued to escalate, and Timothy Pfeiffer wrote Governor Edwards to argue that a state prosecutor should be appointed. Edwards agreed with him, and Beekman didn't oppose the idea. "As far as I'm concerned," he said, "I'd be grateful for any help I could get."

The man chosen for the job was a sixty-five-year-old veteran prosecutor named Wilbur A. Mott, who lived about thirty miles north in the town of East Orange. Mott had spent his career in Newark, beginning as a police judge and later serving eighteen years in the Essex County prosecutor's office. He had a reputation as an astute lawyer and a clever cross-examiner, with a roster of notable murder cases under his belt. These included the 1912 conviction of a philandering Newark man found guilty of poisoning his wife.

Mott believed Gibson's story, or stories, as it were. Despite numerous discrepancies, the main points remained consistent, even as certain details shifted this way or that. Totten and another detective accompanied Gibson on a painstaking reconstruction of her late-night mule ride. They came away from the exercise believing she had indeed witnessed the murders, even if her imagination ran wild in certain retellings. Mott wasn't in a rush to make any arrests. The case still required a lot of work, and Mott knew that before bringing it to a grand jury, he needed to firm things up to a point where he was confident of a quick trial and conviction. In briefings with reporters, Mott answered lots of questions without saying anything very pertinent, but there was one point on which he never wavered.

"Do not think of this case as a mystery anymore," he said. "It is complex, but it is no longer a mystery."

JANE GIBSON HAD A FRAUGHT but mutually beneficial relationship with the press. The Hall-Mills case was her first taste of celebrity, which must have been enticing to a woman with a tendency toward theatrics. Gibson, in turn, sold newspapers. What reader could resist, say, Detective George Totten posing with Gibson's world-famous mule on the front page of the *Daily News*? The trade-off for Gibson was the constant stream of visitors and relentless intrusions into her private life. She'd become something of a freak show, and the public couldn't get enough. Even actual celebrities were enthralled. Asked to name some famous duos he admired, F. Scott Fitzgerald told the *Morning Telegraph,* "Mencken and Nathan, Park & Tilford, Lord & Taylor, Lea & Perrins, the Smith Brothers, and Mrs. Gibson, the pig lady, and her Jenny mule."

At times, the spotlight wore Gibson down. On Halloween morning, she watched four photographers pull up to her farm in a taxicab. One of them stepped out of the car and crossed a rope that Gibson had stretched across the entrance to a dirt lane leading to the house. As the photographer approached, Gibson appeared in her front doorway.

"Stay back there!" she shouted.

Gibson reached behind the door and produced a double-barreled shotgun, kneeling to take aim. As the photographer cautiously retreated, one of his companions leaned out of the taxi and pointed a camera. Before he could even focus the lens, bullets were flying. The photographers scrambled back into the cab, which left a cloud of dust in its wake.

Later, when reporters came to inquire about the incident, Gibson declared, "Yes, I shot at them, and I am going to get some of them yet. The things they print about me are not true. They are liable to get themselves into trouble. The papers that print these things are liable to prosecution and they had better watch out. I told the truth as I saw it and that is all."

Gibson felt so strongly about her honesty that she wrote a poem about it, "Truth Forever." On November 1, the *Daily News* published the poem alongside Harpman's latest.

> *I stand before a multitude*
> *To Judge me as I am,*
> *I know that I have told the truth*
> *And back of that I'll stand.*
> *No matter what befalls me now*
> *My duty I must do.*

I'll stick to what I know is just
And see the whole thing through.
Ah, who's afraid of anyone
When truth is in the heart?
What care I for the liar's tongue
That sends the poison dart?
For truth and justice I will stand
And righteousness for all;
The wicked come and go their way
But in the end they fall.

MEET THE PRESS

Frances Hall was a portrait of reluctance when she appeared at her side door on the morning of Wednesday, November 1, in a heavy black dress and matching scarf. She looked out on the withering garden, inhaled the nippy autumn wind, and marched forward into the yard, lowering herself onto a seat framed by white latticework. Cracking the faintest hint of a smile, Frances surrendered to a small group of newspaper photographers, who'd been invited by Frances's attorney Timothy Pfeiffer. "I can't look in all directions," Frances complained as they barked out commands. She rose from her seat and walked over to a sundial, where she posed uncomfortably. As Frances turned her head, a cameraman pressed his finger and captured a shot that would appear on the cover of the following morning's *Daily News*. Her lips were pressed into a pout, her hair smoothed back in a frizzy gray wave, her eyes magnified by pince-nez glasses that seemed to buckle under the heft of her dark brows.

"I hope that you men are satisfied," Frances snarled as she retreated back to the door, "and I hope you won't bother me anymore for photographs. I haven't been able to leave my house because of you!"

Frances had become been a prisoner in her mansion. She ate breakfast upstairs in the company of Sally Peters, who read the newspapers aloud, censoring anything that might cause distress. She passed her mornings in Edward's large sunlit study, filled with reminders of her husband, from Bibles and hymnals to Edward's modern mahogany desk and his hundreds of secular books: Shakespeare and Wordsworth, Plato and Brieux, *Alice in Wonderland.* Outside, a guard stood watch day and night, discouraging intrusions by journalists. An unnamed friend explained to reporters, "Mrs. Hall suffers a tremendous nervous reaction from the horrible crime and its attendant publicity."

Over the past six weeks, Frances had left the house three times—once on business and twice for questioning at the prosecutor's office. Other than that, she was a shut-in. The intensity of the press coverage would have rattled anyone, but Frances's aversion to the spotlight was amplified by her Victorian inclination toward privacy. With the newspapers in control of her story, Pfeiffer decided it was time for his client to speak for herself.

After the photo shoot, some two dozen journalists marched into Frances's parlor, taking in the mahogany chairs upholstered in red plush and the towering bookcases where classic literature mingled with large volumes on theology. Above the fireplace, a heavy bronze-and-marble clock ticked down the seconds until the agreed-upon interview was to commence. Two stenographers set up by the doorway—Frances footed the $250 fee—and a crew of mimeograph men placed their inky devices on tables covered in newsprint. The typists planned to transcribe the interview in shifts, with one of them rushing over to the mimeograph machines every ten minutes to have the text stenciled and duplicated. Pfeiffer explained the ground rules. No questions were off limits—anything the reporters asked, Frances would answer. The inquiries would be dictated by one reporter from the morning papers and one from the evening papers. Other reporters could jot their questions on slips of paper and hand them to the appropriate representative. They would have fifty minutes. Neither Pfeiffer nor Sally Peters would be present.

Moments later, Frances appeared in a black crepe de chine dress with a light silk scarf draped over her shoulders. She forced an unconvincing smile as Pfeiffer led her to a rocking chair next to the stenographers. Grasping the arms of the chair, Frances sat down, crossed her right knee over the left, and began tapping her foot, clad in a single-strap black oxford.

Julia Harpman gazed upon the woman she'd been writing about for six weeks straight. "Mrs. Hall looks like nobody else in the world," she wrote in a story for the *Daily News*. "Her chin is as wide as the forehead. It is unusually long and is in ill proportion to her short, rather dumpy figure. Her face could easily belong to two persons—so different is its upper half from the lower. There exists an amazing variance between her fine, wonderfully clever, slate grey eyes and her heavy chin, topped by the protruding upper lip of her wide mouth. Her ears are extraordinarily large and they are lobeless. . . . Her cheeks bear no lines carved by care. Her nerves are under perfect control. She seems cold but not hard—like ice, which will melt when exposed to the proper warmth."

Frances adjusted her glasses with her left hand, which bore the weight of a three-diamond engagement ring and plain wedding band. She retained the utmost composure throughout the hour-long grilling without "displaying a single spark of feeling," as the *New York Herald* put it, "with never a tremor of the lips, and without a single tear dimming for an instant the cold, steel gray of her eyes."

"Have you any comment to make, Mrs. Hall, on that part of Mrs. Gibson's statements in which she says you were present on the Phillips farm on the night of Sept. 14?"

"What comment could I make? Of course that was not so."

"You were not there?"

"I certainly was not."

Asked if she believed that Edward had written love letters to

Eleanor, Frances let out a sardonic laugh, as if it the question was preposterous.

"I think it is very unlikely that he would."

"What is your feeling toward your husband?"

"I feel he is true to me."

"What is your feeling toward Mrs. Mills?"

"I do not know what to say," Frances replied. "I have no vindictive feeling."

THE FOLLOWING DAY, WHEN THE interview appeared in newspapers, Wilbur Mott and his investigators scrutinized every word. One thing that stood out was an assertion that Frances and Willie had returned home at 3:30 A.M. after searching for Edward at the church. Two witnesses, night watchman William Phillips and neighbor A. H. Bennett, were prepared to testify they saw Frances return to 23 Nichol Avenue as much as one hour earlier, which seemed a notable discrepancy.

Jane Gibson declared the interview a farce. "That is a lie," she said of Frances's denials. "I hate to fight a woman, but she is fighting me." Gibson, of course, knew a thing or two about lying. In the latest version of her eyewitness account, she clarified that she hadn't actually seen Edward and Eleanor as they were struck down by gunfire. "The story I told the authorities and the story I told to reporters are two different things," she said. "When I get on the stand I will give you a better story than you have had yet."

There was another story for Mott to investigate, this one relayed by a Hungarian reverend named Paul Hamborzsky, a friend of Edward's, who claimed Edward had confided he was considering a trip to Reno to obtain a divorce, after which he would leave the church to be with Eleanor, perhaps going into business with the forty thousand dollars he'd stashed in his safe deposit box. Hamborzsky said Edward told him Frances knew of the affair, and that one of Frances's male relatives "said he would finish me if he ever caught me with Mrs. Mills." Detectives were able to corroborate that Hamborzsky had shared this story with several people shortly after the bodies were discovered, but Mott didn't think it was strong enough to present to a grand jury. The prosecutor stacked all of his chips on Jane Gibson.

Mott's theory of the crime, as far as the newspapers were able to piece it together, went like this: A letter Eleanor had left for Edward in the church was intercepted by Ralph Gorsline, the vestryman rumored to have been on De Russey's Lane with Catherine Rastall the night of the murders. Gorsline claimed to have rejected a come-on from Eleanor, but new rumors suggested it was Eleanor who had rejected him. Bitter and jealous, Gorsline gave the purloined letter to Minnie Clark, the Sunday school teacher who accompanied Edward, Frances, and Eleanor to a picnic at Lake Hopatcong the day before the victims disappeared. Minnie was said to be a rival to Eleanor, who spoke derisively of her. She also happened to have visited Frances on the afternoon of the murders, giving her ample opportunity to slip Frances the letter. With the note in hand, Frances and a male companion went to the Phillips farm to confront the lovers at their suspected meeting place. The confrontation turned deadly, and after the victims were shot, Eleanor's throat was slit in an act of revenge. Or so Mott believed.

As Mott built up the case, Pfeiffer hired an investigator of his own. His name was Felix De Martini, and he had worked for the New York Police Department's homicide squad before opening his own detective agency in 1919. In gathering opposition research, De Martini canvassed witnesses, studied reams of newspaper coverage, and retraced the prosecution's every step. Most days he could be found at the Hall mansion, where he sometimes slept, turning in after his nightly conferences with Pfeiffer, Frances, and Sally Peters.

On Wednesday, November 8, De Martini's eyes lit up as he read a letter addressed to Frances from a woman named Nellie Lo Russell: "Dear Madam, In regard to Sept. 14, Mrs. Jane Gibson was not at the Phillips farm at 10 o'clock." If true, this was just the evidence the defense needed, and De Martini pursued it with haste. He and Pfeiffer drove out to a property on the far side of Gibson's farm, where they found Russell in a decrepit single-room shanty, furnished with little more than a stove, a small table, a chair, and a raggedy old couch, with strings of red peppers hanging from the ceiling and pumpkins in the corner. Russell, a thirty-eight-year-old Black woman and former nurse now employed by a Manhattan dressmaker, had been neighbors with Gibson for almost two years. She told the men that around 10:00 P.M. on the evening of September 14, Gibson arrived at her shack saying she had recovered Russell's missing dog, Prince, now safe and sound back at Gibson's farm. Russell put on her coat and shoes and went with Gibson to retrieve the pup. They chatted for a while, according to Russell, who said that when she got home, she immediately looked at her clock and saw that the time was a few minutes before eleven o'clock. If Russell was telling the truth, this meant she had been with Gibson at the same time Gibson claimed to have witnessed the murders.

The following day, Russell went to Pfeiffer's office in Manhattan and signed an affidavit in the presence of a notary public. Presented with a copy of Russell's sworn statement, the prosecution set out to undermine her credibility. Detectives learned that Russell and Gibson had feuded. Russell's neighbors cast doubt on her story. Gibson, for her part, said Russell had mixed up the date. She produced a day calendar, with a notation about her encounter with Russell scrawled in pencil on the page for September 9. Mott's men examined the entry under a magnifying glass. Flyspecks and smudges covering the pencil marks convinced them the note had been written when Gibson said it was. "Mr. Pfeiffer is a mighty smart lawyer. Mrs. Hall is a very intelligent woman. She has some wonderful New York detectives working for her," Gibson said. "But they overlooked one thing—that they were dealing with a businesswoman, able by bitter experience, to keep track of her affairs."

Mott shared Gibson's disregard. Speaking to reporters on Monday, November 13, he said, "I'm not the least interested in Mrs. Russell. I do not think much of her story."

In fact, Mott was ready to present his case to a grand jury. He announced that the proceedings would begin in one week's time.

THE GRAND JURY

The weekend before Mott's opening statements, Phil Payne traveled to his hometown of Perth Amboy, about twenty minutes
from New Brunswick, for a reunion of newspapermen. Though only
twenty-nine, Payne was arguably the most high-profile guest of the
bunch. He'd become a heavyweight in Manhattan's media scene and
a luminary of the budding tabloid genre, swaggering his way to the
top of the *Daily News*. But Payne never forgot where he came from.
As the *Perth Amboy Evening News* observed on the eve of the reunion,
"little did he think that he would reach the place in the newspaper
world which he holds today, as managing editor of one of the large
New York dailies."

On Saturday afternoon, November 18, Payne checked into the
New Packer House, a four-story hotel where the banquet was to be
held. Hours later, he joined his fellow newspapermen for an elaborate dinner, filled with speeches, toasts, and a serenade by the stage
and film star Florence Reed. Also in attendance that night was New
Jersey State Senator Alexander Simpson, himself a former reporter,
as well as a prominent figure in Hudson County's Democratic machine. Payne and Simpson didn't know it yet, but in the future they

would end up working together on something big, something that would make them enemies of Frances Hall. Coincidentally, Frances ended up in Payne's orbit that weekend, too, albeit not physically. They shared the front page of the *Perth Amboy Evening News,* Payne in an article about the newspaper reunion, Frances in the headline directly above: MRS. HALL DID NOT TRUST RECTOR. It was the first time their names appeared in such proximity, but it would hardly be the last.

While Payne celebrated in Perth Amboy, Julia Harpman put the finishing touches on a story soon going to press. The *Daily News* had assembled a spread on the Hall-Mills case to coincide with the start of the grand jury proceedings. Harpman's contribution, under her signature nom de plume, "Investigator," explored the class dynamics inextricably woven into the saga. It wasn't just a murder mystery, but a tale of rich and poor, of the powerful and the powerless—a tragic melodrama in which working stiffs shared the stage with privileged heirs, cosseted by their lawyers and detectives and private guards. In Harpman's assessment:

Justice carries a short-weight scale in the dingy, little Jersey town with its "hunkie" quarter and its tony section up the hill, where the "man of god" made moonshine love and wrote sophomore sonnets to his "Wonderheart"—his "Gypsy Queen." The law says certain things about equality of rich and poor. But the law speaks with its tongue in its cheek. The law says the rich Mrs. Frances Stevens Hall . . . deserves no more consideration than Clifford Hayes, the young man who was thrown into prison on the unsupported accusation of an irresponsible character. But the eyes of reality see an impassable gulf—a chasm cleft by the sinews of wealth—between the preacher's widow and the swarthy young sandwich cook, who worked, when he did work, in a side-street lunch cart. They picture Mrs. Hall as a dowageresque and haughty incarnation of money's power, unmolested by any prosecutor, notwithstanding allegations no less credible than those for which young Hayes was hustled off to jail. Over all the ramifications of the mystery enthralling the imagination of the nation a web of doubt and scepticism has been woven by the propaganda influence of millions.

Frances found a more sympathetic audience in the seventy-six women who put their names to a letter of support. The signatories included Martha L. Johnson, wife of James Wood Johnson, as well as the famous etiquette expert cum pioneering divorcée Emily Post, who summered in the same vicinity as Frances in Maine. "She is now and always has been a woman of the highest type," the ladies wrote, "above suspicion and above reproach, incapable of thinking, much less of doing evil."

AT TEN O'CLOCK SHARP ON the morning of Monday, November 20, twenty men and three women filed into a meeting room on the first floor of the Somerset County Courthouse in downtown Somerville, about ten miles from the scene of the murders. They hailed from twelve different towns around the county—farmers, merchants, the postmaster of Bernardsville, the reverend of Somerville's First Reformed Church, the superintendent of Hillsborough's Duke estate, the wife of a prominent local contractor. It was, as one newspaper noted, "a mature and, for the most part, gray haired grand jury."

Somerset County Prosecutor Azariah Beekman was skeptical of Jane Gibson's story, and he had opposed taking the case to a grand jury based on the available evidence. But Mott's determination prevailed. They now sought three nameless "John Doe" indictments, one for the man who allegedly fired the fatal shots (whose identity would soon be revealed); one for the woman who allegedly accompanied him to the farm (Frances, most likely); and one for a second man suspected of being an accessory (presumably Ralph Gorsline).

As the jurors took their seats, they saw a large easel on which was displayed a map of the area around the Phillips farm. The prosecutors also passed around photographs of the crime scene, taken by a Somerville photographer after the bodies were removed. A display of the victims' bloodstained clothing chilled the room: Edward's gray-and-black suit, the panama hat, his gold tie clasp with the letter *G* engraved; Eleanor's red-and-blue polka-dot dress, her long brown woolen scarf, the navy-blue turban found near her body.

The mood at the courthouse was electric. State troopers standing guard over the building kept large crowds at bay. A mezzanine encircling the octagonal rotunda was packed with dozens of onlookers, bumping elbows to get a view of the grand jury room below. When George Totten realized the assembled gawkers could peek into the room through a transom, he climbed a stepladder and covered the glass with a swath of black cloth.

The first two days were uneventful. Mott and Beekman ran through a battery of witnesses who described the finding of the bodies and the limited forensics at the scene. They also called witnesses who could place Edward and Eleanor near the Phillips farm, like the trolley operator who drove Eleanor down Easton Avenue, and the women who saw them, one after the other, walking in the direction of De Russey's Lane. Pearl Bahmer arrived from Newark's House of the Good Shepherd in the company of a nun. Ray Schneider, still imprisoned on a charge of perjury, was hauled over to the courthouse through a subterranean passageway from the adjoining jail.

"Did you go up there," Mott demanded, "knowing that [Pearl] was having her period, for the express purpose of lying down on your back, as you did, and [having] her do the vile thing she did to you? Wasn't that why you went there?"

"No, sir," Ray lied. "It was not."

On the third day of the grand jury, the prosecution introduced witnesses who'd heard gunshots and screams on the night of the murders. One of them was Norman Tingle, the man whose wife had seen a falling star from their porch, predicting it was a harbinger of death. "All the shots that I heard were within a minute and a half or two minutes," he said. "I heard either three or four."

When Nellie Lo Russell took the stand, she swore she'd been with Gibson on the night of the murders. Mott countered with a witness named George Seipel, who testified that on the evening of September 14, he twice visited Russell's shack to discuss the sale of a horse. Russell was not home, according to Seipel, who said that on his second visit, he waited for her between 9:30 and 9:50 P.M. The timeline was just enough to throw a bit of doubt on Russell's affidavit, in which she claimed to have gotten home around eight, and that Gibson showed up a few minutes before ten.

The most intriguing testimony of the day came from Emma Voorhees, whose name and story had managed to evade the newspapers heretofore. Voorhees lived on Easton Avenue, a couple of miles up the road from De Russey's Lane. In her recollection of the fatal night, two cars came to a screeching halt in front of her house around 9:40 P.M. She peeked out the bay window in her bedroom and saw several figures, at least one of them female, arguing in the darkness. "What are you doing here?" a man said loudly. Voorhees heard two gunshots fired into the air, like warning shots. The people scurried back into their cars and sped away, heading in the direction of the Phillips farm. "We never thought any more of it," Voorhees told the jurors. Her tale was intriguing, but it wasn't clear what, if anything, the incident had to do with the events at the crabapple tree, where the murders were believed to have occurred around 10:20 P.M.

Toward the end of the afternoon, the grand jury heard from Charlotte Mills, seen around town lately in a stylish new wardrobe. Her makeover included zebra-stripe stockings that were, as one observer put it, the "latest thing from flapperdom." The sixteen-year-old dressed more conservatively for the court, appearing in plain brown stockings that complemented her three-piece navy suit, with a Peter Pan collar and a blue silk tie to match.

"This is your time to talk," Mott implored. "It is your only chance, if you want to have us find out who killed your mother. Now is your time. You may talk freely."

"Well," Charlotte replied, "there is one thing I would like to say, and that is, I think Mrs. Hall knew of the relations between my mother and Mr. Hall." As for Charlotte's father, she insisted he was not jealous of the reverend. "He liked Mr. Hall," Charlotte said. "They were friends."

The prosecutors put this assertion to the test when Jim Mills took the stand next.

"Did you have any concern about who your wife was writing the word 'honey' to?" Beekman asked.

"No," Jim replied. "I did not."

Toward the end of his testimony, Mott asked, "Can you tell this grand jury anything that will help them to find out who it was that foully cut your wife's throat and shot four bullets into her head?"

"No, sir," said Jim. "I cannot. I cannot tell you a thing."

AFTER A FOUR-DAY RECESS, THE grand jury reconvened on Monday, November 27, the longest day of testimony yet, with nineteen witnesses passing in and out of the grand jury room. Louise Geist, soberly dressed in a tailored blue suit with a plain silk velour hat, was questioned by Beekman about the phone call from Eleanor summoning Edward from the house. Could Frances have listened in on a different receiver? Louise couldn't provide a definitive answer, but she believed Frances was on the porch by the time Edward picked up the line. "I didn't see her go out, but I heard the screen door slam," Louise said. The other maid, Barbara Tough, who had worked in the Hall household since emigrating from Scotland in 1916, testified that she never witnessed any marital friction between her employers. She'd been out with a friend that evening after a day off, and although she didn't see Frances or Willie when she returned at ten o'clock, going straight to bed, she assumed they were in the house.

Two of Eleanor's sisters, Augusta Tennyson and Elsie Barnhardt, testified about their knowledge of the affair and the rumors of an elopement. Tennyson said Edward and Eleanor's romance had intensified as early as February. "She said she would give up everything for him," Tennyson told the jurors. Barnhardt recalled an occasion when Frances had said, "Here's to our wives and sweethearts. May our sweethearts remain our wives and our wives remain our sweethearts." Barnhardt had impishly replied, "Here is to our wives and sweethearts—may they never meet."

Ralph Gorsline's testimony, expected to be one of the highlights, turned out to be an exercise in pulling teeth, with Gorsline repeatedly pleading ignorance to any scurrilous goings-on within the church.

"Do you want this grand jury to understand that you don't know anything about this case at all," one juror asked, "or any of the gossip?"

"No suspicion ever entered your mind up to the day of the tragedy?" said another.

"I wonder if Mr. Gorsline has told us everything he has in his mind," echoed a third. "I think Mr. Gorsline has something more to tell than he has told us."

Responding to a question from Beekman, Gorsline said, "I don't go to church to spy upon anybody." To which Mott replied, "What was there in his question that involved spying on anybody?"

Minnie Clark's testimony was a further disappointment. Newspaper reports about the investigation portrayed Clark and Gorsline as Frances Hall's eyes and ears. There was every expectation that Mott would interrogate Clark about the letter she was suspected to have given to Frances, which Gorsline, in turn, was suspected of having first given to Clark. On the contrary, Minnie's time on the witness stand was so brief that, when she walked out of the grand jury room less than five minutes after going in, there was a collective gasp among the reporters and spectators gathered outside.

As Harpman suggested, "Today's proceedings had much of the outward aspects of a Grand Jury whitewashing."

On the fifth and final day of testimony, Tuesday, November 28, Azariah Beekman took the stand to explain how Jane Gibson was able to identify Frances as the woman on the farm. When Frances and her brothers were summoned to the Middlesex County Courthouse on October 17, Beekman said, their questioning was "rather a subterfuge." Gibson, it turned out, was also in the prosecutor's office that day. Beekman had staged the interrogation in order to give her a furtive look at the suspects. Gibson expressed certainty that Frances was the woman she'd seen in the automobile headlights, but she wasn't so sure about Henry Stevens, despite her insistence that Frances had cried out, "Oh, Henry!" Unbeknownst to the public, there was another Henry who'd come under scrutiny.

To explain this twist in the investigation, the prosecution called Detective Ferd David, who had accompanied Gibson to New Brunswick's railroad station one morning. David told the jurors he had instructed Gibson to observe the commuters and "take particular notice" of anyone resembling the man from the Phillips farm. Shortly before the arrival of the seven fifty-five train to New York, David watched from a distance as Gibson focused her attention on one man in particular. After the train pulled away, David asked Gibson if the man was familiar to her. "If I saw him with his hat and overcoat off, I think I could say more about him," Gibson replied. "But he looks very much like the man I saw that night." The man in question was none other than Henry de la Bruyere Carpender, Frances's cousin and neighbor, who looked like a taller and balder version of Henry Stevens. The problem, David explained, was that Henry Carpender had an alibi. He'd been at a dinner party until around ten thirty that night, and his attendance was confirmed by the host.

The jurors were skeptical, expressing doubts about Gibson's identifications and asking David whether it wouldn't have been more prudent to conduct a proper lineup. Couldn't Gibson have been making the whole thing up based on stories she'd read in the newspapers? There was reward money at stake, was there not? Mott grilled David on these same points, to such an extent that it almost seemed as if he was working for the defense.

"In your experience," said Mott, "don't you always consider that bringing two people together and simply asking, 'Is this the man that took your pocketbook,' is the very weakest kind of identification?"

"It certainly is," David conceded. "There is no question about that."

BY THE TIME JANE GIBSON was called to testify, the prosecution's case didn't look very convincing. Mott and Beekman had presented a set of dots without any way of connecting them. But if the jurors heard Gibson's account from her own lips, if they found her to be compelling and credible, maybe that might be enough to persuade them.

Gibson approached the grand jury room dressed in a black suit and matching stockings, with French-heeled shoes that slowed her steps. As she walked across the floor, the spectators in the mezzanine stared down in suspense. Frances Hall had come to the courthouse that day in anticipation of the grand jury's decision. Bundled up in a heavy black coat, she sat between Timothy Pfeiffer and Sally Peters, against a wall directly across from the grand jury room. Gibson came close enough that the two women could have touched. As she disappeared into the doorway, Sally leaned over and whispered into Frances's ear.

Seated before the jurors, Gibson described what she had seen and heard on the night of the murders. The barking of her dog. Her pursuit of the supposed corn thief. The car turning around in De Russey's Lane. Its headlights revealing the faces of "a small woman and a quite tall man." The voices in the darkness. ("Explain these letters!" "Oh, please, please, please!") A gunshot. A woman screaming in terror. Another woman crying out, "Oh, Henry!" The glow of a flashlight, "as if somebody was trying to find something in a hurry." Three more gunshots. Gibson's hasty retreat on her mule. Her subsequent return to the crime scene in search of the missing moccasin. The sound of heavy sobs. The sight of a woman weeping over a dead body in the moonlight.

"I just looked at the face," Gibson recalled, "and then I thought, 'Well, you are old enough to have sense enough not to be out here this hour of the night.' I knew I saw this woman there with the man earlier in the evening."

Gibson testified that she'd seen the same woman inside the prosecutor's office several weeks later, and that she picked the woman's companion out of a crowd at the train station. But then, crucially, she hedged.

"I am asking you now," said Mott, "was Henry Carpender the man you saw that night in De Russey's Lane?"

"I feel that he was."

"I don't know what you mean. Do you mean that you think so?"

"Yes."

"How sure are you?"

"Well, general appearance, to look at him."

"Are you sure enough so you would be willing to have him go to the electric chair for murder?"

"If he done it," Gibson said. "I believe he was the man."

Mott, either out of frustration, or because he had lost all confidence in his own witness, or because he now accepted that the case was hopeless, began to question Gibson as if cross-examining her. Hadn't Gibson originally described the man as having bushy hair? Wasn't Henry Carpender wearing a hat when she saw him at the train station? How could she possibly be sure?

"To see him with the hat off," said Gibson, "that would make me feel perfectly safe."

Mott cited a remark Gibson had made earlier in the investigation, suggesting the man on De Russey's Lane looked like a light-skinned Black man—the implication being that Gibson could have been describing a very tan white man, as befit Henry Stevens's appearance following his summers down the shore.

"Henry Stevens looks more like a colored man in the dark than Henry Carpender does, does he not?"

"Yes, he does."

"Therefore, Henry Stevens looks more like the man than Henry Carpender, does he not?"

"Well," said Gibson, "the face is not the same."

Far from convincing the jury that Gibson's story was accurate, the only thing Mott had convinced them of was that Gibson couldn't identify Henry Carpender as the killer, at least not beyond a reasonable doubt.

"You realize," a juror said, "you have made a very serious charge, don't you?"

"Yes."

"If this grand jury acts on your word, where will the prosecutor stand when it comes to trial, if it should come to trial? Do you suppose you will have another change of mind?"

"No, sir. I do not suppose so."

WHEN GIBSON EMERGED FROM THE grand jury room, nearly two hours after going in, Frances Hall's spine stiffened as she came face-to-face with her accuser. Gibson stared at Frances as she walked by, her clunky French heels hammering the floor. Frances's face did not stray from the jury room door, but her eyes followed Gibson as she crossed the lobby, making her way toward the exit.

A couple of hours later, with no further witnesses to call, Mott and Beekman exited the room. "Here comes the dramatic moment," Pfeiffer whispered. As the grand jury deliberated, crowds thronged the courthouse and the assembled state troopers snapped to attention. Bets were placed in a hotel lobby across the street. Outside the grand jury room, dozens of men and women leaned over the railings on the mezzanine, their eyes fixed on Frances, sitting calmly with her hands folded in her lap. Sally Peters bit her lip and twirled her fingers. Pfeiffer looked down at the floor, his face resting in his hand. Mott and Beekman were called back in. Finally, at 4:23 P.M., the door was flung open and the jurors filed out, their civic duty fulfilled. Reporters rushed inside to learn the decision.

"Are you ready, ladies and gentleman?" the foreman said.

"YESSSSS!"

"For reasons which to them seem sufficient and controlling," said the foreman, reading slowly from a piece of paper, "the grand jury took no action on the Hall-Mills murder case and laid the matter over."

The reporters immediately swarmed Mott, who declined to comment. One of them darted out of the room and broke the news to Frances, who said nothing but allowed herself a fleeting smile. Pfeiffer grasped his client's arm as she rose from her chair. Tears streamed down Sally Peters's cheeks. They hurried Frances out of the courthouse and into a waiting Dodge sedan, "a silent, black-clad figure," as one observer put it, "with her head held high."

The grand jury result was popular in Somerset County, where there was little appetite for a trial at the mounting expense of taxpayers. In New Brunswick, the citizenry clamored for justice. "There can be no thought of surrender, of quitting under fire, in connection with the investigation of the Hall-Mills mystery," the

Daily Home News declared in an editorial, "no matter what the cost and no matter what the length of time that may be involved in that effort."

Later that evening, in the tiny kitchen of 49 Carman Street, Jim Mills was asked his opinion of the outcome while making himself a bologna and cheese sandwich. "That's pretty rotten, and justice has not been done," he said. "Here it is nearly eleven weeks and we're right where we were when it started. But if justice is not done by the state, it will be done by a higher power, and the conscience that has this thing to think over will be punished for its owner. It'll all come out some day, but it's pretty rotten to think the whole thing was thrown down like that. I didn't expect it."

In the *Daily News*, Julia Harpman described the grand jury's conclusion as "one of the most dramatic days in the history of crime—a day replete with thrills the like of which were unknown before the annals of unsolved mysteries were doomed to include the New Brunswick case." As Harpman saw it, the murders were bound to remain a puzzling enigma, "unless there should be a deathbed confession or some equally improbable development."

Phil Payne had just such a development in mind.

14

MADAME ASTRA

In early February, two months after the grand jury session, Frances stood on the platform of New Brunswick's Pennsylvania Railroad station, all bundled up in her winter wraps, carrying a ticket to New York but no luggage. Her train arrived and Frances boarded, leaving behind the horrors of the previous autumn. She looked forward to an extended jaunt through the Continent with Sally Peters, just the balm to ease her sorrows.

Two days later, a small army of photographers swarmed Pier 55, north of Manhattan's West Village. Rumor had it that Frances and Sally were among the eight hundred seafarers who had booked passage on the *Mauretania*, a 790-foot ocean liner bound for the Mediterranean. Journalists stalked the ship, but the pair was nowhere to be found. Two miles up the Hudson River, another boat, the Naples-bound SS *America*, pulled away from the dock. Frances and Sally had managed to keep their names off the manifest, eluding the newspapers. They settled in as their vessel set sail for Italy, a world away from the homicide investigation that had fizzled to a tepid denouement back home.

The mystery that captivated America for the better part of three months had faded from the headlines. In Somerset County, Azariah Beekman and George Totten continued to work the case, but they needed a fresh set of eyes. They found one in Ellis Parker, a celebrated sleuth from the prosecutor's office in Burlington County, fifty miles south. A stout, fifty-one-year-old farm-bred Quaker, known to use words like "thee" and "thou," Parker bore the trappings of a hard-boiled detective: bowler hat, mustache, necktie, briar pipe dangling from the corner of his mouth. He had come to be regarded as an American Sherlock Holmes, with roughly a hundred cases under his belt and an impressive rate of conviction. He would later be called upon to solve the Lindbergh kidnapping in 1932, but some of his recent cases were media sensations in their own right, like the killing of Burlington County carnival impresario "Honest John" Brunen. During the Hall-Mills investigation, there had been calls for Parker to swoop in and solve the mystery. The New Brunswick *Daily Home News* argued that it "would be no reflection on the local force, in a case of such magnitude, to call in additional assistance." Charlotte Mills had made a similar plea in a letter to Parker, writing, "I know that you will not lose any time in clearing up the mystery surrounding the cruel slaying of my mother." Parker monitored the case from the sidelines. "They're following blind trails," he'd said in October. "When this church crime is solved, I believe there will be a solution upsetting every theory so far advanced."

By the end of 1922, Parker was ready to lend a hand. Writing about him in the *Daily News*, Julia Harpman gushed, "The name Ellis Parker today strikes terror to the criminal heart. It symbolizes the majesty of the law. . . . Now he is being urged to take up the badly scattered threads of the Hall-Mills murder and to make an effort to piece together a solution."

Parker had a hunch about who killed Edward Hall and Eleanor

Mills. Harpman's boss, Phil Payne, had the same hunch. Now all they had to do was prove it.

ON THE AFTERNOON OF TUESDAY, January 16, Jim Mills elbowed his way through the crowd at the Capitol Theatre in downtown Trenton and bounded up to George Silzer, the newly elected Democratic governor of New Jersey and successor to Edward Edwards, now a U.S. senator. Silzer had just finished his inaugural address when he set eyes on the skinny man standing before him. Jim introduced himself with an overeager handshake and got straight to the point. "Please," he pleaded, "do something about finding the murderer of my wife." The governor said he was well apprised of the case, and he told Jim that if he had any new information, he should convey it to the governor's secretary, who quickly whisked Jim away. As Jim told a reporter the following morning, "You don't get anything unless you keep agitating."

Jim had always been consistent in his story about the night of the murders. Eleanor stormed out of the house around seven thirty. He worked on some window planters. He walked over to St. John's and closed up. He read the newspaper. Around eleven, he bought a bottle of soda water from the corner store and went to bed. Charlotte confirmed her father's presence at 49 Carman Street as of ten fifteen, when she returned from a visit to her aunt's house. But depending on exactly what time the killings occurred, there was wiggle room in Jim's alibi.

Ellis Parker struck up a rapport with Jim, taking care not to let on that he considered him to be the primary suspect. On the contrary, Parker gave off the impression that he suspected Frances. His only goal, he assured Jim, was justice for Eleanor. During one of Parker's visits to the Mills home, on January 14, he interviewed Jim in the presence of a stenographer.

"Did you see any letters at all? Before the murder?"

"There were two letters in a scarf. . . . Never been in the mail, never dated or signed."

"Who were they addressed to?"

"One was 'Dear,' and one was 'Honey.' She would write things like that out of books, and she would keep it for a while and then take them and burn them."

Parker didn't buy it—he came away from the interview even more determined to establish Jim's guilt, and he wasn't the only one. Phil Payne had also decided to take a closer look at the cuckolded handyman. He told Harpman to ingratiate herself with Jim and look for any "exploitable peculiarities." It didn't take long for Harpman to find one: Jim Mills believed in ghosts.

Jim's proclivity for the otherworldly was hardly remarkable. The 1920s had ushered in a renewed fervor for spiritualism, as humanity grappled with the loss of tens of millions of souls to the Great War and the Spanish flu. RIDDLE OF THE LIFE HEREAFTER DRAWS WORLD'S ATTENTION, declared a headline in the *Sun and the New York Herald*. By 1922, according to the *Daily News*, Ouija boards had "ousted the card table" as the parlor game de rigueur for society figures such as Alice Claypoole Vanderbilt, Elsie de Wolfe, and Theodate Pope Riddle. Sir Arthur Conan Doyle spread the ghostly gospel with a series of books and lecture tours, including a thirteen-date jaunt through the United States that kicked off at Carnegie Hall. The famed Sherlock Holmes author had lost a son to the flu, but only in body. "Kingsley isn't dead," Conan Doyle told the Associated Press, "and it is interesting to note that from such seances the truth about the afterlife is becoming more and more apparent."

Charlotte Mills was a convert. "I am taking up spiritualism and I am going to try to communicate with my mother," she announced to reporters. "I have just finished reading *The New Revelation* by Conan Doyle, and I never before read anything that interested me so much and made me feel so hopeful." Her mother had dabbled in the occult, too. The previous winter, Eleanor had corresponded with an East Indian spiritualist who advertised his services in the newspapers ("Let the stars guide you"). During the murder investigation, the psychic came forward to reveal that Eleanor had asked him whether Edward would get a divorce, and if she should follow him to the Orient. He claimed he had given Eleanor a more dire prediction: that she was doomed to meet an untimely death.

As Harpman soon discovered, the hocus-pocus had rubbed off on Jim. When she reported back to Payne, his instructions were blunt: "Let's pitch to this guy's weakness."

In Payne's estimation, there was only one way to extract a confession from Jim: by scaring him. He hatched a plan to stage a séance in which Eleanor would haunt her husband from the grave. It was precisely the type of cartoonish stunt that tabloid newspapers were made for, and Payne, a wild maestro of the tabloid form, spared no expense in its execution. He ordered his art department to create a letterhead for a mythical seer named Madame Astra. The illustration featured a line drawing of a veiled brunette with large earrings, framed by a mélange of owls, cobras, bats, black cats, toads, and various other creatures. To simulate Madame Astra, Payne called upon Bernardine Szold, a bohemian-looking character from his scrappy pack of female scribes. At twenty-six, Szold had an illustrious future in store, one that would take her to Paris and Shanghai before she settled down in Los Angeles and became a noted socialite and hostess to the Hollywood intelligentsia. To prepare for her role as Madame Astra, Szold visited mystics to pick up on their techniques, and she ventured uptown to Cain's, a warehouse for retired Broadway props. There, she purchased a black velvet backdrop that had been used in the *Ziegfeld Follies*, as well as a plaster pedestal with a green snake coiled around the column, a stuffed tomcat with luminous eyes, a large brass Buddha, and a gold mock throne. The requisite crystal ball was provided by an optician. A set dresser arranged the props in Szold's railroad-style apartment.

In the meantime, Harpman visited Jim Mills, who told her he'd received a strange letter from a New York medium, inviting him to a complimentary appointment at her Manhattan lair. He asked Harpman what he should do.

"I don't believe in spirits," she said, "but if you do, I don't want to advise you against seeing this woman. But watch out for a trick."

"I was afraid of that," Jim replied. "I won't go unless you go with me."

The plan appeared to be working. On a bitter winter's night in February, Harpman and Jim arrived on the doorstep of Szold's apartment, where they were greeted by a dark-complexioned man dressed like a swami, the toes of his satin slippers curled up like scorpions' tails. The man was Szold's husband, Otto Liveright, a literary agent and playwright who had procured his getup from a masquerade shop.

"You stay out," Liveright scowled at Harpman, betraying not a hint of familiarity. "The gentleman must come in alone."

Jim stepped into Madame Astra's den, where he found Szold at a table with the crystal ball. Incense wafted through the room as Jim gazed at the ersatz fortune-teller, glistening with baubles and costume jewelry.

"What do you seek with Astra?" she said, gesturing for Jim to take a seat.

"I've got an invitation."

"Well, what do you wish to know?"

Jim stood there blankly.

"What do you wish to know?"

"Who are my enemies?" Jim replied. "I want to know who my enemies are."

Jim sat down and placed his hands on the orb. Little did he know, his enemies were right there in the apartment. Before moving forward with the séance, Payne had consulted with Azariah Beek-man, who gave the plan his blessing. (What did he have to lose?) Beekman looped in George Totten and Ellis Parker. The three of them, as well as Payne and a stenographer, sat behind the heavy velvet curtain that Szold had procured as a backdrop, quiet as mice.

Szold closed her eyes, pretending to drift into a deep trance, swaying and moaning amid the incense smoke, revealing strange images from deep within the crystal ball. After a sufficiently theat-rical warm-up, she welcomed a woman's spirit into the room.

"Mrs. Mills."

"My wife?!"

"Yes."

As the séance progressed, Szold conveyed elaborate visions of Eleanor. She evoked the dead woman's appearance, her gestures, her mannerisms. When Jim removed one of his hands from the crystal ball, Szold grabbed it and put it back on, warning that he risked breaking contact with the spirit world. Then she went in for the kill: *Was it not true that Jim was responsible for Mrs. Mills death?*

"I never killed her," Jim protested. "I couldn't do anything like that."

Madame Astra persisted in her accusations, but Jim was un-flinching. He maintained his innocence, never once exuding the faintest hint of guilt. Unable to rattle her client, Szold brought the séance to a close, but not before employing one last trick. She peered back into the crystal ball, telling Jim it now revealed the image of a man. A short man, stocky and bald, with a mustache. It was a man Jim recognized, in his mind, as Ellis Parker, who listened from behind the curtain.

"Go to your friend," Madame Astra proclaimed, "and confide in him."

THE NEXT DAY, JIM TOOK a train from New Brunswick to Burlington, a small town on the Delaware River between Trenton and Philadelphia. In his office nearby, Parker was studying the stenographer's transcript when the phone rang. It was Jim, and he urgently needed to see to Parker, who sent a car to the train station right away.

When Jim arrived, Parker took him into a side room. Jim sat down and recalled his strange experience from the previous evening, adding a specious detail: he said that Madame Astra had proclaimed his innocence. Knowing this to be false, Parker tried a bit of reverse psychology.

"Well, Jim," the detective began, "if this spiritualist sent you to me, I can't see how I can help you unless you were guilty, and that you were going to tell me all the facts so that I could tell them to the public, and if the facts are as I believe they are, no jury in the world would ever convict you. In fact, you would have the sympathy of the world. The preacher not only betrayed the trust that you placed in him, but he was a hypocrite before his God. In my judgment, God committed this crime and he used you as an instrument."

It was no use—Jim didn't budge. He chatted with Parker a while longer before leaving to catch a train back to New Brunswick. Afterward, Parker called the *Daily News* and told Payne they should take one more crack at breaking Jim's alibi. Then he typed up a letter to Totten, apprising him of the latest developments. "I wanted to leave the impression on him that I kind of thought he was guilty," Parker wrote. "Just what effect this will have I don't know, but if we don't get the desired effect, some other process has got to be gone over and we will have to keep on as there is no question as to this man's guilt." Parker also indicated he was comparing notes with Frances Hall's private detective. "De Martini telephoned that he would be here on Tuesday," Parker said. "I will see what he knows and has found out."

A few weeks later, per Parker's suggestion, Payne decided to give Jim another brush with the spirit world. He told Otto Liveright to don his guru getup and head down to New Brunswick, reprising his role as Madame Astra's mystical wingman. Julia Harpman tagged along in a chauffeured limousine. They pulled up in front of 49 Carman Street and waited. Jim had gone to the movies that night, so he didn't get home until around ten o'clock. After watching Jim walk up the creaky wooden stairs at the back of the house, Liveright bounded up to his second-floor apartment and banged on the door, which flung open a moment later.

The plan was for Liveright to look at Jim with an evil eye and declare, "You are bad man! Madame Astra, she suffer. You did not told the truth. The spirits are very angry!" But Liveright barely got through the opening of his script before Jim's reflexes kicked in. He grabbed a carving knife and started waving it around at the costumed intruder. Liveright ran back down the stairs and into the car, which sped away into the dark winter's night.

Payne's attempt to solve the Hall-Mills murders was now at an end, at least for the time being. But it was just as well—Payne would soon be consumed by a tragedy of his own.

"A NEW, MONGREL FOURTH ESTATE"

One brilliant spring morning in 1923, sunlight filled the home of Phil and Helena Payne, casting a warm glow on Helena's sickly pallor. For three years, Helena had struggled with Bright's disease, an inflammation of the kidneys. The condition had worsened in recent months, leaving her weak and bedridden. "When the spring comes, I'll be well again," she had said over the long winter. "The sunshine will bring me strength." Alas, as the *Daily News* lamented, "The sunshine came too late." Helena slipped into a coma and died at 10:10 A.M. on Thursday, April 19. Her funeral was held days later at St. Joseph's of the Palisades, where the Paynes had exchanged vows eight years earlier. The public schools in West New York suspended class for ten minutes out of respect for Payne, who served on the board of education. Flags on all public buildings were lowered to half-mast. The color guard of the town's local American Legion post, which counted Helena as a member of the women's auxiliary, led the procession to her burial plot. Julia Harpman's husband, Westbrook Pegler, was one of the pallbearers.

Helena's death set Payne hopelessly adrift. He mourned the children they would never have. He abandoned plans for a new home, which the couple had already commissioned an architect to design. He stayed with his mother-in-law and lay down on the bed where Helena slept as a child. Some nights, on the way home from work, after the paper had gone to press, Payne would creep into St. Joseph's and pray—for Helena's eternal peace, for the strength to carry on without her. He took time off and traveled north to his childhood home of Gravenhurst, the Canadian lake resort where he and Helena had spent their honeymoon and returned each year for a summer vacation. Payne walked to a spot along the water where they had savored so many sunsets. He picked out a large rock and arranged for it to be shipped back home. It was placed atop Helena's grave.

Even in mourning, Payne continued to excel professionally. With the Hall-Mills murders behind him, at least for the time being, Payne steered the *Daily News'* coverage of other sensational crimes, from the murder of showgirl Dorothy King to the exploits of rumrunners along the Jersey shore. He championed the rise of celebrity culture, whether keeping tabs on the gossip swirling around stars like Rudolph Valentino or purchasing the serial rights to novels by F. Scott Fitzgerald. "The tabloid pattern was shaping up," one of Payne's colleagues observed, and Payne had the numbers to prove it. During the week of October 8, as Payne's reporters busied themselves with the divorce trial of hotel impresario William Earl Dodge Stokes and the home runs Babe Ruth was knocking out of the Polo Grounds, the *News* learned it had become the most-read newspaper in the country, with an average weekday readership of 633,578. "There is no newspaper," boasted a celebratory editorial, "morning or evening, in the United States, that has within forty or fifty thousand the circulation of the DAILY NEWS."

In just four years, Joseph Medill Patterson's tabloid had broken William Randolph Hearst's stranglehold on New York City, where Hearst's *Evening Journal* and *New York American*, once the industry's reigning champions, were now in decline. Hearst, a high-rolling kingpin who lorded over the world's largest media conglomerate—twenty-three newspapers read by one in four Americans; the magazines *Cosmopolitan*, *Good Housekeeping*, and *Harper's Bazaar*; a newswire, a features syndicate, a film company, and an animation studio—had initially dismissed the tabloid craze now spreading to rival publishers, such as Cornelius Vanderbilt Jr. and the E. W. Scripps Company. But by the summer of 1924, as tabloids sprouted in Los Angeles, Boston, Baltimore, St. Louis, Des Moines, and Detroit, the ever-competitive Hearst had no choice but to concede his miscalculation—he needed to start a tabloid of his own.

Hearst's intentions were consummated on June 24, with the debut of the New York *Daily Mirror*, a morning paper that one critic derided as "a slavish imitation of the *Daily News* in every respect." Brimming with sports, comics, contests, advice, theater, film, and, of course, crime, the *Mirror* took the tabloid formula and put it on full blast. If the *Daily News* was unashamedly down-market, the *Mirror* was positively vulgar, promising readers "90 percent entertainment, 10 percent information." News stories in the inaugural issue included a wife-slaying, an attempted wife-poisoning, and a dead priest. There was an excerpt from a controversial novel called *Flaming Youth*, a "true story" by an anonymous "Queen of Broadway" who had ensnared a wealthy widower, and "exclusive" body-sculpting advice from Valentino, who appeared shirtless on the cover. With its motto of "short, quick, and make it snappy," the *Mirror* trafficked in all the crude promiscuities of the era, which made it well positioned to challenge the *News*. As *Editor & Publisher* suggested, Hearst's tabloid had "entered the fight with zest."

In a matter of weeks, the fight would become even bloodier: a third tabloid was about to enter the ring.

On July 17, 1924, newspaper editors received a telegram from Bernarr Macfadden, an idiosyncratic media tycoon known for his outlandish flair, espousal of quack medicine, and barefoot walks through New York City. Fifty-five years old and chiseled like a statue, Macfadden stood out as an avatar of Jazz Age eccentricity. He'd embarked on a long and winding journey from the rural wastelands of Middle America to the power circles of postwar Manhattan, where Macfadden—né Bernard McFadden (he changed his first name to Bernarr because Bernard "looked ordinary")—cemented himself as a self-made health buff and publisher of middlebrow periodicals focused on fitness and human-interest topics, including the wildly successful *Physical Culture*. While Joe Patterson was busy establishing the *Daily News*, Macfadden pioneered the confession-mag genre, bringing the world such voyeuristic titles as *True Story*, *True Experiences*, *True Romances*, *True Detective Mysteries*, *Dream World*, and *Ghost Stories*. Now, as the *News* and the *Mirror* locked horns, Macfadden prepared to enter the fray. After his plans were revealed in his July 17 telegram to editors, Payne immediately forwarded the news to Patterson, quoting Macfadden's announcement: "I expect to begin publishing [a] New York daily newspaper that will be human all the way through. Illustrations will be an important feature of this proposed newspaper, and every possible means will be used to make it attractive and appealing. Sensationalism will be used where it serves good purpose but we will not confine our idea of news to murder, suicide and divorce scandal."

Two months later, on September 15, Macfadden's tabloid rolled off the presses at 25 City Hall Place, where Macfadden had purchased the former headquarters of the *Evening Mail*. He named it the *Evening Graphic*, paying homage to a defunct nineteenth-century proto-tabloid known as the *Daily Graphic*. Unlike its respectable predecessor, Macfadden's paper went on to earn a nickname befitting the racy content for which it became famous: the *PornoGraphic*. As one contemporary newsman suggested, Macfadden had given New York "one of the most unusual news-publications it has ever seen." The content was an assortment of typical tabloid fare—crime, celebrity, features, photos, ridiculous contests. And yet the style of the

Graphic was anything but typical. Wherever possible, news stories were written in the voice of their subjects, as told to the *Graphic*'s reporters and editors, aping the first-person style of Macfadden's confession mags: "Friends Dragged Me in Gutter"; "I Know Man Who Killed My Girl"; "We Faced Death Together in Flames." The *Graphic*'s most memorable innovation was an art form known as the composograph, in which the faces of story subjects were super-imposed on body doubles. It was an outrageous way to illustrate sensational news events, like the murder-suicide of socialites Sydney and Frances Brewster, or the bedroom antics of Edward "Daddy" Browning and his teenage bride, Peaches Browning. (They didn't call it the *PornoGraphic* for nothing.)

To celebrate the tabloid's debut, Macfadden visited the *Graphic*'s cavernous fourth-floor newsroom, where staffers hoisted the five-foot-six-inch mogul onto a table. "We are going to publish a news-paper which will publish nothing but the truth. That is our motto," Macfadden began, speaking in an accent that one attendee described as a mix of Old Scotch and Choctaw. "It will be of the people, by the people, for the people. As you know, the people themselves will write a great deal of this paper, and the editors and reporters will help them write it. . . . We will make this publication great because we will be a *crusading newspaper*." He slammed the fist of one hand into the palm of the other. "We are going to keep our crusade for health! For physical fitness! And against medical ignorance! The fight I have made against the use of drugs has made a difference in every drugstore, and we are going to continue it. We will be against prurient prudery. We are featuring a contest in which we will look for Apollos and Dianas. We want perfect mates for a *new* human race, free of inhibitions, and free of the contamination of the small-pox vaccine!"

Later that day, Phil Payne combed through the *Graphic*'s first issue to size up the competition, which he didn't find to be much com-petition at all. "First page contains only one three column picture," he wrote to Patterson, dismissively. "On the whole, paper looks to me like [a] newspaper hash of all combined MacFadden publications."

As far as Payne was concerned, the *Daily News* was superior to its burgeoning rivals in every way, and he felt confident he could fend off their incursions. It was true that Payne didn't need to worry about external forces threatening his standing at the *News*—a conflict was brewing within.

PAYNE'S GRIEF OVER HELENA WAS long-lasting and profound, dragging him into the depths of despair even as his professional life presented every reason for happiness. Eventually, at the urging of his friends and Helena's mother, Payne pulled himself up and got back in the saddle. One of Payne's closest friends, the *Daily News* reporter Francis Farley, inspired something of a personal renaissance, exerting a positive influence on Payne's style and behavior. The old Phil Payne was simple, slouchy, unconcerned with fashion. The new Phil Payne wore expensive suits, prowled the chic haunts of midtown, and rubbed elbows in elite clubs like the Rotary, the Cheese, and the Inner Circle, which parodied him during its annual dinner show at the Hotel Astor, alongside fellow New York luminaries including Governor Al Smith, Mayor John Francis Hylan, U.S. Representative Ogden L. Mills, and *New York World* editor Herbert Bayard Swope. A gossip item in *The New Yorker* noted that Payne had been "bon-vivanting around town quite a bit."

In another personal development, Payne was increasingly spotted in public with Peggy Hopkins Joyce, a flamboyant showgirl whose millionaire marriages—and subsequent separations, most recently from the Swedish count Gösta Mörner—provided endless material for tabloid reporters, including the *Daily News*, where Joyce was a regular on the front page. Payne made good money as a newspaper editor, but not enough to satisfy Joyce's appetite for diamonds and furs. What Payne *was* able to give Joyce, which the fabulously wealthy men in her life could not, was a spotlight in the country's largest newspaper. He showered her with what one contemporary described as "a great publicity campaign," and Patterson wasn't happy about it.

Patterson could be a demanding and sometimes highly critical boss, scolding Payne for a "tendency to question orders" or a "picture [that] looked awful on page one." Patterson warned Payne to dial back the coverage of his lady friend. "I'm tired of seeing pictures of Peggy Joyce in the paper," he snapped. The final straw came one evening in 1925, when Joyce visited Payne in the newsroom, darting around the corridors like a mischievous child. Payne gave her a tour, from the reporters hammering out stories on weathered Remingtons to the monstrous presses that churned out hundreds of thousands of papers every morning. As Joyce marveled at the powerful machines, Payne asked if she wanted to turn them on, leading her to the control panel. She extended one of her soft pale fingers, tapped the start button, and then dramatically recoiled when the presses came roaring to life. "Take me out of here!" she yelled, clutching Payne, who hit the stop key and escorted Joyce back to his office. When Patterson, still based in Chicago, heard about the incident, he was furious. Payne had crossed the line, and his editorship was now at an end.

The news broke in the May 9 edition of *Editor & Publisher*: "Philip A. Payne, managing editor of the *New York Daily News* for the past two and a half years, has resigned from that post, effective June 15." The tabloid's city editor, Frank Hause, a pallbearer at Helena's funeral, was promoted to succeed him. Payne, who was permitted to collect his $11,986 bonus for the year, claimed he had "completed arrangements for a tabloid daily newspaper in another city," and that he would announce these plans after returning from vacation. He left town for Maine and then packed up for a longer trip to Europe, setting sail May 27 aboard the *Berengaria*.

Under Payne's leadership, the *News* had continued to gain circulation. It now sold far more copies than any other American newspaper—roughly eight hundred thousand on weekdays, and on Sundays close to a million, the milestone at which Patterson said he would relocate from Chicago to New York. This runaway circulation growth made Payne a valuable commodity for any zealous newspaper publisher, and one such publisher wasted no time in snapping him up. He hadn't even returned from his European sabbatical when Hearst's announcement went out: "Philip A. Payne, who resigned last month as managing editor of the *New York Daily News*, will become managing editor of the *New York Mirror*."

The change—set to take effect July 1, upon Payne's return from the Continent—was seen as a major escalation between the warring tabloids. A year after its launch, the *Mirror*'s circulation had climbed to nearly three hundred thousand. But what good were three hundred thousand copies when your rival sold nearly a million? Hearst wasn't interested in second place—he ordered Payne to take on the *News*, and Payne was more than happy to oblige.

BY THE TIME PAYNE'S ALLEGIANCE shifted, New York's tabloids had become an inexorable force in the rapidly changing media landscape, which also faced disruption from radio and film. "The tabloid picture paper has attacked intrenched eight-column journalism and threatens to become a new, mongrel Fourth Estate," suggested an article in *The Nation*. While proponents celebrated the tabloids' brevity, irreverence, and "youthful crusading spirit," as one disciple put it, the futsy old guard scorned their circulation-obsessed tendencies toward vulgarity and sensationalism. In one of the more contemptuous assessments, a *New Yorker* writer sneered: "With unction and spurious gravity, they disclose slave rings which are at best nebular; they prowl among the unhappy memories of victims who, by a certain twist, may be romanticized; they employ such items of the news as seem suited to their purpose as pegs upon which to hang breathless suggestions of unsuspected deviltry; they gird on their armor for ringing crusades upon matters that are trivial; they play upon the prurience of their handmade audience with any instrument that comes to hand, and upon their cupidity with stupidly opulent contests; they are unrestrained in the publication of gruesome photographs; they hold it old-fashioned to attempt the recording of the actual news; they publish editorials which are amusingly diffuse and shrewdly based upon trifling matters; they are the biggest money makers in the publishing business; and they are growing fast."

Growing fast was Hearst's primary mission, and Payne executed it with gusto. For starters, he doubled down on reader contests, the front line of the tabloid wars. One of his more nonsensical creations was a so-called "Big Dough Man" contest, in which hundred-dollar prizes were awarded for inane one-liners. "My friend is a big necker from Spooner, Wis." "My friend is a big hat man from Derby, Conn." And so on. To advertise the stunt, Payne sent a heavyset gentleman into the streets of Manhattan in an outfit dyed to resemble greenbacks. "We want people talking about our tabloid," Payne told *Editor & Publisher.* "Thus we send out a fat man for thousands to see, laugh at, and talk about on Broadway. Thus we try often to lead off the paper with something we know no other newspaper will play. It may be a triviality, yes. But it will be interesting and it will not be so overplayed that the news suffers. The success of a tabloid, as well as the standard size newspaper, depends on its complete, if compact, coverage of the news. Leave out the news and circulation will drop. In building mass circulation, however, trivialities are exceedingly important, because so frequently they are more interesting than the current great events."

Not all of Payne's efforts were trivial. He continued to champion women journalists, such as Helen Hadakin, the paper's first female reporter, whom Payne sent into the Holland Tunnel to chronicle its construction firsthand. He hired a young writer named Micheline Keating on the strength of her breakout novel, *Fame*, for which Payne had acquired the second serial rights. Like Julia Harpman before her, Keating became a dogged crime and features reporter under Payne's tutelage, covering Jazz Age sensations like the Peaches and Daddy Browning scandal, Charles Lindbergh's transatlantic flight, and the funeral of Hollywood heartthrob Rudolph Valentino, whose death at age thirty-one following an emergency appendectomy sparked a tabloid tour de force.

Payne was an advocate for his employees and a staunch defender of their work. When police officers roughed up *Mirror* journalists covering a textile strike in New Jersey, Payne filed suit over injuries and damaged cameras. When Canadian censors banned the *Mirror* due to "objectionable material," Payne declared, "We are negotiating with government officials in Ottawa now, and hope to have the ban lifted shortly."

Payne reserved his strongest ire for targets of the *Mirror*'s newspaper crusades. One such target was Harry Kendall Thaw, the disgraced railroad scion and murderer of renowned architect Stanford White. Thaw had been released from his second stint in an asylum despite an alienist's testimony that he abused rabbits while institutionalized. He'd gone back to live in his hometown of Pittsburgh, but when he began popping up at stylish Manhattan nightclubs and Broadway revues, like the *Ziegfeld Follies* and Earl Carroll's *Vanities*, Payne made it his business to drive Thaw out of town. One evening in September 1925, Payne assigned a *Mirror* reporter to follow Thaw to the exclusive Del Fey Club on West Forty-fifth Street, where the reporter's scrubby attire hindered his entry. The reporter called Payne—himself once a scrubby newsman, now an influential figure in New York society—to ask what he should do. Payne frequented the Del Fey and was friendly with the venue's famed hostess, Texas Guinan. "I'll come down myself," he said, hanging up the phone.

At Payne's request, the Del Fey's headwaiter seated him at a table close to Thaw's, positioning the men back to back. The scene wasn't too dissimilar from the evening of June 25, 1906, when Thaw brandished a pistol inside Madison Square Garden's crowded rooftop dinner theater and fired three shots at White from close range, killing him instantly. At the Del Fey, where the luminous guest list that night included the writer Michael Arlen, the actress Ethel Barrymore, and the heiress Gloria Gould Bishop, several patrons gasped when Thaw's hand disappeared into his pocket, only to emerge with a handkerchief. The hostess came over and whispered in Payne's ear that Thaw had been frisked upon entry. Feeling confident he wouldn't be shot, Payne approached his quarry for a chat. "That conversation," Payne later said, "convinced me that the man is insane and ought to be locked up."

The *Mirror's* coverage of its Thaw encounter was merciless. WHY IS HARRY THAW FREE? the front page roared on September 18. "Harry K. Thaw, who is not a potential murderer, but a nationally established murderer, is staggering about Broadway, his bloated face and protruding eyes marking him as he reels about the night clubs of the roaring forties." In an update the following day, the *Mirror* crowed: "Harry has suddenly decided to visit his sick mother, whose illness has not hitherto caused any of the many wrinkles in his bloated face. The Mirror has won. It has removed Harry K. Thaw from Broadway as a menace to society, sane or insane. . . . If he comes back to New York the Mirror will renew its campaign to get him away."

Recapping the episode, *Time* magazine's media columnist wrote, "Whether Mr. Thaw is, after all, a slobbering degenerate or merely an old man infected with a disgusting and pathetic lust for pleasures which youth alone can make charming; whether or not the Mirror had any higher purpose in its denunciations than the enlargement of an already huge circulation—matters little. The whole episode merely furnished one more example of how a smart editor can make sensationalism the light that illumines his paper's exceeding morality."

PAYNE AND THAW CROSSED PATHS again several months later, in February 1926, but this time, Thaw wasn't the one who ended up in the *Mirror's* crosshairs.

The venue was the Earl Carroll Theatre on Seventh Avenue and Fiftieth Street. The occasion was a party in honor of Carroll's financier, William R. Edrington, a millionaire Texas oil magnate. The crowd, which arrived in limousines and top hats, included Shirley Booth, a rising Broadway star; Condé Montrose Nast, owner of *Vanity Fair* and *Vogue*; Irvin S. Cobb, one of the highest paid journalists in the United States; and Vera Cathcart, a headline-making British countess. In all, several hundred people filled the ornate theater—eating, drinking, dancing, taking swigs from their hip flasks, and ogling girls from the *Vanities* cast, who pranced around in skimpy bathing suits and negligees. The main floor had been converted into a dining room, with an orchestra, a buffet table, a hot dog stand, and a bar on the stage. To the right of the bar lay a bathtub, from which guests filled their glasses to the brim. Taking a sip as she mingled with a *Mirror* reporter, the countess remarked, "Good champagne!"

Around 4:00 A.M., Payne was preparing to leave when the evening's host darted up to him.

"Don't go yet," Carroll implored. "I'm going to put on a wow of a stunt!"

Payne watched as the bathtub was moved to center stage and refilled with what appeared to be more alcohol. A girl with bobbed black hair and "the face of an angel," as one admirer put it, emerged from the wings. Her name was Joyce Hawley, a seventeen-year-old model and aspiring *Vanities* cast member, whose courage had been stimulated by several rounds of drinks backstage. Wearing an orange chemise that clung to her lithe frame, Hawley daintily approached the tub under the glow of a spotlight. A woman near the front of the stage tossed Carroll a green jacket, which he held in front of Hawley as if she were changing behind a dressing-room curtain. Her slippers came off and her lingerie dropped to the floor. As Carroll swept aside the coat with a flourish, several guests caught a glimpse of Hawley's breasts as she lowered herself into the tub and propped her feet over the edge, wine dripping from her pale toes. Carroll looked out at the crowd, beaming with satisfaction. "Gentlemen," he yelled, "the line forms to the left!"

A gaggle of men in dinner jackets elbowed their way toward the tub, retrieving glasses from a nearby table and holding them up to a spigot that had been fitted into the drainpipe. Some of them patted Hawley on her head and shoulders. One man tickled the soles of her feet. After a few minutes, tears streamed down Hawley's cheeks, at which point the bathtub was wheeled offstage. The show was over, and so was the party. Payne and the other remaining revelers exited the theater and staggered into the dawn.

The following morning, Wednesday, February 24, the *Mirror* published a vivid account of the scene Payne had witnessed. It was picked up by newspapers all over the country. ORGY OF WINE IN N.Y. RIVALS ANCIENT ROME, one headline declared. The exposé prompted an investigation by federal Prohibition agents, who set out to probe what the *New York Times* described as an "all-night bacchanalian orgy," resulting in Carroll's indictment. Payne took the stand during Carroll's trial a few months later. He swore he'd obtained Carroll's blessing to report on the shenanigans, even though Carroll's parties were understood to be off the record.

"May I print the story?" Payne had asked.

"Go as far as you like!" Carroll replied, according to Payne.

The Earl Carroll bathtub scandal turned into a media circus. It was also a major scalp for the *Mirror*, which, under Payne's leadership, had become a threat to the *News*. After riding the coattails of two rich and powerful men, Payne now had his own power to wield. He was channeling that power in pursuit of an even bigger story for the *Mirror*, a cloak-and-dagger investigation quietly unfolding in New Brunswick, New Jersey. If it came to fruition, it would be the biggest story of Payne's career. As one of his friends put it, he was "showing the world how tough he could be: he was going to scoop the town."

"INVESTIGATION A"

Three months after the bacchanal at Earl Carroll's midtown theater, George Totten sat across from Phil Payne in a small town fifty miles away, wondering what had brought the acclaimed editor of New York's *Daily Mirror* to Totten's dinky office in Somerville. A lot had changed in the three years since Payne, Totten, and Azariah Beekman teamed up, unsuccessfully, to force a confession out of Jim Mills, with a fake séance organized by Payne's *Daily News* journalists. For one thing, Beekman, who became a judge upon the conclusion of his term as Somerset County prosecutor, had died a month earlier, stricken with apoplexy while enjoying a night in Manhattan. "He was untiring in his effort to run down those guilty of perpetrating the Hall-Mills murder case," Beekman's obituary noted, charitably omitting his shortcomings in the investigation. "The fact that these were never brought to justice was always a source of disappointment to him." Totten had been pushed out by the new prosecutor, Francis Bergen. He'd filed an appeal with New Jersey's Civil Service Commission, claiming he'd been dismissed "on account of politics" after three decades as a county detective, but the commission had yet to issue a ruling on Totten's fate.

Payne, meanwhile, had become an even bigger player in the national media, making waves with the *Daily Mirror*'s ferocious tabloid coverage. He gazed out the window of Totten's office and took in the quietness of Main Street, recalling the mayhem that had descended on this sleepy New Jersey town four years earlier, when a grand jury declined to indict Frances Hall for the murder of her husband and his mistress. Payne then turned to Totten and began to speak.

"Ever hear that, about a year and a half after the murders, Louise Geist married a man named Arthur O. Riehl?" Payne asked, pulling a sheaf of papers from his breast pocket and laying them on Totten's desk.

Totten said he'd heard that Geist, the Halls' former maid, had married Riehl, a twenty-nine-year-old tradesman, but that the couple didn't live together. Payne gestured at the documents on Totten's desk, explaining that one of his reporters had uncovered a damning allegation from Riehl. According to Payne, Riehl claimed that on the evening of September 14, 1922, Louise and Peter Tumulty, the Halls' gardener and chauffeur, had accompanied Frances Hall and Willie Stevens to the Phillips farm, where they witnessed the murders. Riehl further claimed Louise had received five thousand dollars in exchange for her silence, and that she'd told him the officials in Middlesex County "were always taken care of" for quietly obstructing the investigation.

"What do you think of *that*?" Payne asked.

"So darned clumsy that I can't understand your paying any attention to it," Totten replied. "Don't forget that Middlesex County officials only *assisted* Somerset County. They didn't collect any evidence that wasn't available to everybody working on the case. Carbon copies were made of all the statements and distributed to everybody who took any part in the investigation. How could the Middlesex County officials prevent Mr. Beekman, Mr. Mott"—the special prosecutor—"and Colonel Schwarzkopf of the New Jersey

State Troopers from breaking the case? Can't you see the thing's preposterous?"

Payne smiled. "We've got the names of the witnesses they tried to buy off," he said, speaking slowly. "I've investigated this story thoroughly. Furthermore, we've come across a Burns detective who has proof that Ralph Gorsline and his girlfriend were in De Russey's Lane that night, and met Mrs. Hall and her cousin there—not only met but spoke to them—and we've got something else up our sleeves that's the real berries."

Totten could hardly conceal his skepticism. "That must've been quite a large company there at the farm that night," he said, sarcastically. "Mrs. Hall and Tumulty and William Stevens and his cousin and Ralph and the girlfriend. With Dr. Hall and Eleanor that would make nine—a regular convention! Does Louise corroborate her husband's story?"

On the contrary, Payne conceded: Louise had denied the whole thing.

"Well," Totten said with a shrug, "it's your funeral. You know I'm out of the game. What do you want with me?"

Payne told Totten he wanted access to the investigative files, which would enable the *Mirror* to compare its new reporting to the statements and testimony from 1922. Totten had also kept in touch with some of the witnesses who'd testified before the grand jury, which made him even more of an asset to the *Mirror*'s investigation. He and Payne talked it over. The more they talked, the more Totten warmed to Payne's proposal. What did he have to lose? He was sixty-one years old, recently ousted from a job to which he'd dedicated three decades of his life. Moreover, Payne was happy to compensate Totten for his services, and he could use that money if he lost his employment appeal. After a couple of hours, it was a fait accompli—Payne left Somerville with Totten's promise to assist the *Mirror* in any way he could.

PHIL PAYNE WASN'T THE FIRST one to take another crack at solving the murders. In the summer of 1924, as Bernarr Macfadden was laying the groundwork for the *Evening Graphic*, the *Graphic*'s recently hired editor, Emile Gauvreau, had come up with an idea that would put the *Graphic* on the map right away. "We hoped to revive the Hall-Mills murder case of 1922, reconstruct the crime, accuse certain people of it in our first issue and bring about a trial," Gauvreau later recalled. He assigned the story to Thomas Meares, an enigmatic reporter with an English accent, a pipe often in hand, a distinguished mustache, and, supposedly, a glass eye. Day after day, Meares traveled to New Brunswick, where he struck up a rapport with Jane Gibson, loosening the Pig Woman's lips with cash from his generous expense account. He spoke derisively of Gibson's grammar and diction but firmly believed her story, which he re-created for an office mate back in the newsroom. "I hear voices, *voices*. Such shouting. Terrible words—oh, they said awful things, terrible. Then they said, *Why did you write those letters?* Then I hear shots. . . . I see Mrs. Hall. I seen her by the lights from another car. By the crabapple tree, I see—" Meares paused and asked his colleague, "Do you believe her?"

In late August, as the *Graphic*'s launch date neared, Macfadden's attorney contacted Azariah Beekman to discuss the story. In the meantime, Gauvreau and a private investigator visited New Brunswick, where they spoke with Gibson and other locals, taking stock of Meares's reporting. Back in New York, Gauvreau met with Macfadden and Fulton Oursler, the chain-smoking editor in chief of Macfadden Publications, to determine whether they should publish an article in the *Graphic*'s debut. "A solution of the mystery would have attracted tremendous attention to our new paper," Gauvreau wrote of the meeting. "But using assumption as evidence is a dangerous matter, and in an eleventh-hour talk with Fulton Oursler . . . I voted against the story as something which, I was certain, would lead to disaster. Oursler, though disappointed in our preparation in this enterprise, agreed with me and Macfadden concurred."

Meares chased the story for another few months, taking it all the way up to New Jersey's attorney general, Edward L. Katzenbach, who received a letter from Beekman asking about the possibility of unsealing grand jury records. Katzenbach said he would look into it—but he had better things to do than involve himself in some reporter's improbable quest to revive a two-year-old cold case. By October, Meares was growing impatient. "While I don't want to rush you," he told Beekman, "I feel that I must point out to you that my time is very valuable, and that I am anxious to finish up this case as soon as possible, as there are other cases which demand my immediate attention." Meares went so far as to propose that Katzenbach appoint an attorney who could serve as a "special assistant" to Beekman, in order "to deal with the case and investigation on behalf of the state." By mid-November, with no smoking gun to be found, Gauvreau killed the story for good. Undeterred, or perhaps obsessed, Meares wrote to Katzenbach one last time, on November 17, 1924: "I personally am just as interested as ever, and it is my hope and desire to be able to assist you in the future in definitely clearing the matter up. It is possible that I may sever all connections with this paper in the near future. However that may be, you may rest assured that my services are always at your disposal and I hope that we may jointly be able to accomplish something worthwhile in the above connection."

The *Graphic*'s pursuit of the Hall-Mills case stopped there. But a year later, as Payne settled into his new job at the *Mirror*, aware of the *Graphic*'s efforts, he picked up the bread crumbs that Meares left behind. To Payne's mind, it was not satisfactory that the case should gather dust among the annals of unsolved crime. He also knew what it would mean for the *Mirror* if they could achieve what the *Graphic* had not.

The first step was a bit of reconnaissance. For this, Payne enlisted his trusted friend and colleague Francis Farley, who had joined Payne at the *Mirror*. Farley traveled to New Brunswick and returned with a notebook full of intrigue that convinced Payne they were onto something. With the séance fresh in his mind, Payne had gone into the exercise focused on Jim Mills. But Farley's reporting took things in a different direction. They now believed Jim had nothing to do with it, and that powerful influences had conspired to obscure the truth. Probing the murders anew would require a significant investment, in terms of both time and manpower, and there was no guarantee the investigation would bear fruit. But Payne came to the following conclusion: "A newspaper can win the public if it can prove public officials are derelict in their duty because of moneyed interests, and then can push such a case to conclusion to see that justice is done."

Payne assigned the story to a seasoned thirty-eight-year-old reporter named Herbert B. Mayer, a New Orleans–born veteran who had fought on the front lines of France. Like Francis Farley, Mayer had worked for Payne at the *News*, and he knew his way around a high-profile case, having covered the murders of socialite Joseph Bowne Elwell and showgirl Dorothy King. Payne swore Mayer to secrecy, keeping only a small number of *Mirror* employees apprised of the investigation. Mayer then disappeared from the newsroom and began working out of a hotel uptown. Whenever someone inquired as to his whereabouts, Payne would reply, "He's sick."

When Mayer first began snooping around New Brunswick in the winter of 1926, doors slammed at every turn. "The Hall-Mills case? I wouldn't dare talk to you about that," he was told, or, "We are absolutely forbidden to discuss that." But Mayer persisted. With the assistance of two other reporters from the *Mirror*, he began to pick up subtle clues. He learned, for instance, that Frances and Edward Hall had employed a cook in 1922, a trusted servant named Mary Gildea who was present at 23 Nichol Avenue on the night of the murders. Why hadn't Gildea's name come up during the original investigation? Another development concerned Peter Tumulty, the Halls' gardener and chauffeur. In 1922, Tumulty said he had only been employed by the Hall family for three weeks at the time of the murders. But a postman told Mayer that Tumulty had in fact been accepting mail at the Hall home for at least eighteen months. One day, two *Mirror* reporters posing as members of Frances Hall's "private legal department" paid a visit to George Seipel. In 1922, Seipel had aided the prosecution by undermining Nellie Lo Russell, the defense witness who swore Jane Gibson had lied about her whereabouts on the murder night. But Seipel had also given testimony favorable to Frances, saying Gibson had offered him a hundred dollars to corroborate her story. Speaking now to the undercover journalists whom he believed to be in Mrs. Hall's employ, Seipel said that Frances's private detective, Felix De Martini, had promised to "fix him up" after the grand jury hearings.

By far the most damning dirt Mayer dug up was Arthur Riehl's allegation against Louise Geist. Apart from Jane Gibson's testimony, it was the only other accusation placing Frances at the crime scene, and it was exactly what Payne needed to blow the case wide open.

SOME STORIES ABOUT PHIL PAYNE'S revival of the Hall-Mills investigation are so outrageous it's hard to tell what's real and what's apocryphal. He supposedly flirted with a plan to lure a suspect— Jim Mills?—to a rural cemetery, where a *Mirror* journalist, cloaked in a white robe to simulate the ghost of Edward Hall, would emerge from a freshly dug grave and proclaim, "You killed me! God knows you did. I want you to confess the truth right now and cleanse your soul!" Another hard-to-believe stunt that may or may not have taken place involved luring this same unnamed suspect, described in the only surviving account as a "little man whom newsmen found childlike in simplicity," to a dinner party at an oceanfront cottage Payne had rented in Manhattan Beach, Brooklyn. There, several *Mirror* journalists posing as thugs ordered the man to take a seat in the

The first article about the murders—published in the September 16, 1922, edition of New Brunswick's *Daily Home News*—foreshadowed the media circus to come.

The Hall and Mills families lived blocks apart but inhabited different worlds, as evidenced by their respective domiciles. The Hall home, at 23 Nichol Avenue, was a gloomy Victorian mansion prior to its top-to-bottom makeover in 1926.

Before her brutal murder in September 1922, Eleanor Mills had "dreams as big as the earth."

De Russey's Lane, the dusty country road that led Edward Hall and Eleanor Mills to their deaths.

Throughout the fall, starting the day the bodies were found, crowds descended on the site of the murders, corrupting the crime scene and turning it into a carnival.

❖

The crabapple tree where the corpses were artfully arrayed, before
and after throngs of murder tourists got their hands on it.

❖

The newspapers were filled with frumpy, unflattering photos of Frances Hall. She commissioned a set of glamour shots to burnish her image in the press.

The ever-eccentric but often amiable Willie Stevens, with his signature walrus mustache.

Detective George Totten and prosecutor Azariah Beekman with the victims' clothing—and looking quite sanguine despite their lack of progress in the investigation.

Rev. E. W. Hall | Mrs. Eleanor Mills | Mrs. Frances Hall | James Mills | Willie Stevens

Charlotte Mills | Raymond Schneider | Pearl Bahmer | Clifford Hayes | Unknown

Whodunnit? A murderers' row of the victims and suspects.

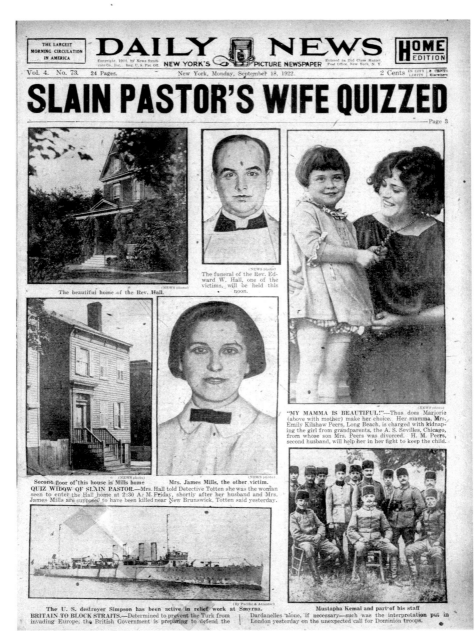

THE LARGEST MORNING CIRCULATION IN AMERICA

DAILY NEWS

NEW YORK'S PICTURE NEWSPAPER

Copyright, 1922, by News Syndicate Co., Inc. Reg. U.S. Pat. Off.

Entered as 2nd Class Matter, Post Office, New York, N. Y.

HOME EDITION

Vol. 4. No. 73. 24 Pages.

New York, Monday, September 18, 1922.

2 Cents IN CITY LIMITS 3 CENTS Elsewhere

SLAIN PASTOR'S WIFE QUIZZED

—Page 3

(NEWS photo)
The beautiful home of the Rev. Hall.

(NEWS photo)
The funeral of the Rev. Edward W. Hall, one of the victims, will be held this noon.

(NEWS photo)
Second floor of this house is Mills home

(NEWS photo)
Mrs. James Mills, the other victim.

QUIZ WIDOW OF SLAIN PASTOR.—Mrs. Hall told Detective Totten she was the woman seen to enter the Hall home at 2:30 A. M. Friday, shortly after her husband and Mrs. James Mills are supposed to have been killed near New Brunswick, Totten said yesterday.

(NEWS photo)
"MY MAMMA IS BEAUTIFUL!"—Thus does Marjorie (above with mother) make her choice. Her mamma, Mrs. Emily Kilshaw Peers, Long Beach, is charged with kidnaping the girl from grandparents, the A. S. Sevilles, Chicago, from whose son Mrs. Peers was divorced. H. M. Peers, second husband, will help her in her fight to keep the child.

(By Pacific & Atlantic)
The U. S. destroyer Simpson has been active in relief work at Smyrna.

BRITAIN TO BLOCK STRAITS.—Determined to prevent the Turk from invading Europe, the British Government is preparing to defend the

Mustapha Kemal and part of his staff
Dardanelles alone, if necessary—such was the interpretation put in London yesterday on the unexpected call for Dominion troops.

Edward and Eleanor, pictured beside their respective homes, share the front page of the *Daily News*, which pioneered the tabloid form with an emphasis on photography.

DAILY ☀ NEWS. **FINAL EDITION**

THE LARGEST MORNING CIRCULATION IN AMERICA

Copyright, 1922, by News Syndicate Co. Inc. Reg. U. S. Pat. Off.

NEW YORK'S PICTURE NEWSPAPER

Entered as 2nd Class Matter Post Office. New York N. Y.

Vol. 4. No. 106. 28 Pages. ★ ★ ★ New York, Thursday, October 26, 1922. 2 Cents IN CITY LIMITS | 2 CENTS Elsewhere

MRS. HALL ACCUSED

Page 2

This exclusive and extraordinary photograph shows the Rev. Edward W. Hall, slain New Jersey rector, surrounded by members at an outing. At extreme left, lower row, is Mrs. Addison (Minna) Clarke, close friend of the Halls and Mrs. Mills.

Mrs. Hall (left) and Mrs. Mills posed for this photo at an outing.

MRS. HALL ACCUSED.—Mrs. Jane Gibson, in a statement in the hands of New Jersey prosecutors, has stated that Mrs. E. W. Hall was at scene of double murder on fatal night.

REUNITED.—George Cline, acquitted of murder charge, was reunited with wife and children last night, his brother-in-law, Charles Scullion (left), joining them.

The Reverend Hall was popular with the women of St. John's, as this photo of a church outing at the Jersey Shore, top, makes plain. Below, Frances and Eleanor in happier times.

What reader could resist George Totten posing with the world's most famous mule, Jenny? Her theatrical owner, Jane Gibson, is pictured on the opposite side of the page. Between them, Eleanor Mills.

The pioneering tabloid maestro Phil Payne, pictured in his office at the *Daily News* before he jumped to Hearst's *Daily Mirror*, where he revived the case.

❖

Three covers from the *Mirror*'s swashbuckling Hall-Mills crusade, including the front page that brought the case back to life.

Describing the Pig Woman's hospital-bed testimony, the *Mirror*'s Herbert Mayer wrote, "No more dramatic, no more powerful scene, has been staged ever in an American courtroom."

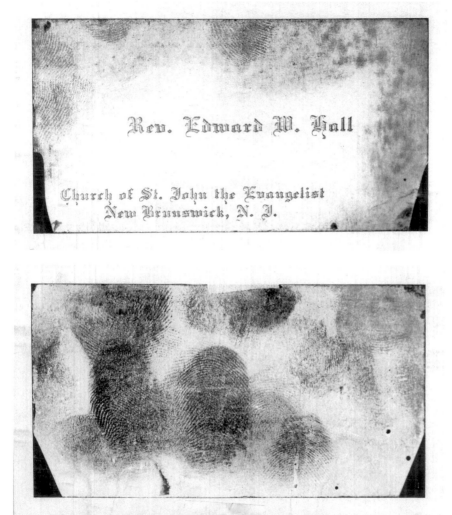

Edward Hall's infamous calling card, allegedly bearing the
fingerprints of Willie Stevens.

Jim and Charlotte Mills, reading the *Daily Mirror*, which became their ally in pursuing justice for Eleanor.

The former Hall home and St. John the Evangelist, May 2022.

To this day, Edward and Eleanor haunt the Somerset County Courthouse, where visitors can glimpse the clothing in which they were murdered, including Edward's famous panama hat.

middle of a cold room, where they attempted to extract a confession by threatening him with ropes, chains, and blunt instruments. The inquisition went on for an hour before coming to an abrupt and malodorous conclusion. One of the *Mirror* reporters ran over to a phone in another part of the cottage and called Payne. "He shit his pants!" the reporter exclaimed. The reporters then took the soiled suspect to a hotel room in Upper Manhattan for a warm bath and fresh clothes. They called a taxi and sent him back to New Brunswick with their apologies. Or so the story goes.

By late spring, the *Mirror* was putting the finishing touches on its investigation with the help of George Totten, who provided copies of unpublished records from 1922. On June 1, Totten met Payne at the Hotel Empire on Broadway and Sixty-third Street. Arthur Riehl joined the group, as did a notary public, who took down Riehl's statement. The affidavit went as follows: Riehl said he met Louise Geist while employed as a deputy sheriff in Union County. What he didn't tell Louise was that, in addition to his official duties, he was "voluntarily working" on the Hall-Mills case "to see whether I could break the case myself." They began dating, one thing led to another, and on September 2, 1924, they married. The newlyweds continued to live separately, Riehl explained, because Louise "was particularly anxious not to let her mother know." Riehl said he learned Louise was a member of the women's division of the Ku Klux Klan. He also said that "when she had some liquor in her," she "used to boast of her part in the Hall-Mills case." Louise would malign the authorities, bragging, "I was too smart for them. They couldn't get anything out of me."

Riehl said his estranged wife claimed that Edward and Frances Hall "were not on good terms," and that Edward was known to "entertain" at the Phillips farm. "She intimated to me, although she would never directly admit, the fact that Dr. Hall himself had had relations with her." According to Riehl, Louise's off-the-record account of the fatal night bore little resemblance to her official statements and testimony. She claimed Edward had left the house that afternoon around three o'clock, absconding with "a large amount of money" and telling Louise that "he would be gone for a couple of days." There had been no call from Eleanor summoning Edward under the guise of a confusing medical bill. In reality, Peter Tumulty had driven Frances, Willie, and Louise to the Phillips farm around ten o'clock, although Louise didn't explain how they knew when and where to find the adulterers. "Louise said she and Mrs. Hall wore black dresses but she would never tell me who did the actual killing," said Riehl, adding that Louise "would never wear black again if she could help it."

Riehl said he asked Louise about a house she had purchased after the murders. Louise's deceased father, he suggested, must have left a good bit of life insurance for her to have been able to afford it.

"No, he did not. I paid most of that," Louise replied. "I put in five thousand dollars for the place."

"*Five thousand dollars?* Where did you get so much money?"

"I always know how to get it."

Riehl continued, "This and other things she said led me to believe that the money came from the Hall-Carpender families." He claimed Tumulty had bought a house, too, and that Louise had said, "He paid for most of it out of that matter." Louise also told Riehl that one of Totten's counterparts in the Middlesex County prosecutor's office, Detective Ferd David, "was always taken care of, and that it was his job to stop anybody from 'breaking the case.'"

The couple separated in November 1924, after Louise learned the truth about Riehl—that he was an armchair detective desperate to solve the Hall-Mills mystery. Furious that she had been duped, Louise claimed she had previously been married to a man from New York, and that the marriage had never been annulled. "Shortly afterward," Riehl said, "I began to be aware of the fact that I was being followed by strange men, and I recognized one of the men as Felix De Martini." Before signing the affidavit, Riehl concluded,

"I believe that Louise Geist Riehl is thoroughly cognizant with the facts which led to the killing of the Reverend Dr. Hall and Mrs. Eleanor Mills, and was a participant in, or accessory to, that crime; that she is a bigamist and a perjurer from her own confessions to me; and realizing these things, I intend to ask the state, through legal channels, for annulment of my marriage to her."

One month later, just after midnight on July 1, Riehl's annulment petition was filed in a Trenton courthouse. Somehow, the petition disappeared before reaching the eyes of journalists, conveniently protecting the *Mirror*'s scoop. Payne took the *Mirror*'s Hall-Mills dossier to New Jersey's newest governor, A. Harry Moore, a protégé of Frank Hague, the Democratic Party boss from Hudson County, where Payne was a prominent and well-connected resident. On Monday, July 12, Payne spent an afternoon in Trenton with Moore and Edward Katzenbach, the attorney general. Payne presented the *Mirror*'s findings, and Moore promised that the authorities would investigate them. The governor, grateful for the *Mirror*'s legwork, assured Payne that he would get the inside track on any major developments. This mutually beneficial arrangement reflected a well-established tradition, exemplified by the Hearstian yellow journalism of the late nineteenth century, in which newspapers actively interfered in criminal investigations. Though frowned upon by modern standards, such close coordination between police and the press seemed well-suited to the lawless climate of the 1920s, and Payne relished the benefits it provided for his growing tabloid.

The *Mirror*'s findings now filled two large briefcases weighing fifty-two pounds. Payne kept the documents locked away in a steel filing cabinet in his office, and he secured a set of duplicates in a bank vault downtown, labeling them "Investigation A." By the third week of July, Payne was ready to publish his exposé. The governor had been looped in. Four lawyers had combed through every single word. There was only one thing left to do: Herbert Mayer left for New Brunswick to approach Frances Hall for comment.

"A TISSUE OF DISGUSTING LIES!"

Try as she did to recede into obscurity, Frances Hall could not escape the glare of the press. In April 1925, the *Daily News* wrote about her return, on the SS *Conte Verde*, from another trip to Italy, noting, "She wore a heavy veil to prevent her recognition." In June, a *News* photographer captured an image of Frances at the funeral of Edward Hall's mother, her face hidden by mourning garb. Toward the end of the year, the twenty-five-thousand-dollar renovation of her mansion was duly reported on, as were rumors of a new marriage. She'd been spotted often in the company of one Dr. Lane Cooper, a childhood friend and professor of English at Cornell University. After the *Daily News* wondered aloud on its front page, HALL MURDER WIDOW WED?, Frances refuted the gossip, declaring to reporters, "There is nothing to these reports of my marriage to Dr. Cooper. I denied them three weeks ago. Beyond that, I won't make any statement."

Months later, in the summer of 1926, the bell rang at 23 Nichol Avenue, now fully remodeled in red brick and stucco. Frances answered the door and smiled at the gentleman standing before her. The man introduced himself as Herbert Mayer, a reporter for the

New York *Daily Mirror*, who had come to speak with her about a story the newspaper was about to publish. The warm pleasantries of their initial greeting cooled to an icy chill as Mayer detailed Arthur Riehl's allegations against Frances's former maid. Describing the interaction, Mayer later recalled, "I have seen 30 men executed. I have seen men go into battle, too, and have seen women gripped by tragedy. But no human being I ever saw before seemed so nervous as Mrs. Hall." Mayer remembered reading about the time Frances had faced several dozen reporters in her parlor in 1922, responding to their queries with stoic resolve. This did not seem like the woman now standing before him in the doorway of her mansion.

"It is all rubbish—all disgusting, awful rubbish!" Frances snapped. "Who is this man, Riehl? I didn't know Louise was married. It is all rubbish, a tissue of disgusting lies!"

"But Mrs. Hall," Mayer prodded, "we came to see you about this for publication and to quote exactly what you said. Riehl's story will be published. His statements are on file in a court of record. We have come all the way out here to give you an opportunity to meet these statements and to deny them and—"

"They are rubbish. All rubbish."

"Won't you please answer a question or two, Mrs. Hall, or deny his charges?"

"I won't talk for publication. I won't be interviewed," Frances insisted, shutting the door in Mayer's face.

Nothing Frances said could have stopped what was to come. As the sun rose on the morning of Friday, July 16, the investigation Payne had worked on for eight months finally saw the light of day: HALL-MILLS MURDER MYSTERY BARED. On the front page, an artist's rendering depicted Frances kneeling over Edward and Eleanor's dead bodies. The coverage unfurled over five pages inside the paper, including a cartoon about Edward and Eleanor's love affair. There were photos galore—Edward on the beach, barefoot in a tank top; Frances cloaked in her gloomy mourning shrouds. "Evidence is in the hands of the New Jersey authorities directly accusing Mrs. Hall and her brother of being at the murder scene the night of the crime," Mayer wrote. "In addition to this, there is a mass of equally startling evidence gathered by the Daily Mirror in an exhaustive investigation and turned over to the authorities. The nature of this demands the reopening of the entire case." The exposé had it all: Riehl's charges against Louise Geist. Claims that witnesses were bribed. An allegation that Ralph Gorsline lied to the grand jury. The following quote from Jim Mills: "Last time, the thing was quashed. Everybody in town, at least 90 percent of them, knows that it was the Hall money that quashed it." The *Mirror* noted that George Totten had assisted during the "latter phases" of the investigation. That same day, it was reported that Totten lost his appeal to be reinstated as Somerset County's chief detective. He was officially a free agent.

After the *Mirror* hit newsstands, reporters at the chancery court in Trenton demanded access to Riehl's annulment petition, but it was nowhere to be found. Hours later, the missing documents magically turned up in a clerk's desk drawer. Payne's proximity to state officials presumably helped ensure that the petition remained hidden until the publication of the *Mirror*'s story.

Reporters rushed over to Louise Geist's house outside of New Brunswick, where she declared Riehl's affidavit "an absolute falsehood." Geist said her attorney advised her to "refuse to have anything to do with the Daily Mirror and their story, and I acted on his suggestion."

The following day, Geist gave an interview to a *Daily News* reporter, who had planted himself outside her home until she invited him in. "I know his statements were made to get even with me for leaving him and to get money by having a New York newspaper write more of this mess," she said of her estranged husband. "For the last two weeks, a New York newspaper man tried to get me to say that I suspected Mrs. Hall. As God is my judge, I think she is just as innocent as I am. When they say that Mrs. Hall and her brother were driven to the scene of the murder on the night of the tragedy, they lie. I was in the house and I saw no one leave it. . . . I defy prosecutor Toolan to bring Riehl face to face with me and in his presence have Riehl prove his statements as contained in the petition." John Toolan, the Middlesex County prosecutor, who had been an assistant prosecutor during the 1922 proceedings, agreed with her. "I have investigated the statements made in the annulment proceedings," he said, "and I cannot find one thing upon which to base an official investigation." In a jab at its rival, the *News* concluded: "Despite sensational stories in a New York paper, there is little likelihood of any further investigation of Riehl's statements. . . . Although newspapers have had criers in New Brunswick for twenty-four hours, selling extras purporting to have solved the murder, this town has given little thought to the so-called murder sensation."

PHIL PAYNE WAS UNFAZED BY his critics. Newsstands throughout New York and New Jersey were stripped bare of the *Mirror*'s July 16 edition, and Toolan's dismissiveness mattered little, considering that Governor Moore had enlisted detectives from his native Jersey City. Herbert Mayer described them as "some of the most brilliant members" of the city's detective force, chosen for the assignment by Mayor Frank Hague himself. The *Mirror* additionally claimed that some of its most "startling" evidence had been withheld from print at the governor's request. For Moore, this new investigation was a chance to remedy the national embarrassment of 1922, bolstering his political fortunes and bringing glory to his state, which would seem to explain why he was willing to pull out all the stops in pursuit of so-called Jersey Justice.

Payne, meanwhile, was so confident in the *Mirror*'s reporting that he sent a telegram to Frances Hall's attorney Timothy Pfeiffer daring him to sue: "This is a challenge to you as Mrs. Hall's legal representative to bring a criminal libel action against me personally if the statements published in today's DAILY MIRROR accusing Mrs. Hall are not correct."

In the coming weeks, the *Mirror* unleashed a barrage of follow-ups: HALL CASE WITNESSES GRILLED; MRS. HALL'S SPIES; HALL BRIBERY IS REVEALED. While these articles contained little in the way of new concrete information, they supplied ample intrigue. One particularly juicy morsel posited that a state trooper who investigated the original case "was said to have solved the mystery" but "vanished as though from the earth about the time that Mrs. Hall went to Italy." Overall, though, the *Mirror* simply weaved a web of suspicion by reiterating details that didn't add up, no matter how circumstantial. Why had Frances gone to Italy of all places, the only country without a U.S. extradition treaty for homicide? Why was the cook, Mary Gildea, never put forward for questioning, even though she was present in the Hall mansion on the night of the killings? Why had Peter Tumulty been portrayed as a new employee when he in fact appeared to be a long-trusted servant? Describing the "succession of startling neglect by some officials" during the 1922 investigation, the *Mirror* suggested that a "hidden hand" had "blocked solution up to this time of the so-called mystery."

The *Mirror* also took a closer look at Frances Hall's private detective, Felix De Martini. Rather than endeavoring to solve the murders, De Martini had been retained for a "purely defensive" undertaking, employing a fleet of twenty operatives to dig up dirt. One of De Martini's men said he'd been ordered to infiltrate an auto company where Jane Gibson's husband worked: "De Martini told me to go out and work under cover and learn what people were saying about Mrs. Hall." Another operative claimed he "went out and got the dope on Mrs. Gibson." Several witnesses recalled "being approached by strange men who spoke of money in connection with their testimony." Jim Mills relayed his own experience with De Martini's crew, telling Herbert Mayer, "De Martini and his detectives kept after me for two years. They followed me around and they put men to work alongside of me and apparently were in some way trying to connect me with the murders. Of all those who might have committed the crime, I was the only one who was questioned at length. The reason of this, of course, is that I was poor." Jim's eyes welled with tears. "Mrs. Hall never speaks to me anymore," he said. "Whenever she sees me, she walks on the other side of the street or passes by me without looking. . . . She wrote a letter to Charlotte after the killing telling her that she would be looked out for, but Mrs. Hall never did anything for the girl." In an editorial, the *Mirror* showered Jim with sympathy: "High-priced lawyers and detectives surrounded Mrs. Hall when she became a suspect. Prosecuting officials sworn to do their duty equally for rich and poor were very considerate in their treatment of Mrs. Hall. They are still considerate. But Jimmy Mills—the same officials have browbeaten and badgered him. He had been dragged before a Grand Jury and subjected to a grueling examination. He has been fingerprinted like a felon and hounded by private detectives. . . . Mrs. Hall was a suspect at the time of the murder. She is more of a suspect now than ever before. . . . Until the persons involved in this crime are brought to trial, Jersey Justice is something to sneer at instead of to admire. There is evidence enough to warrant arrests now."

In reality, much of the *Mirror*'s evidence was conjecture, and Timothy Pfeiffer acted as if the whole thing was preposterous. "It is nothing more than a summer sensation for the newspapers," he claimed. "It will blow over soon."

Pfeiffer couldn't have been more wrong: the investigation was gathering strength. Governor Moore's Jersey City detectives diligently worked the case, now with cooperation from Somerset County Prosecutor Francis Bergen. Arthur Riehl was questioned further. Previous witnesses were reinterviewed, and new witnesses spoke out for the first time. Neighbors of Nellie Lo Russell backed up Jane Gibson's account, saying they had not seen Gibson anywhere near Russell's shack on the night of the murders. One of De Martini's men swore that "at no time in his work was he instructed . . . to try and find the murderers of Dr. Hall and Mrs. Mills, but that on the contrary, the effect of De Martini's instructions to him were such that he understood clearly that all that was wanted was information which favored Mrs. Hall." Detectives consulted with Payne and pored over the evidence, including ten affidavits compiled by Mayer and his team. On the evening of Tuesday, July 27, they reached a decision: Frances Hall was to be arrested, and the *Mirror* would get a front-row seat.

The following day, Payne traveled to Somerville, where Prosecutor Bergen drew up two warrants, one for each victim. Around nine thirty that evening, Bergen contacted a Somerset County judge to sign off. Since Frances resided in Middlesex County, where the warrants were to be served, the imprimatur of a Middlesex justice was required as well. Payne rode with the authorities to the home of a judge in Dunellen, a town north of New Brunswick, where the countersignature was obtained. The group then sped away in the rain toward 23 Nichol Avenue, warrants in hand.

Around a quarter to midnight, two police cars pulled up in the vicinity of Frances's house, parking at a discreet distance. A crew of state troopers slipped out of the vehicles and furtively surrounded the dimly lit Hall mansion. Dressed in plain clothes, they crept toward the house and stationed themselves at every point of egress. A light rain drizzled down as Payne watched Captain John Lamb of the state police and two Jersey City detectives climb the front steps. They lingered for a moment and then pressed the doorbell, disturbing the silence of the night. A servant answered and Willie came down, recognizing Captain Lamb as one of the men who had questioned him in 1922.

"Hello, Willie," said Lamb. "I came here to see Mrs. Hall right away. I have important business of an official character."

Willie called upstairs to his sister, who appeared a few minutes later.

"Good evening, gentlemen," she said. "Your visit is rather a late one. I suppose you want to question me again?"

"I have a warrant calling for your arrest," Lamb explained. "I have been instructed to take you to Somerville at once."

As Lamb showed Frances the warrant, she asked to phone an attorney, Russell Watson, a family friend and counsel for Johnson & Johnson, who arrived ten minutes later. Watson read the warrant and informed his client she had no choice but to comply. Willie watched in distress.

"You can't take my sister out of here at this time of night!" he demanded, lips trembling. "You can't take my sister away!"

Frances gathered her things and emerged from the house with Elovine Carpender, who escorted Frances toward Captain Lamb's car, bound for the Somerset County Jail. Willie, on the verge of tears, pulled a pipe out of his pocket and stuck it between his lips, like a baby with a pacifier. As Payne watched from the curb, a taxi driver remarked with a grin, "Deez rich guys can get a long way with their money."

The *Mirror* had prepared an article about the arrest, carrying Payne's byline. All that was left to do was update it with the details Payne had gathered during his police ride-along. As the *Mirror* put the finishing touches on its story, other newspapers learned of the arrest and scrambled to catch up. At five o'clock in the morning, a journalist from the *Mirror* called the city desk of another New York paper pretending to be a tipster.

"Have you heard about Mrs. Hall's arrest?"

"We just got it a few minutes ago. What have you got on it?"

Payne laughed in the background. He had finally achieved what he first set out to do three years earlier at the *Daily News*. He had succeeded where the *Evening Graphic* had failed. It was a boon not just for the *Mirror*, but for every newspaper in America, all of them now poised to capitalize on the public's ravenous interest in the Hall-Mills saga. In his article, Payne boastfully proclaimed that the

Mirror had "solved" the "most baffling crime of the century. . . . With this dramatic arrest came the official declaration that the mystery of the Hall-Mills murders is at an end."

Despite Payne's braggadocio, however, the end of the mystery was nowhere in sight.

THE ARRESTS

As Frances walked into her mansion on the afternoon of Friday, July 30, a *Daily News* photographer darted across the lawn and pointed his camera. Timothy Pfeiffer, trailing behind, lunged at the photographer and struck him with one of the bags he was carrying for his client. Frances had already posed that day for a swarm of cameramen while exiting the Somerset County Jail on a fifteen-thousand-dollar bail bond. Couldn't they allow her a moment of peace?

If nothing else, Pfeiffer's attack on the photographer underscored his loyalty. He'd been a trusted counselor to Frances for nearly four years, not only advising her on legal matters, but managing her interactions with the press. He was as much her public relations director as her attorney. But now that Frances faced a homicide trial for the second time in four years, she required the additional services of a heavyweight defense lawyer. For that she settled on Robert H. McCarter, an influential Republican and former state attorney general whose stature in the legal field was matched by his good breeding. Sixty-seven years old, with silver hair retreating from a hard-boiled mug, McCarter hailed from a noted New Jersey family of Scottish and Irish descent. He was now at the pinnacle of his career, with degrees from Princeton and Columbia Law School, and corporations were said to pay upward of one thousand dollars a day for his services. Frances was sure to get her money's worth.

On the other side of the ring was State Senator Alexander Simpson, whom Governor Harry Moore appointed as special prosecutor in the case, with assistance from the Somerset County prosecutor, Francis Bergen. Apart from a common heritage, Simpson was the polar opposite of McCarter, as well as thirteen years younger and a good deal shorter, measuring in at a diminutive four foot eleven. Simpson ran in the same Democratic political circles as the governor, and he was a fellow consigliere to Jersey City mayor and Democratic Party boss Frank Hague, who had lent his best detectives to the investigation. With boundless energy, a dramatic panache, and wavy brown hair, Simpson had graduated from Jersey City's public school system and, like McCarter, studied at Columbia Law School, although he couldn't afford to complete his education there. Instead, Simpson advanced his legal training by working for a judge, bringing in extra money as a freelance reporter for newspapers including Pulitzer's *New York World*. It was Simpson's journalism background that brought him to the same reunion of newspapermen that Phil Payne had attended in 1922. Senator Simpson was no doubt familiar with Payne, a fellow Hudson County resident whose job as a big-shot editor came with access to big-shot politicians.

In Simpson's career as a state lawmaker, he championed an array of liberal causes, from bills supporting organized labor to the legalization of Sunday motion pictures. As an attorney, his résumé included difficult homicides like the Lamp Black Swamp murder, a wife-slaying that rocked Hudson County in 1907. The *Daily Mirror* described Simpson as "one of the most brilliant criminal lawyers in the East, and an able opponent for McCarter." In another article, the *Mirror* suggested that Simpson represented the "masses," and McCarter the "classes."

Simpson set up shop in Jersey City and traveled as needed to Somerville, where the state troopers were headquartered. His team fanned out to interview dozens of witnesses, some from the original investigation, others who spoke for the first time. Tips and leads poured in, many of them frivolous or downright kooky, others deemed worthy of pursuit. You couldn't walk down Somerville's main drag without bumping into reporters—lounging under trees outside the courthouse, gorging on peach and blackberry pie in the local eateries, or gossiping in the lobby of the Somerset Hotel. Simpson made sure the press never wanted for information. Publicity, he believed, was just what the investigation needed, and he served it up liberally. "Three men and one woman are deeply involved in this case, and the evidence against them is positive," he told journalists in early August. "I am absolutely convinced that Jane Gibson tells a truthful story."

Others were not so convinced. "The facts discovered by the Mirror were inflated beyond their actual worth for the simple reason that the name of Hearst has always possessed a peculiar ability to stampede political office holders," wrote a correspondent for *The New Yorker*. "Whatever is true, I believe that the authorities are quite as far at this moment from the conviction of the crime as they were four years ago. I do not believe that the Mirror's evidence is of any actual value, except of course as it serves the purposes of sensational journalism."

THE ALLEGATIONS THAT ARTHUR RIEHL first aired in the *Daily Mirror* no longer appeared to be at the heart of the inquiry. Simpson barely skimmed Riehl's claims when he interviewed Louise Geist at the Jersey City courthouse on August 5. He was more interested in establishing whether Frances had eavesdropped on Eleanor and Edward's phone call on the night of the murders.

"I saw that she had the receiver," Louise conceded.

"When you were watching her, she had it up to her ear?"

"Yes."

Nor was Peter Tumulty quizzed about whether he'd driven anyone to the crime scene. Tumulty told a detective the Halls had hired him as a gardener six weeks before the murders and that he'd only begun working as Frances's chauffeur in the days following Edward's death. (The *Mirror*'s reporting suggested he'd been employed much longer; Tumulty's son told a detective in 1922 that his father had previously been a chauffeur for one of the Carpenders.) The last time Tumulty saw Edward alive, he said, was when he washed the family's green Case car on the morning of Edward's disappearance. Tumulty also swore he'd never "been approached" about concealing knowledge of the murders, not that he had any knowledge to conceal.

In other interviews, officials focused on the sloppy nature of the 1922 probe.

"Didn't you think it was strange that no autopsy was held?" morgue owner John Hubbard was asked.

"We could have kept the bodies all right," Hubbard replied. "We could have kept them if necessary."

Similar questions were put to the undertaker, Samuel Sutphen.

"Didn't you think at the time that it was rushing matters a little?"

"I surely did. They were very anxious to get him back to New Brunswick," Sutphen said. "It looked as if they wanted to get the body out of Somerset County so that Somerset County officials would not perform an autopsy."

Charlotte Mills, now twenty and working an office job at a motor company, sat for a deposition on August 10. Like other witnesses, she described being badgered by Frances Hall's detectives. "De Martini trailed me all over," she said. Charlotte also revealed that her mother, before disappearing on the evening of September 14, had clipped an article from the *New York World* and placed it on Reverend Hall's desk at St. John's. The article carried the byline of Percy Stickney Grant, an Episcopal priest whose writings espoused a belief that divorce should be accessible to the clergy. The implication was obvious—Eleanor had at least pondered the possibility that Edward might separate from his wife.

The case took a dramatic and unexpected turn on the stormy afternoon of Thursday, August 12, when Captain Lamb and two Jersey City detectives arrived at the Hall mansion yet again—this time to inform Willie Stevens that they had obtained a warrant for his arrest. "My God," Willie exclaimed. "I didn't expect this!" Frances helped Willie pack a small bag with toiletries, shirts, and an extra suit. Lamb also had a warrant for Henry Carpender, whom Tumulty retrieved from the train station shortly after five o'clock. When Carpender arrived at the Hall mansion, he took the warrant in his hands and read it over nonchalantly, flashing a cool smile. "Never mind, Willie," he reassured his cousin. "It's all right."

News of the arrests spread quickly, and it wasn't long before a crowd formed in front of 23 Nichol Avenue. Frances phoned the New Brunswick police and asked them to send a patrolman to keep journalists off her property. One of these was Grace Robinson, a mild-mannered but plucky *Daily News* reporter whose slight frame belied a fearless demeanor. Julia Harpman had branched out into writing about movies and working on splashy features. Since July, she'd been in France covering Gertrude Ederle's historic attempt to swim the English Channel, which meant Robinson was now the tabloid's star crime correspondent. Clad in a rain-soaked summer dress, Robinson lingered near the curb with two other reporters, deadline fast approaching. An officer informed the trio they were being taken into custody for loitering. "I can't move," Robinson snapped. "There is going to be an arrest in a few minutes, and I've got to have the story!" The reporters were released after a brief detention, but they didn't make it back in time to witness Henry Carpender and Willie Stevens entering a car bound for the Somerset County Jail. The grounds for Henry and Willie's arrests were not made public, but as usual, Phil Payne had the inside scoop: "The character of this evidence is known to the DAILY MIRROR, but is not published at this time in order not to embarrass the authorities. This evidence, however, will be published exclusively in the DAILY MIRROR."

On August 27, the *Mirror* made good on its word: HALL DEATH PRINT. Beneath the startling front-page headline was a large reproduction of two fingerprints—or, rather, side-by-side images of the same alleged fingerprint. On the left, a print of Willie Stevens's index finger, taken after his arrest. On the right, a print obtained from Edward's calling card found at the murder scene. Attention was drawn to several "ridge characteristics" that the prints appeared to have in common; forensic experts were prepared to testify that the prints were identical. The calling card, it turned out, had been collecting dust in the office of a fingerprint expert tracked down by the *Mirror*. George Totten believed it was the same card he'd found "propped up on an angle" near Edward's foot, "supported by weeds on tufts of grass." The *Mirror* had obtained the card "some time ago" and turned it over to the prosecution. "The card will be one of the state's most vital pieces of evidence," Herbert Mayer wrote. Other reporters were furious when they saw the *Mirror*'s exclusive. "If *your* paper dug up something like that and gave it to me," Simpson told them, "you would have an exclusive story and pictures too."

The previous afternoon, Simpson had revealed the calling card at a bail hearing, sending gasps through the crowded courtroom. Willie fiddled with a yellow pencil and leaned forward as Simpson laid out his theory of the crime. "Did she mean murder? No," the senator said. "I think Mrs. Hall meant to confront these people, but she was involved in this thing and murder was done right before her eyes." Simpson pointed at Willie, invoking Jane Gibson's description of the man she'd seen at the Phillips farm. *"This man,"* the prosecutor continued, as Willie's face contorted into a rage, "who has been described as a colored man . . . with his kinky hair and dark complexion. I can demonstrate that this man, Stevens, was on the scene of the crime the night of the murder, near enough to put a card at the feet of the dead man." Bail was denied.

Weeks earlier, at a preliminary hearing, Gibson testified that she'd seen Henry Carpender with "a glistening thing" in his hand moments before the shots were fired. This new detail appeared to firm up the most crucial part of Gibson's story from 1922, in which she said she heard a woman cry out, "Oh, Henry!" Back then, detectives originally suspected Henry Stevens, but they shifted their focus to Henry Carpender after Gibson picked him out of a crowd. Now, Simpson had found a glitch. Anyone who knew Henry Carpender knew that his relatives didn't refer to him as Henry, but by his nickname: Harry. Could the other Henry, Henry Stevens, have been at the crime scene after all? Simpson intended to find out.

IN ADDITION TO THE ARRESTS, the press occupied itself with a flurry of smaller developments, some more fruitful than others. A trove of missing statements from the 1922 investigation turned up, discovered by Azariah Beekman's brother. He had taken the statements to the authorities, but only after Phil Payne ratted him out for trying to sell them to the *Daily Mirror*. Additionally, a man named Robert Earling came forward claiming he'd seen Jane Gibson riding her mule down De Russey's Lane on the night of the murders, which corroborated Gibson's timeline. John Stillwell, a chauffeur who had driven the funeral party to Edward's interment, described seeing a scratch on the left side of Frances Hall's face when she briefly pulled up her veil on the ferry ride back from Brooklyn. A Jersey City detective interviewed Paul Hamborzsky, the Hungarian reverend and friend of Edward Hall's, who claimed in 1922 that Edward had received physical threats. Reiterating his earlier statements, Hamborzsky said, "He admitted to me he was in love with Mrs. Mills and he couldn't give her up, and he was having lots of trouble at his house, and all the members of Mrs. Hall's family hated him, and Henry threatened him and said, 'If you don't give up Mrs. Mills,

I'll show you what I'll do with you!'" Edward, according to Hamborzsky, talked about getting a divorce and running away with his mistress, adding, "I am in fear of my life." All of this was helpful to Simpson's case, but it was time to reel in a bigger fish.

In early September, Simpson drove down the shore to personally interview the men who claimed Henry was on the beach in Lavallette at the time of his brother-in-law's murder, on September 14, 1922. The more these men talked, the less Simpson believed Henry's story. None of the witnesses could say, beyond a shadow of a doubt, that they'd seen Henry fishing under the moonlight that evening. Henry fished lots of nights, after all. The most important detail of Henry's alibi concerned a bluefish, reeled in by a man named Arthur Applegate. Henry said he'd gone into his house to retrieve a scale to weigh it. He'd even shown the authorities his fishing diary, documenting the catch. Speaking now with Simpson, Applegate couldn't swear that he'd caught the bluefish on September 14, nor could he furnish any supporting details about the night in question.

"Detectives or reporters questioned me and formed the idea in my mind that that was the night," Applegate said.

"And without these detectives," Simpson continued, "you could not say as to the night the fish was weighed?"

"I could not."

Another local told Simpson he *believed* he was fishing with Henry on the night in question, but that he didn't recall anything about a bluefish. This witness, Simpson told reporters, "directly contradicted Applegate on a vitally important matter."

Henry Stevens was one of several people who'd come under fresh scrutiny. Detectives also reacquainted themselves with Ralph Gorsline and Catherine Rastall, the choir members long rumored to have been in the vicinity of the Phillips farm when the killings took place. Questioned on September 9, Gorsline and Rastall stuck to their original stories: Gorsline left the YMCA, bumped into Rastall on the street, and gave her a ride home. But within twenty-four hours, investigators had broken them down. Rastall cracked first, admitting she was in Gorsline's car on the lovers' lane adjacent to the farm. She said that about fifteen or twenty minutes past ten o'clock, they heard voices, then a woman's scream, then four gunshots: "We both agreed not to say anything about it." The detectives showed Gorsline her statement. "Well, I'll talk," he said. "Do you know what I am doing now? I am ruining my life. I have a wife, a thirteen-year-old daughter, and a nice home. I am going to lose all of them." After four years, Gorsline finally admitted, "I know Mrs. Gibson's statement concerning the shots and screams and moaning is true, because they coincide with what we saw and heard."

Grace Robinson of the *Daily News* paid a visit to Gorsline's shingle-and-brick abode, where she introduced herself to a tall woman with dark hair and matching eyes. "We have nothing to say," the soon-to-be-former Mrs. Gorsline barked, as the door slammed in Robinson's face.

Separately, an affidavit was obtained from a private eye who had investigated the case for the Burns Detective Agency. He recalled a visit one day in the fall of 1922 from a "tall, lanky fellow," later identified as Gorsline, who showed up at the agency's offices in the Woolworth Building and relayed a "weird story." The affidavit did not specify the nature of this story, but it would soon be revealed.

Simpson now felt confident he could secure an indictment. But no one expected the moment to arrive as quickly as it did. On Wednesday, September 15, exactly four years after the bodies of Edward Hall and Eleanor Mills began to decompose beneath a crabapple tree, a grand jury met to decide whether Frances Hall, Henry Carpender, and Frances's brothers should be indicted for murder. Thirty witnesses, one afternoon, and ten minutes of deliberation later, the jurors reached a decision: all four suspects would stand trial.

AFTER THE GRAND JURY PROCEEDINGS, Simpson and his men raced down to Lavallette to arrest Henry Stevens.

"What can I bring with me?" Henry asked.

"Well, you can take nothing with you with which you might inflict a wound, such as a silver pencil."

"How about my fountain pen?"

"That's all right."

"How about a safety razor?"

"Bring it along, but they may take it."

According to the state's theory, Edward had been confronted about the affair and warned to cut it off, but he and Eleanor secretly planned an elopement, possibly to Germany. Frances somehow learned about their Thursday-night rendezvous and went to the Phillips farm with her two brothers and Henry Carpender. Willie, unbeknownst to the others, carried a gun. Amid a quarrel, Willie brandished the pistol. Tempers flared. Overcome by anger, Henry Stevens grabbed the weapon and opened fire. The shots rang out between 10:18 and 10:22 P.M. The suspects fled, but one or more of them later returned to the crime scene, where Eleanor's throat was severed and the bodies were carefully staged.

If the murders had indeed unfolded in this manner, then what, or who, was the catalyst? To answer this question, investigators turned to yet another familiar character from the earlier saga, Minnie Clark, perhaps the only congregant whose devotion to St. John's rivaled that of Eleanor Mills. In 1922, Clark was barely questioned during the first grand jury inquiry, despite a tenacious rumor that she had been a mole, suspected to have intercepted Eleanor's love letters and given them to Frances. Clark was afforded no such courtesy by Simpson, who believed she knew more than she let on. Questioned by one of Simpson's detectives on September 17, Clark admitted she had visited the Hall home on the afternoon of the murders, joining Frances for a glass of raspberry drinking vinegar and a jar of mixed pickles. But she denied ever finding any of Edward and Eleanor's love letters, or seeing any of their love letters, or exchanging gossip with Ralph Gorsline, another suspected spy, about any such letters. Simpson didn't buy it. A few weeks later, police showed up at Clark's house, where they found her in the upstairs bedroom, wrapped in a pink kimono and apparently feigning an illness. A doctor was summoned, and after he confirmed Clark was the picture of health, her arrest commenced as planned. She was charged as an accessory to murder and released on five thousand dollars' bail.

Felix De Martini, who'd been accused of harassing and intimidating witnesses, was arrested in Brooklyn on the same charge. But he fought his extradition to New Jersey and was released to serve as a witness for the defense. A trial date for Frances, Willie, and Henry Stevens was set for November 3. Simpson decided to hold a separate trial for Henry Carpender, who maintained he was at a dinner party on the night of the murders. "It is my firm conviction," Carpender said, "that Senator Simpson has determined not to try me with my cousins for the sole reason of endeavoring to deprive them of the benefit of the proof that Mrs. Gibson committed perjury when she testified that she saw me at the scene of the murder."

As Simpson and McCarter prepared for their showdown in court, new developments continued to unfold. Eleanor's body was exhumed a second time for yet another autopsy. Jim Mills wept on his knees beside the grave site as her remains were pulled from the earth. "Oh God, let justice be done!"

The most sensational breakthrough involved Henry Dickman, the missing former state trooper referenced in one of the *Mirror*'s earlier reports. He'd surfaced in August at the U.S. Army disciplinary barracks on Alcatraz Island in San Francisco, where he was being held for desertion. In late September, Dickman was brought back east and remanded to an army prison on Governors Island, New York City. In his cell there, he was interrogated by a special investigator identified in news reports as "Detective X," alternately described as a onetime Scotland Yard operative and a former agent of the United States Department of Justice. Dickman told Detective X that when he'd questioned Henry Stevens about his alibi in 1922, he found Henry to be "evasive in his answers." As Dickman put it, "I was impressed with the fact that he had knowledge which he was not disclosing." Dickman also claimed that county officials had, on several occasions, instructed him to "lay off" when "it seemed that I was developing a lead." He said Louise Geist "told me that Mrs. Hall listened in and heard the whole conversation," and that "Charlotte Mills told me that the letters that passed between her mother and Dr. Hall were placed in a big Bible that was kept in the big room where the Bible class was held."

The biggest shocker involved an alleged meeting between Dickman, Henry Carpender, and Azariah Beekman at Beekman's office in March 1923. "We can make it worth your while to get out of the case entirely," Dickman recalled Beekman saying, as Carpender pulled a checkbook from his pocket. In Dickman's telling, he promptly removed himself from the compromising situation, only to be summoned to Beekman's house several weeks later. The two men chatted for a while, and when Dickman got up to leave, Beekman said, "When you go out you will find a letter in the mailbox. Take it." Dickman opened the envelope and counted twenty-five one-hundred-dollar bills. This time, he cast his scruples aside and accepted the money. He resigned from the state police and hit the road, bouncing around between Montreal, New York, and Miami before joining the army in December 1924.

Simpson didn't specify the nature of Dickman's allegations for the newspapers. "I won't discuss the statement beyond saying that it is too sensational to be published in full," he told reporters. "My opinion is that the story should come out in open court—from Dickman on the witness stand."

AS THE TRIAL DREW NEAR, Frances acknowledged it was in her best interest to rekindle a relationship with the press, or at least the journalists who might be counted upon for a sympathetic portrayal. One afternoon, amid a sudden downpour, Timothy Pfeiffer invited a reporter inside the Hall home to take shelter from the rain—a respectable writer from Frances's preferred paper, the *New York Times*. Frances greeted the newsman warmly and surprised him with an impromptu interview. "My chief worry has been reporters, but really the photographers have been the terrors," she said. "On some of the really hot days, however, I felt quite sorry for them. One day, in particular, I debated whether to send them out some cold lemonade or turn the hose on them, but I was afraid that it would be misinterpreted either way."

On another occasion, as Frances left a hearing at the Somerset County Courthouse, she offered two reporters a lift to New Brunswick. She ordered her driver into the rear of the Dodge and took the wheel herself, chatting amiably with her passengers as they motored about the countryside.

"I have just about reached the conclusion that New Jersey is not a fit place for decent people to live," Frances sighed. "I don't know whether I shall continue to live here or not."

"Do you plan a trip to Europe when the trial is over, Mrs. Hall?"

"It is impossible for me to make any plans at the present time," Frances replied with a smile. She fell silent as the Dodge chugged along, passing roadside hot dog vendors and dusty gas stations and vegetable stands. "I used to be a good American, and I am still a good American, but—" Frances paused, shaking her head. "I am getting skeptical."

The charm offensive achieved its desired effect. After interviewing Frances at 23 Nichol Avenue one day, Grace Robinson wrote, "Mrs. Hall showed herself to be a totally different sort of person than she usually has been painted. She is not cold nor austere, though by birth and breeding she should have been. Instead she glows with a passionate love of color and beauty."

These flattering portraits held no sway with the *Daily Mirror*, which was enjoying rapid growth: 418,527 copies on average during the month of September, fewer than only five other morning or evening papers in all of America, though still well short of the *Daily News'* one million readers. The *Mirror* lambasted the "innocuous" interviews Frances had been doling out. Frances disliked journalists in general, but she especially despised those who worked for the *Mirror*, a seedy rag that had instigated her current predicament. Her antipathy spilled into public during an interview in the home of one of her cousins, Sydney Carpender. Denying the long list of allegations lodged against her, Frances called the case "a malicious persecution of myself and my family instituted by a tabloid to increase its circulation, and abetted by politicians to advance their own ends." For the first time, Frances responded to every bit of mud Payne's tabloid had slung at her. "The *Daily Mirror* sent Arthur Riehl to [an] attorney who, without knowing its true purpose, drew Riehl's petition for the annulment to my former maid from a typewritten statement which Riehl brought with him. The *Mirror* then used the irrelevant and scandalous portions of the petition attacking me and my family as the basis for its defamatory campaign. . . . The tabloid repeatedly and recently has stated that I fled to Italy to escape extradition. I made trips abroad only to obtain every necessary relief and relaxation after the horror I had been through. I went to Italy because I wanted to go to a place that was warm and beautiful. The fact that one couldn't be extradited from that country I didn't even know about." Frances additionally claimed that her fortune had never exceeded $300,000—far less than the $1.7 million she was reported to have been worth in 1922—and that she "can't imagine where all the stories of family wealth came from unless inspired by the tabloid." The bottom line: "The tabloid is still in full charge of the investigation."

Payne didn't take these insults lightly. He sent a telegram to New Brunswick's *Daily Home News*, which published Payne's missive on its front page the following morning: "Before the Mirror began publishing stories which were partly responsible for the present investigation, Mrs. Hall and Henry Carpender were told of the facts in possession of this newspaper and asked for statements. They refused to reply. . . . The Mirror repeatedly gave Mrs. Hall the opportunity of publicly answering certain questions. She has not done so. The offer remains open. Now that a trial is near, Mrs. Hall and her staff of lawyers are resorting to the same sort of propaganda they used four years ago in an effort to divert suspicion from themselves and to arouse public sympathy."

In response, Frances told the *Daily Home News*, "It is not necessary for us to discuss our side of the case in the newspapers. As I have stated before, we will only be too glad of the opportunity to appear in court and answer the charges that have so falsely been made against us. But that will be in a court of law. We do not care to try the case in the newspapers. I have already stated my opinion of the *Daily Mirror*, and I do not wish to go into that any further."

Four years after the murders, on the eve of what the *Mirror* foreshadowed as "the greatest criminal trial this country has ever known since the Harry Thaw case," Phil Payne and Frances Hall were now enemy combatants. In a matter of weeks, they would come face-to-face in a courtroom, but Payne felt like his work was already done. "Whatever the outcome," a *Mirror* editorial declared, "the crime is at last and for the first time thoroughly sifted, and thereby New Jersey retrieves its position of rigid and impartial law enforcement for high and low alike."

As he had demonstrated time and time again—with his séance stunt, his Harry Thaw crusade, the Earl Carroll bathtub exposé— Payne would stop at nothing in pursuit of a story that was sure to sell newspapers. Perhaps the excitement of circulation-building was starting to get the best of him.

TRIAL OF THE CENTURY

By early November, as Frances Hall and her brothers prepared to face a jury of their peers, Somerville transformed from a provincial backwater into the most heavily scrutinized town in the United States. Nowhere else, it was said, could you expect to find so many journalists in one place, except perhaps for the national political conventions, or the signing of the peace treaty at Versailles. More than two hundred reporters, editors, and photographers—from New York and New Jersey; from Washington and Massachusetts; from Pennsylvania and Kansas and Tennessee—had arrived to chronicle the proceedings, which even the most seasoned among them called "the great story of a generation." Somerville would be their home for the next several weeks, which meant lodging was now the borough's most precious commodity. The *Daily News* reserved a whole floor of the Somerset Hotel, the lobby of which doubled as a social club for visiting scribes. Other New York papers took out leases on entire homes, whose rents soared to five hundred dollars a month. An enterprising property owner welcomed thirteen employees of the *Daily Mirror*, who shared the house with a single black cat.

Landlords weren't the only ones profiting from the influx. It was a boon to those who trafficked in bootleg liquor and games of chance, as well as to Somerville's legitimate entrepreneurs. One haberdashery owner reported that overcoats, shirts, neckties, and socks were flying off his shelves. "Business is good," he said. But there was also resentment that powerful Hudson County politicians, at the urging of a troublemaking tabloid, had inserted themselves into local affairs. "To believe that one sensational New York newspaper could cause all the recent proceedings and expense," an editorial in the *Somerset Democrat* bemoaned, "does not sit well with Somerset County taxpayers."

Among the hordes of journalists tramping around Somerville were the beat reporters who had been following the story for months, including Herbert Mayer of the *Mirror* and Grace Robinson of the *News*. The *Evening Graphic* sent Leo Casey and Jack Miley, "both wonderful reporters," a colleague recalled, "our purpose having been not only to report the aroused sensation, but to make it plain, should a conviction not seem likely, that *we, we, we*, the *Graphic*, were quite innocent of having brought this trouble to Mrs. Hall, her brother Willie, brother Henry, and cousin Henry de la Bruyere Carpender."

In addition to their own staff, news outlets commissioned guest correspondents, employing ghostwriters as needed. The Post Syndicate secured the byline of Ethel Stevens—wife of Henry—and the *Mirror* boasted that its lineup would include Charlotte Mills, who had already produced a series of autobiographical articles for the Famous Feature Syndicate. Also on the Hearst tab was Richard Enright, a mystery author and former commissioner of the New York City police. The *Graphic* gave a column to the Reverend Dr. John Roach Straton, who proclaimed in his God-fearing prose, "Anyone that strikes a blow at the sanctity of the marriage vow undermines the foundations of the nation." Editors additionally sought out superstars like Theodore Dreiser and Mary Roberts Rinehart, only to blanch at their staggering day rates, although the novelists Fannie Hurst and Edna Ferber would end up parachuting in briefly. Dorothy Dix, the famed advice columnist and crime reporter, arrived in Somerville with a thousand-dollar weekly syndication agreement, and Frances Noyes Hart was assigned to the trial for the Washington *Evening Star*, an experience that would culminate in her pioneering 1927 courtroom novel, *The Bellamy Trial*. The dean of the Hall-Mills press corps was Damon Runyon, a dapper literary newsman and future author of the stories that inspired *Guys and Dolls*. Employed by Hearst's Universal News Service, Runyon was heralded by the *Mirror* as "the greatest of all descriptive reporters."

In a curtain-raiser before the start of the trial, Runyon observed that the spectacle had "taken on some of the aspects of a big sports event." It wasn't merely a metaphor: a telegraph switchboard used two months earlier during the world heavyweight fight between Jack Dempsey and Gene Tunney had been installed in the courthouse basement, with a staff of twenty-eight operators at the ready. Four stenographers were on hand to record every word of the proceedings, hourly transcripts of which would be churned out by a bevy of mimeograph machines. At the local telephone exchange, eight additional switchboard operators were brought in to handle the increased volume of calls, including from the extra lines installed in hotel rooms and private homes. Inside the three-hundred-capacity courtroom, folding chairs replaced swivel seats to accommodate as many as 130 members of the press, who spoke of the trial as if they'd never seen anything like it.

"It's got the Thaw case beaten by a mile," one journalist marveled.

"It is the most fascinating and interesting case I have ever written about," another concurred. "It has a combination of every element that makes a murder case great."

As the opening arguments loomed, Willie and Henry passed the time in their jail cells, Willie immersed in a book on metallurgy and Henry making his way through a twenty-year-old volume of magazines with stories about fishing and hunting. Henry Carpender, whose trial was scheduled for a later date, buried his nose in detective novels. Free on bail, Frances drove to Princeton for a session with a professional photographer. She returned with twenty-two portraits to be distributed to newspapers all over the country, hoping editors would use these instead of the unflattering pictures already in circulation.

On the morning of Wednesday, November 3, Frances stepped out of her doorway, sucked in a breath of fresh air, looked up at the clear blue sky and the bright autumn foliage, and said, "It is a lovely day, isn't it?" Projecting confidence, she posed for the photographers camped out in front of her house and stepped into a car headed for Somerville, where hundreds of spectators greeted her, craning their necks as she disappeared into the Somerset County Courthouse, made of gleaming Alabama marble in the neo-Palladian style.

Inside, sun illuminated a stained-glass skylight above the courtroom, which had the feel of a large chapel, or a small amphitheater. Shortly after 10:00 A.M., sixty-four-year-old Justice Charles W. Parker and thirty-nine-year-old Judge Frank L. Cleary, both tall and lean, took their seats behind the bench. The defendants entered, joining seven attorneys and one private detective huddled around the defense table. Reporters took note of the squirrel-fur collar on Frances's black silk coat, which matched her pocketbook and shoes. The widow's outfit was accented by gray silk gloves and a pearl stickpin jutting out of a black ribbon hat. Her brothers wore dark suits, Willie's emblazoned with a gold watch chain across his vest. "He somehow made me think of a successful delicatessen dealer," Runyon wrote.

After jury selection—six farmers, two clerks, a superintendent, a mason, a blacksmith, and a teamster—Alexander Simpson took the floor, a "sartorial sensation," as one reporter described him, whose outfits became a highlight of the trial. For his opening arguments, the pint-size prosecutor wore a colorful dress shirt and a pin-striped suit tucked into black leather spats, which gave him the look of a jockey. As he rose to face the jury, suspense gripped the tightly packed courtroom, filled with reporters and family members and a few dozen ordinary townsfolk lucky enough to nab seats. The two lead attorneys for the defendants, Robert McCarter and State Senator Clarence Case, studied Simpson as he launched into his opening argument. He sketched out the contours of the case and his theory of the crime, running through all the evidence and witnesses that had been accumulated over the past four years. He described Eleanor as "a woman in humble circumstances" who "longed to live a big life," and Edward as a "very fine-looking man" who "found he was in a chill, cold household." Frances, in turn, was a "strong, proud woman, wounded perhaps as much in her pride as in her affections." Simpson outlined the state's theory of the crime and, in closing, glared at the jurors and said, "You may draw guilt or you may draw innocence, but surely you have to draw the conclusion that, with this evidence, it is perfectly right—nay, it would be wrong *not to* put these three defendants on trial."

Simpson marched back to his seat and the court adjourned for lunch. The trial of the century had begun.

THE FIRST FEW DAYS WERE a mix of familiar faces and dramatic surprises. One unexpected attendee was Jane Gibson's mother, Salome Cerrener, present not in the company of her daughter, but as a guest of the defense, telling anyone who would listen that the Pig Woman was a no-good liar. It was all too much for Gibson, now reportedly suffering from cancer. After an emotional confrontation, Gibson collapsed and was taken to the local hospital, where she was treated for a blood infection, teetering on the edge of death. At Simpson's urging, Gibson was soon transferred to a larger and better-equipped hospital in Jersey City. Whether she would recover, and whether she would be well enough to testify, was anyone's guess.

One by one, witnesses paraded through the courtroom: George

Totten, Peter Tumulty, Minnie Clark, the chauffeur who'd observed a scratch on Frances's cheek, the man who'd seen Gibson riding her mule on De Russey's Lane, another man who said he saw a Dodge parked near the farm around midnight, Eleanor's sisters, Jim's brother, and so on. The biggest surprise was the introduction of two mystery witnesses, husband and wife John and Charlotte Dickson, who had an intriguing story to tell about the night of the murders. At 8:30 P.M., they said, a man came to the door of their home in North Plainfield—about seven miles from the crime scene as the crow flies—agitated and confused, thinking himself to be in the town of Bound Brook, and looking for directions to the Parker Home, an old-age facility close to the Phillips farm. The Dicksons told the jury they escorted the man to a nearby trolley station and parted ways at eight forty-five. They remembered the time because the man had pulled out a large open-face gold watch. Asked to identify the man, Mr. Dickson rose from the witness stand, walked over to the defendants, and placed his hand on Willie Stevens, who sat with a puzzled look on his face as half the courtroom rose to its feet. "There were audible gasps of astonishment," Grace Robinson observed.

Another fascinating moment came when the jury heard from Ralph Gorsline—now separated from his wife—who described hearing gunshots between ten and ten thirty as he sat in his seven-passenger Apperson touring car with Catherine Rastall. The shots were followed by a tortured moaning. "As if something, somebody, whoever was doing it, was endeavoring to stop the moaning," he said. After four years of lying about his presence near the crime scene, Gorsline had finally come clean. But there was something Gorsline would not concede: he firmly denied visiting the Burns Detective Agency.

"Have you ever been in there?" McCarter asked Gorsline on cross.

"Never in my life."

"Did you ever meet a man by the name of William Garven?"

"No, sir."

Garven, the agency's former New York manager, insisted otherwise, testifying that Gorsline visited the agency on October 1, 1922. During this meeting, according to Garven, Gorsline not only admitted to being on De Russey's Lane, but said he had encountered Henry Stevens carrying a revolver. In Garven's recollection of the story, Henry scared Gorsline away by firing two shots into the dirt. "What the hell are you doing here? This is none of your affair! Get the hell out of here!" Simpson asked Gorsline to step forward. "That is the man," Garven swore.

Reporters were especially interested in the testimony of Henry Dickman, the former state trooper. Earlier, Simpson had refused to divulge Dickman's allegations for the newspapers. Now they heard it all from Dickman's own lips. He told the jury about accepting a twenty-five-hundred-dollar bribe from Henry Carpender and Azariah Beekman, in return for disappearing from the case. The defense, in turn, took the wind out of Dickman's sails by portraying him, rather accurately, as a shady character who had deserted from the U.S. military. But his testimony intrigued the courtroom all the same.

In another titillating moment, a woman named Marie Demarest testified that she'd seen Minnie Clark and Ralph Gorsline furtively snooping on Edward and Eleanor in Buccleuch Park. It was the first public corroboration of Clark and Gorsline's alleged spy craft. Demarest also claimed to have seen Henry Stevens in New Brunswick at 9:45 A.M. the morning after the murders, contradicting Henry's timeline. "It was that gentleman right there," she said, pointing at the defendant, who had claimed he took a train to New Brunswick after learning of Edward's death in the afternoon.

When it came time to hear from Louise Geist Riehl, whose estranged husband had by now dropped the annulment petition that helped set the trial in motion, the courtroom's ears pricked up once again. In questioning Louise, Simpson attempted to establish that Frances had listened in on Edward and Eleanor's phone call on the night of the murders, when they arranged a time and place to meet. Louise had answered the call in the second-floor hallway before Frances picked up a phone downstairs, at which point Louise indicated that the call was for Edward. In her numerous conversations with detectives, some of them separated by four years, Louise had given varying indications of whether she'd seen Frances hang up the phone. During a deposition months earlier, she had admitted to fluctuations in her memory. But now, as Simpson pressed Louise on this crucial point, she held firm in her response, telling the jury with certainty that Frances had "placed back the receiver and turned around and walked out."

"You said nothing at all to that grand jury about Mrs. Hall putting up the receiver," Simpson pointed out.

"They undoubtedly did not ask me."

Louise may have answered honestly. Or she may have altered her story to spite Simpson, who had dragged her back into a matter she was all too eager to forget. Whichever the case, she succeeded in riling the prosecutor: reporters could see the displeasure on Simpson's face.

ON NOVEMBER 9, AS RAIN lashed the windows and wind shook the barren limbs of trees outside the courthouse, the proceedings took a morbid turn. A physician named Otto Schultze exhibited a mannequin's head made of wax and papier-mâché, using a red crayon to mark the spots where three bullets had entered Eleanor's face. He then made a sweeping motion to illustrate the cutting of Eleanor's throat. But that wasn't the most gruesome part: Schultze explained that when he performed Eleanor's third and final autopsy, on October 26, he discovered that her tongue, larynx, and windpipe were missing. The implication was that whoever was responsible for this mutilation must have harbored a burning animus toward the talented soprano.

"These were all organs of singing, weren't they?"

"Yes."

Charlotte Mills hurried out of the courtroom, unable to bear the display. "I would rather have been stricken blind at that moment than to have looked at the vivid demonstration," she wrote in her newspaper column. Charlotte sobbed through her own testimony, identifying several letters written in her mother's hand, describing a large book in the study of St. John's where Eleanor and Edward exchanged love notes, and recalling her last conversation with her mother just a few hours before the murders. "She came from church, went up to the house, got a nickel to phone, and went around the corner to [use the] phone, and told me to wait," Charlotte said. "That was the last I saw of her."

When Charlotte's father took the stand, in a wrinkled gray suit, he was subjected to a cross-examination that one observer described as "sinister in its implications." In preparation for the trial, the defense had searched high and low for any shred of evidence that might lead jurors to ponder whether Jim Mills should have been indicted instead of the defendants. Timothy Pfeiffer had gone so far as to write to Bernardine Szold, the former *Daily News* reporter, now living in Paris, who had portrayed Madame Astra four years earlier. In his letter, Pfeiffer asked Szold whether there was any truth to a "rumor" that Mills had confessed during the séance. When Phil Payne caught wind of this, he tried to beat Pfeiffer at his own game. "Please cable Pfeiffer immediately," Payne wired Szold, "asking what he will pay you to return here and testify you heard Mills make [a] confession." If Pfeiffer had complied, Payne would have been able to expose him for bribing a journalist to fabricate evidence. He didn't take the bait, but that didn't stop the *Mirror* from printing Pfeiffer's letter to Szold alongside an article confirming that the séance had yielded no such result: "Never during those long hours did Mills weaken once."

Lacking real evidence against Jim Mills, Robert McCarter resorted to insinuation. Mills owned a shoemaker's knife, didn't he? "Yes." He and Eleanor "had a few words" on the night she disappeared, no? "We didn't have no few words at all." Wasn't it "a fact" that Jim found some of Eleanor's love letters the day before she was killed? "No, sir." Wasn't it odd that Jim didn't inquire with the police or hospital when he realized Eleanor was missing? "My wife used to go away sometimes a day or two." McCarter also asked Jim about the five hundred dollars he had received in 1922 for the letters sold to the *New York American* by Florence North, the family's former representative.

"That is one of the Hearst papers?" McCarter asked.

"I think so."

"And the New York *Mirror* is also a Hearst paper, is it not?"

"I object to this!" Simpson cut in. "We are not trying the *Mirror*, nor are we trying Mr. Hearst. . . . If Mr. Hearst can stop murder, he is doing good work."

A GOOD PORTION OF THE trial focused on the fingerprints found on Edward Hall's calling card, which made for hours of esoteric testimony. Fingerprinting was still a relatively new field. The study of ridge impressions as a means of identification dates back to ancient China, but it wasn't until the late nineteenth century that fingerprint evidence slowly began to be incorporated into homicide investigations. The FBI, under J. Edgar Hoover, had established a national fingerprint bureau only in 1924, and even among experts, there were no uniform standards for confirming an identification. The prosecution's witnesses were prepared to testify to five similarities between Willie's fingerprint and the print on the card—a seemingly low bar. Still, the card was Simpson's best evidence, and he called on several fingerprint experts to support it. One was Lieutenant

Joseph Faurot, a veteran New York police inspector who had previously testified, in 1911, during the first American trial in which a conviction was obtained exclusively with fingerprint evidence. Another was Lieutenant Edward Schwartz, a Newark police official who assisted in the 1922 investigation. Schwartz had taken possession of Edward's calling card after the first grand jury, and he held on to the card until turning it over to Payne in the summer of 1926. These experts did not flinch in their belief that Willie Stevens had left his mark. Faurot, who had studied fingerprinting among the more advanced European police agencies, showed the jury twenty enlarged photographs of the prints, explaining how the highly unique arch pattern found on the card was a dead ringer for Willie's. "Draw your own deductions," he told the jurors. "You need no expert. After this examination you will be as expert as anybody else." Schwartz wholeheartedly agreed. "The card contains the left index finger of William Stevens," he said.

To counter this testimony, the defense sought to cast doubt on the card's authenticity, arguing there was no way to prove it was the same card found near Edward's foot, or that Willie's fingerprints had not ended up there by some innocent means, or that the card hadn't been corrupted or tampered with. To clarify for the jury how the card had found its way into the case, Simpson called the one man who could articulate the chain of events.

Phil Payne took the stand late in the morning on Friday, November 12, lowering himself into the old oaken chair beside the judge's bench and leaning forward. Frances Hall sneered at the editor, with his slick suit, his self-assured grin, his round face and Coke-bottle glasses. Payne had earned more of Frances's contempt than any other figure in the case, except perhaps for Alexander Simpson, who moved in close, mindful that Payne was hard of hearing.

"You are editor of the New York *Daily Mirror*?" Simpson began.
"Yes."

"Do you know Mr. Schwartz, who is the fingerprint expert of the Newark Police Department, or was until recently?"

"Yes, sir."

"Did you ever see this card before?"

"Yes, sir."

"Where did you first see this card?"

"In Newark, in a hotel."

"Who had possession of the card when you first saw it?"

"Captain Schwartz."

"Do you remember the date?"

"No. Approximately it was around the first week in July."

"Did you give him any financial consideration, or anything of value, for the card?"

"Nothing of financial value."

Simpson stepped back and gave McCarter the floor. The defense attorney slowly approached the stand, keeping a noticeable distance while questioning his partially deaf witness. Payne repaid the discourtesy by cupping his hands to his ears or asking McCarter to repeat himself. More than once, he stifled a yawn.

"When did you become acquainted with Mr. Schwartz?" McCarter asked.

"Several years ago," said Payne.

"How did you learn that he had this card?"

"He told me."

"Where did he tell you that?"

"In Newark."

"Where?"

"Walking down the street together."

"How did you happen to meet Schwartz walking down [the] street?"

"I did not meet him walking down there. I met him by appointment."

"Where?"

"At the same hotel. I think it is called the St. Francis."

"Why wasn't it a good place to meet at his office, right down at police headquarters?"

"Better ask him that."

Payne leaned on his arm, his replies dripping with sarcasm. He told McCarter he'd had three or four meetings with Schwartz before Schwartz agreed to relinquish the card, which was given to Payne in a taxicab. Payne's close friend and colleague Francis Farley was present for the handoff as well.

"You say you gave him nothing whatever for the card?"

"Nothing financial, no."

"Well, if it was not financial, what did you give him?"

Payne paused, staring blankly at the ceiling.

"Why don't you answer me?"

"I can think while I answer just as well as you can think while you ask me a question."

"Does it require a great deal of thought to tell me what it was?"

"No."

"Then why don't you answer?"

Payne leaned back in his chair and smiled.

"I told Schwartz—"

"I have not asked you what you told him," McCarter snapped. "I asked you what you gave him!"

Straightening up to deliver his response, Payne replied, "I told Schwartz that if he could help clear up this crime, he was doing a service to the state of New Jersey. That was the only consideration he got."

McCarter's face turned red as laughter filled the courtroom. Payne went on to explain that he had wrapped the card in wax paper and locked it away in a steel filing cabinet in the *Mirror* offices. He acknowledged that his cameramen had photographed it for publication, and that Herbert Mayer had taken the card to be examined by Faurot, who was vacationing in the Catskills.

"You commanded that it be sent to Faurot?" McCarter suggested.

"I did not command," Payne sneered. "I am not the queen of Rumania."

"Oh! You are the queen of the *Mirror*?"

"Unfortunately, I am not. My sex is masculine."

The courtroom erupted in laughter once again—not even Justice Parker could conceal a smile. McCarter then asked Payne if he had given any directions to the police.

"I do not direct the police," Payne replied. "I'm not the state of New Jersey."

"Oh, aren't you?"

"You have a funny idea of what the state is."

"You know your function is not to criticize me!"

"Nor is *your* function to criticize *me*. All you have to do is ask questions."

Justice Parker, now stern, pounded his gavel on the bench. Payne bowed his head in deference. Frances scowled. McCarter changed gears.

"How much money has the *Mirror* spent on this investigation that you have conducted?"

Simpson shouted out an objection, which the judges sustained.

"Is it not a fact that your compensation from the *Mirror*," McCarter continued, "is a flat sum plus a bonus or something of that character, depending upon the extent of the circulation of the paper?"

"Objected to!"

The question was again overruled.

"Where is your residence, Mr. Payne?"

"West New York, New Jersey."

"That is in Hudson County?"

"Yes."

"The same place the governor lives," Simpson interjected.

"The same place *Frank Hague* lives," the Republican defense attorney parried, suggesting undue influence by Hague, the Democratic Party boss.

"Yes," said Simpson, "and a good county because he lives there, too."

"Does the court think it is proper for counsel to make remarks like these?" McCarter pleaded.

"The court," said Parker, admonishingly, "thinks the whole dialogue is improper."

McCarter had had enough of Payne's derision, but Simpson requested a redirect.

"You were asked a great many questions about your interest in this matter," he said. "Have you any interest whatever?"

"Yes," said Payne. "I want to see this case cleared up the same as any other citizen of New Jersey would want to see it cleared up."

"You say you have not any interest," McCarter interjected. "Have you any principle?"

"Just as much as you have, Mr. McCarter, to ask me that question."

For the last time, Parker silenced the chuckles that fluttered through the courtroom. Payne stepped down from the witness stand, satisfied that he had put on a good show. "It was amusing to hear his answers turn Mr. McCarter's questions into smashing boomerangs," Charlotte gushed in her column. "His snappy replies kept cracking and sparkling around Mr. McCarter's poor head. Like fireworks until he seemed all befuddled."

Payne's testimony had been the liveliest of the trial thus far. But he would soon be overshadowed. Some thirty miles away, in a Jersey City hospital room, the state's star witness was on the mend.

"I HAVE TOLD THEM THE TRUTH, SO HELP ME GOD!"

Jane Gibson lay in a hospital bed, feverish and weak. Since collapsing during the opening hours of the trial fourteen days earlier, amid a quarrel with her estranged mother, Gibson had been convalescing in a Jersey City medical facility, treated for a constellation of ailments including cancer and kidney disease. Throughout the day, physicians had sparred with Alexander Simpson, who was eager for Gibson to be discharged. Gibson's testimony was the linchpin of the state's case against Frances Hall and her brothers, the prosecutor argued, and her presence in Somerville could be delayed no longer. When Gibson's doctors insisted their patient was too ill to endure the roughly thirty-mile ambulance ride from Jersey City, Simpson threatened a writ of habeas corpus to compel her transportation to the courtroom. But the doctors held firm. Instead, Simpson ordered two of his detectives to speak with Gibson in person. They appeared at her bedside early in the evening, finding the once robust Pig Woman pale and weary. Unable to rise, even to a sitting position, Gibson smiled at her visitors, who asked whether she could muster enough strength to testify the following day. The detectives apprised Gibson of her doctors' concerns, emphasizing that she would be making the journey at her own risk. Gibson looked them in the eyes and said, "I can testify, and I want to."

The next morning, an ambulance pulled away from Jersey City Hospital with a nurse and a physician monitoring Gibson's condition. A police car and several officers on motorcycles led the procession, which also included six cars full of reporters and photographers. Driving at a glacial ten to fifteen miles an hour, per the physician's orders, the caravan inched through Jersey City and Newark, Springfield and Scotch Plains, Plainfield and Bound Brook. All along the route, onlookers crowded the roadside as if watching a parade.

"Oooh, the Pig Woman!"

"Do your stuff, Jane!"

Gibson's doctor stuck his head out the ambulance window and yelled to the traveling press corps: "Mrs. Gibson is doing very nicely!"

After three hours and forty-five minutes, the ambulance pulled up to the Somerset County Courthouse, where hundreds of spectators had gathered under a light rain. They erupted in excitement as the ambulance backed up to the courthouse steps. Four officers lifted Gibson, covered in blankets from head to toe, out of the vehicle and into the building. The courtroom was more crowded than usual, with people snugly packed against the back wall. Bailiff John Bunn shouted at the standees to clear a path, and the officers gently lifted Gibson from the stretcher and placed her onto an iron-frame hospital bed facing the jury. Gibson's doctor stood at the ready with his stethoscope, monitoring her pulse and temperature. A nurse pulled the covers from Gibson's face, which had been drained into a ghostly pallor that accentuated the color in her blue eyes and wispy brown hair. She was but a shadow of the gun-toting pioneer woman who had captured the public imagination four years earlier. "Her hands," Damon Runyon observed, "look too frail today to have done the manual labor incidental to farm work."

Bailiff Bunn silenced the courtroom as Justice Parker and Judge Cleary took their seats. Alexander Simpson stepped forward and placed his hand on the footrail of Gibson's bed. "If it pleases the court," he said, "the State produces the witness, Jane Gibson, and asks to have her sworn." Simpson quickly corrected himself, using Gibson's married name: "Jane Easton."

From the front row, a gnarled old woman dressed in black peered at the witness, mumbling aspersions. "She's a liar," Gibson's mother blurted out. "A liar, liar, liar. A *liar*, that's what she is! Ugh!"

Gibson's hand rested weakly on the Bible. Asked whether she solemnly swore to tell the truth, the whole truth, and nothing but the truth, her reply was barely audible: "I do."

It was agreed that the court stenographer would repeat Gibson's answers for the jury after her testimony was complete. And with that, the interrogation commenced.

Gibson began by recounting the events that brought her to the Phillips farm that night, a story familiar to anyone who had followed the case over the past four years. It all began when Gibson set out on her mule, Jenny, pursuing a wagon believed to contain stolen corn. When the wagon turned from De Russey's Lane onto Easton Avenue, disappearing out of sight, something else caught Gibson's attention.

"An automobile came in the lane a little ways and I saw two people."

"A man and a woman, or two men, or what?"

"I saw a white woman and a colored man, and she didn't have no hat on."

"Did you know who she was?"

"I see her face before but I did not know who she was."

"Now you have learned who she was?"

"Yes. Mrs. Hall."

"Have you learned who the man was who was with her?"

"Stevens."

"Which Stevens?"

"Willie Stevens."

Frances and Willie, according to Gibson, stood by the road as the car turned around in the lane. Gibson and Jenny trotted over to the intersection of Easton Avenue to look for the wagon, but it was nowhere to be seen. They turned around and rode back down De Russey's Lane, into the farmland and fields. That's when something pricked up Gibson's ears. She tied Jenny to a cedar tree and trudged through the darkness on foot.

"I heard mumbling voices toward the left of me. Men's voice and women's voices. I stood still. They were coming closer all the time."

Gibson could make out some of the words: "Explain these letters! Goddammit!"

"Somebody was hitting, hitting, hitting," she told the jury. "I could hear somebody's wind going out, and somebody said, ugh. Then somebody said, 'God damn it, let's go.' Then somebody threw a flash toward where they were hollering."

"A flashlight?"

"Yes. And I see something glitter, and I see a man, and I see another man like they were wrestling together."

The nurse leaned over to dab cream on Gibson's dry lips. The doctor checked her pulse. Simpson jingled some coins in his hand while he waited.

"Did you see any faces there?"

"Yes, I see two faces."

"Who were they?"

"One was Henry Stevens."

Gibson's memory had apparently improved since the grand jury four years earlier, when she could not swear which of the two Henries she had seen. Now she was certain she'd seen both of them, but Simpson said it wasn't necessary to identify the other of the two faces, and Henry Carpender's name therefore went unspoken.

Carpender was, however, sitting in the courtroom for the first time during the trial.

"Did you see Willie Stevens there?"

"No."

"After you saw Henry Stevens's face, did you hear anything?"

"Yes. The light went out and I heard a shot."

"Then what did you hear?"

"Then I heard something fall heavy. Then I run for the mule."

"Did you hear a woman's voice after you heard the shot?"

"One said, 'Oh Henry,' and the other began to scream, scream, scream so loud. 'Oh my! Oh my! Oh my!' So terrible loud."

"Did you hear anything in the way of shots after the first shot?"

"That woman was screaming, screaming, trying to run away or something, screaming, screaming, screaming, and I just about got my foot in the stirrup when—Bang! Bang! Bang! Three quick shots."

"Then what did you do?"

"I stumbled over a stump and I ran home."

"When you say you ran, do you mean that *you* ran, or that the mule ran home?"

"The mule ran home."

Back at the farm, Gibson sat in the house for a while, pondering what she'd witnessed, unable to shake the feeling that something wasn't right. She decided to go back, the moon now high and bright. Arriving at the scene, as she tied Jenny to a tree and scoured the underbrush, she thought she heard an owl screeching.

"I crossed over the lane right at the cedar and I seen a big white-haired woman doing something with her hand. Crying. Bending down, facing something."

"Did you see who it was?"

"Yes. The woman I seen in the lane earlier in the evening."

"The same woman you say was Mrs. Hall?"

"Yes."

As Simpson retreated to his seat, Gibson's attendants fluffed her pillows. It was time for the cross-examination and she would need all her wits about her. The defense put forth Robert McCarter's co-counsel, State Senator Clarence E. Case, a slender forty-nine-year-old Republican and Somerset County native. It wouldn't be Case's last tangle with the prosecutor—Case would later lead an investigation into Simpson's friend Frank Hague and the Hudson County Democratic machine. His first line of attack was to point out inconsistencies between Gibson's trial testimony and the various statements she had previously given to detectives.

"Did you not tell Mr. Totten and Mr. David that while you were riding your mule along De Russey's Lane, you saw the flash and heard the shots?"

"No, I did not."

"Did you not say to them that after you saw the flash and heard the shots you proceeded on home without getting off your mule?"

"No."

"Or anything like that?"

"No."

"Did you not tell them that while you were on your mule, and before you reached home, you found that you had lost your moccasin and kept on riding home?"

"No."

"Did you not tell them that, one reason why you returned to the scene of the tragedy on that night, after you had once been there, was to find your lost moccasin?"

"I don't remember."

The doctor checked Gibson's temperature.

"Do you remember," Case continued, "that on or about the seventeenth of October, 1922, you were at the prosecutor's office in New Brunswick, and given an opportunity to identity Mrs. Hall, William Stevens, and Henry Stevens? . . . Were you able to identity either Mrs. Hall, or William Stevens, or Henry Stevens?"

"I was not supposed to identify anybody."

Case pivoted to Gibson's testimony weeks earlier at the preliminary hearing, where she had described seeing a man with a "glittering" object in his hand. Case asked Henry Carpender to come forward.

"Is this the gentleman that you then identified?"

"That is one of the men."

"You did not say anything about there being any other man there, at that hearing, did you?"

"Nobody asked me."

Case had planted seeds of doubt by calling attention to some of the shifting details in Gibson's numerous accounts of the murder night. The next step in his strategy was to eviscerate Gibson's character.

"You were sworn here today, I think, as Jane Easton?"

"Both Easton and Gibson."

"Which is your name?

"Both."

"Your name is Jane Easton and it is also Jane Gibson?"

"I acquired that name from having a farm. They always got Gibson's farm products. People got calling me Mrs. Gibson and I never said nothing."

"You took title to your farm under the name of Jane Gibson, did you not?"

"I sure did."

"Therefore, if you took title to the farm as Jane Gibson, how do you explain what you have already said? . . . How do you get the names Gibson and Easton?"

"My marriage name."

"And by your marriage name, you mean that you were married to a man named Easton?"

"I was."

"When and where were you married to him?"

"Nineteen nineteen."

"Will you tell us where you were married?"

"I don't remember that."

"Do you remember the name of the city or town?"

"No."

"Your maiden name was Eisleitner, was it not, Mrs. Gibson?"

"I never used Eisleitner."

"But your father's name was Eisleitner, was it not?"

"Yes."

"You called yourself Mary Eisleitner, didn't you?"

"I never used the word 'Eis.' Always Leitner."

"You permitted yourself to be known as Mary Leitner?"

Objection!

"That was my maiden name. I had a right to use it."

"You were baptized Mary, were you?"

Objection!

"Mary Jane Leitner."

"And you were called at various times Jane Easton and Mary Easton, were you not? And Jessie Easton?"

"Well, my hubby called me that, Jessie. He liked that name."

"And you were also called, were you not, Janet Hilton?"

"No."

"Were you not also called, with your permission, Anna King?"

"No, sir."

Simpson cut in to clarify that the witness must have been mistaken in giving 1919 as the year of her marriage. Her son, William, was now twenty-two years old, and she had married in 1900. Gibson acknowledged the error.

"How many husbands have you had?" Case continued.

"I have had one husband that I can remember."

"And that is who?"

"William H. Easton."

"Do you remember Mr. Kesselring?"

"I remember his name, yes."

"You lived with him as his wife, did you not?"

"No, sir, I did not. I lived in the house."

"Were you not married to Frederick Kesselring in Paterson on the thirteenth day of August, 1890?"

"I don't remember anything about such a marriage."

"Do you remember that Mr. Frederick Kesselring obtained a decree of divorce from you from the Court of Chancery in the State of New Jersey, on the grounds of adultery?"

"No. That is mixed up with somebody else. That man was a married man and had a wife and baby."

"Have you ever known a man named Harry Ray?"

"No."

"You never lived with Harry Ray?

"I never lived with—how many should I have? A dozen? Such talk!"

Case picked up a faded sepia photograph and handed it to Gibson. She squinted at the image from her sickbed.

"I ask you if the young woman that appears in that picture is not yourself."

"Does that look like me?"

"Just tell me, please, whether it is or not."

"It cannot be my picture."

"You were at one time a singer in a concert hall, were you not?"

OBJECTION!

"No, sir."

Gibson grew agitated and her doctor suggested the testimony come to an end, but Case wasn't done with the witness yet. He returned to Gibson's story of the murder night, drilling down on every detail of her tale, conveying to the jury how implausible it all sounded. As the cross-examination finally drew to a close, Case had one final stone to cast.

"Now, Mrs. Gibson, you have made quite some money, have you not, from your connection with this affair?"

"Money?"

"Didn't you get paid a large sum of money by the newspapers?"

"I didn't get large sums of money from any newspapers. These snappers come along—zippo!"

"In January or February, 1923, did you not tell Mr. Ellis Parker that you had received seven hundred dollars from the newspapers?"

"I never did tell him no such thing."

"Did you not, in the month of March, 1923, exhibit yourself and your mule Jenny at the Marine Million Dollar Circus, at the armory, Broadway and Sixty-sixth Street, New York?"

"That was a charity affair. To help the marines. I did not get a penny out of it."

"Didn't you also exhibit yourself in Perth Amboy for money?"

"No!"

After a grueling four hours, the most theatrical testimony of the trial had come to an end. In putting Gibson on the stand, Simpson had counted on her testimony being compelling enough to assure the jury of its authenticity. McCarter and Case, on the other hand, had counted on Gibson's testimony being such a mess that no twelve men in their right minds would believe a word of it. It appeared that one of the two sides had made a safer bet. "No more dramatic, no more powerful scene," Herbert Mayer wrote in the *Daily Mirror*, "has been staged ever in an American courtroom."

Before she was wheeled back to the ambulance, Gibson looked over at the defendants sitting in the front of the courtroom, surrounded by their high-priced lawyers and well-heeled relatives. Summoning every ounce of her dwindling strength, Gibson raised herself slightly from the bed, lifted one of her wasted white hands, and pointed a finger at Frances Hall, who twisted her lips into a contemptuous smile as Gibson's voice rose to a shrill cry.

"I have told them the truth, so help me God!" she wailed. "And you *know* I've told the truth!"

"A SORT OF GENIUS"

By the time the prosecution rested, its case looked more precar-
ious than it had at the beginning of the trial. Jane Gibson had
already failed to convince a jury of her fantastical story in 1922.
Now that the defense had ripped Gibson's credibility to shreds, it
appeared even less likely she would convince a jury now. Still, with
three major witnesses yet to testify, and many lesser ones, anything
could happen. Putting defendants on the stand is always a risk, but
McCarter and Case must have figured there was little downside.
The eldest of the Stevens siblings, they decided, would go first.

"Henry Stevens to the stand!" Bailiff Bunn cried out on the
morning of Saturday, November 20.

Henry settled into the witness chair and folded his hands across
his vest, one thumb resting on the other. Two months in a jail cell
had robbed the shore-dweller of his sun-kissed complexion, but
there was still a hint of tan. Ever the rugged outdoorsman, Henry
had cleaned up nicely for the trial: white linen shirt, collar thick
with starch, dark suit pressed to perfection, a striped black-and-
blue tie that Damon Runyon complimented as a "nifty bit of haberdashery." His salt-and-pepper hair and matching mustache were

carefully groomed, his droopy jowls freshly shaved. Someone who didn't know any better might have mistaken Henry for a Wall Street guy, like his cousin Henry Carpender, as opposed to a modern-day Teddy Roosevelt. Behind a pair of amber-rimmed glasses, Henry's eyes swept the room before meeting the gaze of his attorney, Clarence Case, second-in-command for the defense. It happened to be Henry's fifty-seventh birthday, a fact that was established before Case asked Henry to tell the jury what he was doing on the evening of Thursday, September 14, 1922.

Henry said he ate dinner at 6:00 P.M. before walking onto the beach to catch fish. It was around dusk when a fellow fisherman, Arthur Applegate, approached with a large bluefish, which Henry offered to weigh with his pocket scale. Henry cast his line back into the surf and was joined by a neighbor, William Eger. They fished together until around nine, when Henry trudged to his oceanfront colonial to clean off the evening's catches. He then walked back to the shoreline, where the fish had apparently stopped biting. Henry gathered up his rod and tackle box and invited Eger to join him for a drink. Back at the house, Henry reached into an icebox and pulled out two beverages. "Ginger ale, root beer, some soft drink," he recalled, "and we talked two or three minutes, and then Mr. Eger went home." It was now ten o'clock, and Henry read the newspaper before going outside around eleven to make sure the garage was closed. His next-door neighbors, the Wilsons, were still awake, and he called over with some small talk. Then he stepped inside and went to bed. He was back on the beach the next morning by the crack of dawn, fishing for bait. Contrary to the testimony of Marie Demarest, Henry said he didn't travel to New Brunswick until Saturday afternoon, when he received an urgent telegram from Edwin Carpender informing him that Edward Hall was dead.

"Were you, on the night of September 14, 1922," said Case, "at or near the vicinity of De Russey's Lane or the Phillips farm?"

"No."

"Were you, on Thursday, September 14, 1922, or Friday, September 15, 1922, at or near the City of New Brunswick?"

"No."

"Now, Mr. Stevens, did you in any way, directly or indirectly, participate in the killing of either Edward Hall or Eleanor Mills?"

"No."

"Did you procure that to be done by anyone else?"

"No."

"Have you any knowledge relating thereto?"

"No."

"Cross-examine."

Alexander Simpson's voice filled the courtroom as he rose and approached the witness. He began with a dagger to the heart of the defendants.

"You say Mr. William Stevens is your brother?"

"Yes."

"Is he your full brother?"

"Yes."

"Where was he born?"

"Aiken, South Carolina."

"You know there is no birth record of him in the church in South Carolina where there is a record of yourself and your sister, do you not?"

"No, I do not."

Frances and Willie stewed as Simpson slung mud on their family honor, sullying a proud lineage of Revolutionary War heroes, pioneering entrepreneurs, and faithful American Christians. The picture Simpson painted could have been the plot of some dark Victorian novel about shameful family secrets. It wasn't merely Willie's parentage that Simpson cast doubt on, but his race. Jane Gibson insisted she'd seen a "colored" man on De Russey's Lane that night. Simpson now suggested that Willie more than resembled someone with African blood.

"You say he is your full brother, and is by the same mother as you?"

"Yes."

"He is not by a mulatto?"

"No."

"He has the same father and mother as you?"

"Yes."

"Can you explain the difference in your faces?"

"I cannot."

Henry tensed up in the witness chair, clenching a knee, and glared at his inquisitor. If Simpson had intended to rattle the defendant with these insinuations, he was unsuccessful. Henry's composure did not desert him, and as the testimony progressed, Simpson failed to nudge his witness into anything resembling a statement of guilt. Yes, Henry admitted, he was a good marksman, but he didn't bother with pistols, only shotguns, had never fired an automatic in his life. His relationship with his brother-in-law was always "friendly and cordial," he said, no bad blood between them. He knew nothing of any love affair, or love notes, or secret rendezvous on a lovers' lane. He'd missed his sister's wedding because he was on the road, working, and his absence by no means indicated an objection to the marriage. "I wanted my sister to be happy, and if she wanted to marry Mr. Hall it was perfectly all right." He was indeed the only relative Frances would have addressed as Henry, but Gibson was either lying or mistaken—he wasn't on the Phillips farm that night, and he didn't know Edward had been murdered until seeing the newspaper on his way to New Brunswick two days later. He'd never spoken to anyone named Henry Dickman—in fact he was in Florida when the former state trooper claimed to have questioned Henry near his home in Lavallette. It was true he hadn't visited Frances while she was locked up for two days after her arrest, nor had he visited Willie in the jail before joining him there. But Henry swore he did "everything I could, in talking to people about the case, to tell them just what my sister was, how I knew she was innocent, how I knew that any of her family had nothing whatever to do with it."

"You say now it is not a fact that the reason you kept away from the jail," said Simpson, "was you were afraid somebody would identify you as being around New Brunswick at the time of the murder? That is not the fact, is it?"

"That is not the fact."

Simpson asked Henry to describe, in detail, the cutting of a freshly caught bluefish. The prosecutor then brought forth the effigy of Eleanor's head, instructing Henry to demonstrate on the mannequin's throat how such an incision would be made.

"A bluefish," Henry said, balking at the exercise, "is nothing like that at all. It is a different shape in every way."

Over the next two days, the defense trotted out a dozen witnesses placing Henry in Lavallette on the night of the murders. Several of these witnesses, including Arthur Applegate, conqueror of the six-pound bluefish, had previously told detectives they couldn't swear to the date they'd seen Henry fishing on the beach. They now testified that their earlier statements were in error, even as Simpson, on cross, highlighted discrepancies in their accounts. "Some of them couldn't remember anything else in particular," Damon Runyon wryly observed, "but they all remembered Mr. Applegate's 'blue' and Henry Stevens' weighing of the piscatorial trophy."

Outside the courtroom, the defense mounted a counterattack on Simpson's allegation of Willie's bastard birth. In a statement to the newspapers, the attorneys said Willie had been born to his rightful parents in Aiken, South Carolina, on March 13, 1872, and baptized on June 16, 1872, at St. John's in New Brunswick, where the blessed event had been logged in the church register. "The despicable character of the thoroughly malicious persecution by The Daily Mirror of Mrs. Hall and her two brothers, and of the equally malicious persecution of Mrs. Hall and her two brothers by Senator Simpson," the statement roared, "was never better illustrated than by the opening questions asked by Senator Simpson in his cross-examination of Henry Stevens."

Henry had proven to be a formidable adversary for Simpson. But if there was anyone the defense had cause to worry about, it was Willie—the childlike oaf who pretended he was a firefighter; the grown man who still lived with his younger sister, drawing a modest allowance because he couldn't be trusted to manage his own affairs.

"Is he normal mentally?" Simpson asked Willie's physician, Dr. Lawrence Runyon, who testified on his patient's behalf.

"Not absolutely, but he is able to take care of himself," Dr. Runyon replied. "He is brighter than the average person."

"Well, is he brighter than the average person, a sort of genius in a way, I suppose?"

"Yes, that is just what I mean."

WILLIE'S FACE LIT UP WHEN he was called to testify at 2:40 P.M. on Wednesday, November 23. The teddy bear of a defendant bounded up to the stand, wiping the grin off his face while the oath was administered. He sat down and looked upon the hundreds of eager faces in the courtroom, who studied Willie's neatly coiffed bush of black hair, his brownish-gray suit and matching silk tie fastened into a tight knot, the walrus mustache that added a layer of texture to his otherwise doughy face. Frances stiffened nervously, but Willie, blinking behind his thick oval glasses, looked happy as could be. He settled into the chair, perched an elbow on one of its arms, and cupped his round chin into the palm of his hand as Clarence Case began questioning him.

"Mr. Stevens, how old are you?"

"I am forty-four."

"Did I understand you to say that you were forty-four?"

"Yes."

"Isn't it fifty-four?"

Willie flashed a smile, amused by his own mistake. His testimony had gotten off to a rocky start, but he wasn't about to squander the opportunity to prove his seriousness. In the minutes that followed, to everyone's surprise, Willie disabused his audience of the notion that he was a blithering idiot. The first order of business was to puncture the testimony of John and Charlotte Dickson, who'd claimed a man identical to Willie showed up at their house on the night of the murders seeking directions to the area near the Phillips farm. According to the Dicksons, the man they believed to be Willie wore a derby hat and an open-face gold watch but no glasses. He spoke with a stutter and told them he suffered from epilepsy. ("I am an ep-ep-ep-epileptic.") Willie set the record straight: never wore a derby hat, couldn't see the hand in front of his face without glasses, had no history of epilepsy, and clearly did not speak with a stutter. As for the timepiece in question, Willie handed it to his counsel.

"A *silver* watch and chain?" Case pointed out.

"Yes, sir."

Willie took back the watch and compared its time with the courtroom clock before returning it to his vest pocket. He then craned his neck to exchange a reassuring glance with his siblings. Frances met his eyes with a loving smile.

Case's questioning commenced with a discussion of the .32 caliber Iver-Johnson revolver Willie had owned for at least fifteen years. As far as Willie could recollect, a bullet last escaped the chamber about a decade previously, perhaps longer, although he admitted he would occasionally load the gun with blanks on the Fourth of July. Asked whether he had observed anything unusual in the relations between Frances and Edward in the weeks leading up to the murders, Willie replied, "No, sir, I did not." As for the night of the murders, Willie maintained he'd gone to his room after dinner to smoke and read. He did not leave his room until Frances summoned him around two thirty in the morning to look for Edward. "I immediately got dressed and accompanied her down to the church," he said, assiduously describing their route.

"Mr. Stevens," Senator Case said a few minutes later, "I want to ask you whether you were present at or had anything to do with the murder of either Mr. Hall or Mrs. Mills."

Willie leaned forward, as if to emphasize the words about to come out of his mouth.

"Absolutely nothing at all."

"Do you know anything about it?"

"No, sir, I do not."

Case walked back to the defense table as Simpson rose for his cross-examination. Willie had fared well with his own counsel. But there was every reason to doubt he could survive an attack from the tiny pit bull of a man now approaching him. The courtroom spectators couldn't help feeling as if they were about to witness a bloodbath, and yet they were in for another surprise. Eschewing his usually bellicose manner, Simpson spoke in soft, friendly tones. Willie, in turn, received the prosecutor with a warm smile and deferential courtesy. "No, sir." "Yes, sir." "I do not recollect, sir." He was a crowd-pleaser.

"Are you quite sure that you did not arrive in an automobile with your sister in Easton Avenue on the night of the murder," Simpson asked, "around half past nine or ten o'clock, and stand in the light of an automobile while a woman on a mule went by?"

"I never remember that occurrence."

"You would remember it if it occurred, wouldn't you?"

"I certainly would."

"Your relations with your sister were very close, weren't they, very affectionate?"

"Yes, sir."

"You tried to do everything that she wished you to do?"

"I did."

"And you were concerned with her happiness, weren't you?"

"I was."

"And if you had known that Dr. Hall and Mrs. Mills had an

affair and that Mrs. Hall was losing her husband, would not that have caused you a great deal of concern?"

"Probably it would."

"You would want to help your sister in any way you could?"

"I would."

Simpson handed Willie the card that allegedly bore his finger-print.

"And you did not take a calling card like this, the same as this, with your left hand behind it, your thumb in front like that, and put it at the feet of Dr. Hall after he was murdered?"

"Positively no."

As the cross-examination progressed, Simpson returned again and again to Willie's account of his movements on the night of the murders. One detail in particular aroused Simpson's suspicion—the part where Frances and Willie walked past the Mills residence on their way home from the church but made no inquiry there.

"You have had a good deal of experience in life, Mr. Stevens, and have read a good deal, they say, and know a lot about human affairs. Don't you think it sounds rather fishy when you say you got up in the middle of the night to go and look for Dr. Hall, and went to the house where you thought he was, and never even knocked on the door, with your experience of human affairs and people that you met, and all that sort of thing, doesn't that seem rather fishy to you?"

Case shouted out an objection, but Justice Parker allowed the query. Turning to the judge, Willie said, "The only way I can answer it, your honor, is that I don't see that it is at all fishy."

Simpson persisted, once again asking Willie to describe, step by step, minute by minute, his walk with Frances from their home to the church, in search of Edward.

"Now, your honor," Case objected, "there must be a limitation somewhere. This is the third time that is being requested. It seems to me the questioner is stringing out time for some reason."

"This is a perfectly legitimate cross-examination," Simpson shot back. "I have a perfect right to test the accuracy of the story. I am not doing this with the idea of wasting time at all, but to show whether or not, by reason of peculiar mentality . . . he has not been taught this story and has learned it by rote."

"We will let him tell it once more," Parker agreed.

"May I say a word?" Willie interjected.

"Certainly," said Parker. "Say all you want."

"All I have to say is I was never taught, as you insinuate, by any person whatsoever. That is my best recollection from the time I started out with my sister to this present minute."

Willie had bested his opponent. Ninety minutes after his testimony began, court adjourned for the day.

THE FOLLOWING MORNING, GLOWING ACCOUNTS of Willie's testimony filled the newspapers, like five-star reviews of a Broadway premiere. "The defendant, whom even the defense were concerned about," said the *New York Times*, "had proved the surprise of the trial. He had told a straightforward story in precise language, and, by turns urbanely polite or profoundly grave, he had deftly eluded the nets spread for him by Senator Simpson." Grace Robinson was similarly effusive in her report for the *Daily News*, suggesting that Willie had denied his involvement "so earnestly and with such a show of hurt and astonishment in his wide blue-gray eyes that at times it seemed absurd that anyone had ever tried to link him with the slaying. . . . Mrs. Hall's so-called sub-normal brother exhibited more wisdom than most of the long procession of witnesses who have come to the stand. . . . He astonished the jammed courtroom by his mental clearness, his traces of culture and his courage." Even Phil Payne's partisan *Daily Mirror*, which might as well have been on Simpson's payroll, couldn't help but fawn. At the top of its front page, the *Mirror* declared, WILLIE IS A GOOD WITNESS.

Readers regarded Willie with the same fascination as they did Jane Gibson—two offbeat characters who may or may not have been truthful but were undeniably entertaining. Frances Hall, with her frumpy looks and stodgy disposition, never quite engendered the same likability. Still, Frances's testimony was, in many respects, the most highly anticipated of the trial, now in its fourth week. She was the centerpiece of the whole outrageous affair, the axis around which every facet of the mystery seemed to revolve. Phil Payne's tabloid crusade had turned Frances's world upside down. Now she had no choice but to swallow her pride and swear upon a Bible that she wasn't the cold-blooded murderer portrayed in Payne's filthy newspaper. She had three days left to prepare.

THE VERDICT

Frances would have loved nothing more than to spend Thanksgiving of 1926 in the comfort of her own home, reminiscing with Willie by the fire, toasting their health and good fortune. Instead, she joined her brothers in the Somerset County Jail. Despite the dreary setting, they enjoyed a veritable smorgasbord: roast turkey with chestnut dressing, candied sweet potatoes, mashed potatoes, creamed onions, cranberry jelly, asparagus salad, and plum pudding. In another two days, Frances would be called to the witness stand. For now, she would feast.

In the days leading up to Frances's testimony, the jury heard from an array of defense witnesses. Agnes Storer, the organist at St. John's, testified that Ralph Gorsline, according to her records, would have been at choir practice on the day he was said to have visited the Burns Detective Agency, where he allegedly spoke of encountering Henry Stevens near the murder scene. Three Episcopal clergymen swore there were no scratches on Frances's face in the days after the murders, contrary to what the prosecution had learned from both a chauffeur and a newspaperman. The defense returned to the arcana of fingerprinting with its own forensic experts, who made a case for why the print on the calling card did *not* in fact belong to Willie Stevens—which experts to believe? Felix De Martini gave his side of the story, saying he'd billed Frances Hall $5,090 for 121 days of work. The swarthy detective denied bribing or threatening any witnesses, including Gibson, although he did admit to having Jim Mills tailed. Asked why he had never interviewed Gibson, De Martini replied, "I didn't believe her story. It sounded ridiculous." The same sentiment was conveyed by a dozen of the Pig Woman's neighbors when asked about Gibson's reputation.

"Is it good or bad?"

"Bad."

Finally, as the trial spilled into the weekend on Saturday, November 27, it was Frances's turn to bare her soul. Spectators filled the halls of the courthouse, many of them carrying sandwiches and drinks to avoid surrendering their seats at lunch. They flooded the courtroom as soon as its doors swung open, filling every collapsible canvas chair that had been set up to accommodate the eager mob. The standing-room-only crowd was larger than usual, and the majority of observers were women, from vaunted society ladies to bored housewives and curious schoolgirls.

"Mrs. Hall," said Robert McCarter, "will you take the stand?"

Frances rose swiftly and walked over to the witness stand, wearing nothing to suggest a hint of fashion other than a small pearl necklace peeking out of her collar. After swearing on the Bible, Frances settled into the witness chair and clasped her left hand with her right, her fingers tapping away. She leaned back and glanced at her attorney, whose white hair and kind face inspired comparisons to a man of the cloth, or a schoolmaster, or the late Woodrow Wilson. He set the stage with a tedious history of the venerable Stevens family, then carefully waded into more delicate matters.

"I want to ask you this question, Mrs. Hall, whether during your husband's life, so far as you knew or observed, your husband was a devoted husband."

"Absolutely."

"Did you at the time you learned of his death notice the slightest change or alteration in his demeanor or conduct toward you?"

"Nothing whatever in any possible way."

Nor had Frances detected any behavioral abnormalities, she said, during the Halls' vacation to Maine—never mind that Edward spent the retreat channeling his extramarital passions into a secret love diary. Edward's sisters, seated in the front row and still loyal to the accused, listened attentively as Frances defended their brother.

"Had he been a devoted husband up to that time?"

"Absolutely."

McCarter asked Frances about Eleanor's phone call to Edward shortly before he disappeared. Frances confirmed that Louise Geist had answered the phone, but she denied, contrary to the prosecution's theory, that she herself had listened in.

"I simply put the receiver back again without hearing who spoke."

"You did not hear a thing?"

"I did not hear a thing."

Frances proceeded with her usual self-possession, not that she needed much of it—McCarter was so gentle that the word "murder" did not escape his lips. He spared his client an additional torment by seeing to it that photographers were excluded from the courtroom. One such individual managed to sneak in, and when Frances noticed him, furtively pointing his lens, she promptly alerted the judges. Justice Parker squinted into the crowd and, finding the offending cameraman in the third row, saw to it that he was escorted from the courtroom. Toward the end of Frances's testimony, McCarter took a dramatic pause and turned to face the jury, pulling his client's gaze in their direction.

"Now, Mrs. Hall," he boomed, slowly, "did you kill your husband and Mrs. Mills?"

"I did not."

"Did you play any part whatever in that dreadful tragedy?"

"I did not."

"Did you participate in any way?"

"I did not."

With no further questions, McCarter made a fist and pounded it into the opposite hand, taking a slight bow to signal that the floor was now Simpson's. The prosecutor had been lounging in his chair with a hand pressed to his forehead. As he sprang to attention, Frances leaned forward as if bracing for impact.

"When you got up," Simpson said, referring to the morning after Edward's disappearance, "you telephoned police headquarters?"

"I did."

"You were looking for information about your husband?"

"Yes."

"You thought you would get it from the police?"

"I thought I would hear of any accidents."

"Accident was in your mind?"

"Yes."

"But you said to the police, 'Have there been any casualties?'"

"Doesn't that mean accident?"

"Weren't you looking to see if the dead bodies had been found?" Simpson pressed. "If you used the word 'casualties,' and you had accidents in your mind, why did you use the word 'casualties'?"

"It means accidents," Frances replied. "It is the same thing."

"It also means death, doesn't it?"

"I do not know that it does."

"So, with your understanding of the meaning of the word, you telephoned police headquarters, you did not give your name, and you asked for casualties? You thought, you say, maybe there had been an accident, maybe your husband had been hurt in an automobile accident?"

"Yes."

"Did you telephone to a single hospital in New Brunswick all day Friday?"

"No."

"Yet you were frantic over the disappearance of your husband?"

"I was."

"Why didn't you stop in some hospital if you thought your husband had been in an automobile accident?"

"Because if he had been in any accident and taken to a hospital, I would have been notified. He was well known."

Willie glowered at Simpson as the prosecutor insulted his sister. Their sparring held the courtroom rapt, but the afternoon was slipping away. Justice Parker glanced at the clock hanging over the doorway, the hands of which tilted to the number four.

"Have you very much more?" he asked.

"A great deal more," replied Simpson. He had only questioned Frances for about twenty minutes, but further cross-examination would have to wait—court was adjourned until Monday.

IF FRANCES HAD SPENT THE remainder of the weekend collecting herself, summoning strength for the showdown ahead, there was no indication of it when Simpson resumed on Monday. If anything, Frances appeared more sullen than she had two days earlier, her dreary mien unaffected by the late autumn sunlight beaming in through the windows. Simpson, looking flashy as ever in a broad-striped dress shirt, had no intention of softening his offensive. He'd handled Willie with kid gloves; Frances was in for a bare-knuckle brawl.

"You now say that you did not tell Mr. Toolan, or anybody in the Middlesex County prosecutor's office, that in your conversation with the husband of the murdered woman, you said, 'They have been together' and 'They have been murdered'?"

"I did not say anything of the kind."

"What did you say to Mr. Mills when you first met him about their having been together?"

"I did not say anything about their having been killed."

"You did not know they had been killed?"

"I knew nothing whatever about it."

"And Mr. Mills did not say to you, 'Do you think they have gone to Coney Island?' And you did not reply, 'No, they have been together, and they have been murdered'?"

"No, I did not say that."

"Or any words to that effect?"

"No."

Frances spoke in hushed tones, rendering some of her answers inaudible. McCarter interrupted and asked her to speak up.

"Mr. Mills told me Friday morning that his wife was absent," she elaborated in a louder pitch, "and I knew Mr. Hall went to speak with her Thursday night."

"If your husband," said Simpson, his words dripping with sarcasm, "who, as you say, was so loyal and devoted and had your confidence, was out all night, you knowing nothing wrong about him, you would not put him away in the presence [of] some other woman who had also been away all night, perhaps at her relatives' or somewhere else, you would not place your husband with her, would you?"

"The first thought," Frances insisted, "was they were to meet that evening, as he said he was going to speak to her, and my only thought was that there had been some automobile accident. They might have been killed or injured in some way right nearby."

"Didn't you overhear the telephone conversation, and didn't you hear the appointment made to meet at the place where they were subsequently murdered?"

"I did not hear that telephone conversation."

"How could there be any automobile accident if he did not take the car?"

"Other automobiles in the city might run over people."

The questioning went around in circles—Simpson challenged Frances's assertions, and Frances strained credulity with her replies. How was it that a grieving widow had never so much as mentioned her beloved husband in any of the letters she'd written from Italy just months after Edward's death? "I don't know." Why had she told someone, the day before Edward's body was discovered, that the reverend was "out of town," if she in fact had no idea where he was, and suspected he might be dead? "It seemed the proper way to put it." If she was so distraught the morning after Edward disappeared, how did she have the presence of mind to attend to so mundane an errand as a ten-dollar check deposit? "I don't remember the deposit." McCarter steadfastly blurted out objections, and the audience soaked it all up like a Shakespearean drama. The more Frances squirmed, the more Simpson twisted the knife.

"This man who had been your husband," the prosecutor sneered, "to whom you were devoted, whom you had never suspected, whom you lived with, who met a violent death, you let the body of that man lie in [a] common undertaking shop all of Saturday night, all of Sunday, all of Sunday night, never went to see him, had his remains brought to the church for burial, without anybody except the mute from the undertaker's shop as pallbearers, didn't you?"

"I don't think there were any pallbearers," Frances said. "If they were, they were the vestrymen. I am not sure."

"You do not even remember whether there were any pallbearers?"

"I do not."

Simpson moved in closer and, recalling Frances's objection to the newspaper photographer two days earlier, said, "You were very much—and I say this without any offense—you were very much more concerned in looking at the man you thought was taking your picture than in remembering the details of your husband's funeral."

Frances endured the blow with dignity, catching herself before exhibiting a rare show of emotion. But her iron façade was beginning to crack. For more than four years, Frances had refused to admit her husband's betrayal. His relationship with Eleanor Mills was not a reality that the widow cared to acknowledge, at least not publicly. Perhaps she simply chose not to hear the rumors, see the letters, listen to the witnesses who had shared so many salacious details about the protracted affair, the planned elopement, the brazen affections exchanged right under her nose. For a proud Victorian woman who remained fiercely protective of her privacy and loyal to the mores of her class, whose aversion to scandal was stronger than her commitment to truth, it was, perhaps, easier to deny reality than to accept it. Or maybe the former Sunday school teacher was just an exceptional liar.

After two hours of relentless interrogation, Simpson finally managed to cure his witness of the delusion that Edward Hall had been an honest and faithful spouse.

"You never had your suspicions aroused enough to believe that there might be any kind of attachment between your husband and Mrs. Mills?"

"I had absolutely no such thought."

"Didn't you say," Simpson pressed on, "that you did not even believe it after the letters were found?"

"I am not sure of it now."

"You don't believe it now?"

"I am not sure of it."

"After you have heard all these letters read," Simpson pleaded, "you even now say there was nothing between them, between your husband and Mrs. Mills? That is your opinion, is it not, you say it now, after having heard these letters read, there is nothing wrong, there was nothing wrong between your husband and Mrs. Mills? After hearing all this evidence?"

Frances gripped the arms of the witness chair, swaying ever so slightly as the color rushed out of her face. Her response came in a slow and halting tone.

"After hearing all this evidence," Frances said, her blue-gray eyes welling with tears, "there must have been something going on I knew nothing of."

The admission forced her not only to concede that her marriage was a sham, but to do so in front of the press and the public and the eyes of the law. She had been born with honor; now, regardless of what the future held, she would live out her days in shame. Marrying a man of God seemed like the best decision she could have made as an aging heiress—a means to enrich her social position while eschewing the life of a spinster. Instead, it may have been the worst decision Frances Hall ever made.

Before releasing the witness, Simpson took one last opportunity to portray Frances as a cold and uncaring woman.

"Charlotte Mills was one of your scholars in the Sunday school?"

"Yes."

"The girl, about sixteen, had lost her mother?"

"Yes."

"Yet, when she came to see you, you would not let her in the house to talk to you?"

"I did not see her when she came."

"Well, you refused to see her."

"I asked Mr. Pfeiffer to see her."

"You did not see her?"

"I did not see her."

"That is all."

Frances took leave of the witness stand and rejoined her coterie of lawyers and kin. Willie stood up and hugged his sister, causing her lips to tremble. Gazing at the once proud widow from the press gallery, Grace Robinson thought: "She was Tragedy enthroned."

IN THEIR CLOSING ARGUMENTS a few days later, Robert McCarter and Clarence Case floated their own theories about who might have killed the minister and the choir singer. Ray Schneider, for instance. "Assuming that he did not commit the murder," Case insinuated, "he at least had opportunity to rifle the dead man's pockets and take his gold watch and chain . . . and to sprinkle the calling cards about—the cards that included the one later claimed to bear the fingerprint of Willie Stevens." Or maybe it was the Pig Woman, mistaking Edward and Eleanor for corn thieves. "This crime may have been committed by Mrs. Gibson herself," Case told the jury, leaning in close. "Oh, gentlemen, I don't say it is so, but I say to you that it is within the realm of possibility, if not probability." McCarter made the case against Jim Mills. "I am not here to vindicate or scold that dead couple, they have their own account to make with their creator," he said. "But I am here as a man with red blood in his veins to question the innocence of a husband who placidly admits his wife to be absent for forty hours without raising a finger to find out where she is or what has happened to her, except to say to Mrs. Hall, 'Perhaps they have eloped.'"

McCarter saved his most poisonous venom for Phil Payne, who had appeared in court earlier in the day but was now absent. Recalling the late-night arrest of his client, and showing no sympathy for Payne's auditory impairment, McCarter pointed to the press section and wailed, "That Mephistopheles, who was here this morning, and who has not the courage to sit here this afternoon, that man who has his satanic hand in front of his ears to hear what he wants to hear, with his photographers and with his reporters, comes first to Somerville and then . . . goes to Mrs. Hall's house at midnight and surrounds the house, and some state trooper, with I don't know how many escutcheons on his coat—Bang! Bang! Bang! 'Madam, you are under arrest for the murder of your husband four years ago. We could not even wait until tomorrow morning. We will take you at ten o'clock at night, and we will take you over to Somerville and take you up to some Justice of the Peace up here, and after we have done with you there we will land you in the jail, and we will have Payne's photographers, who are following you, take your picture as you go in.' My gracious! What good newspaper stuff that is."

McCarter posited that the print on Edward Hall's calling card, which Payne had obtained from the fingerprint expert Edward Schwartz, was a fraud. "Four trips to Newark by Philip Payne to see this man, and without any authority from Somerset or Middlesex County, he then and there deliberately handed over that card to Philip Payne. It was not 'til Mephistopheles took the stand, and had his ears forward for the purpose, that it appeared that Schwartz did not want to see him at his office, but told him to go up the street to the St. Francis Hotel. . . . [Then] they take a taxicab, and go where no man saw them, and the card is slipped out of Schwartz's pocket and put into Payne's pocket. For any consideration? Oh no, oh no. Payne isn't spending any money. Payne and the *Mirror* are not interested financially in this matter. They are doing this so that justice may be vindicated."

McCarter's screed about the card carried on at length. Later, after learning of McCarter's comments, Payne sent the attorney a telegram responding to the suggestion that he lacked the courage to bear the censure in person: "Dear Mr. McCarter. You're right, I didn't have the courage. I was afraid if I came to court while you were summing up, I'd die of old age or boredom before you finished."

The following morning, as the closing arguments continued, Payne made sure McCarter could see him. He took a seat in the press section behind the jury and listened as McCarter lambasted Jane Gibson's "theatrical display." McCarter called Gibson's testimony a "humbug prepared under the guidance of Philip Payne, who sits here to witness it all." He went on for several minutes flaying Payne and the rest of the prosecution's "galaxy of witnesses." Senator Case then brought the closing arguments to a fiery conclusion. He spoke to the jurors as a fellow Somerset County man, railing against the external political forces that had entered the case, and suggesting that the powers in Jersey City were "running the whole show." In a nod to the journalists furiously taking notes, Case articulated his "respect for newspapers and the work they accomplish, and the men and women who are connected with this work—most of them." Case paused and looked at Payne. "Of course, there is no assurance that snides will not get into reporting and newspaper service," he said. "No newspaper should undertake to do what this sheet they call the *Mirror* has undertaken to do."

Perhaps no one enjoyed the attacks on the *Mirror* as much as Payne's former employer, which had been running a not-so-subtle message alongside its coverage each day: "For the BEST account of the Hall-Mills case, read the DAILY NEWS. The unbiased truth, FAIR TO BOTH SIDES. Not propaganda."

ON FRIDAY, DECEMBER 3, SPECTATORS stuffed themselves into the courtroom one last time. Simpson had moved for a mistrial based on thirteen affidavits—including one from Charlotte Mills—that alleged inappropriate conduct among members of the jury, from nodding off in court to engaging in conversations about the trial that revealed a prejudice against the prosecution. The keeper of a local hotel where the jurors were staying complained about several of them in a letter to the court. But it turned out that Herbert Mayer of the *Daily Mirror* had typed up the letter and given it to the complainant to sign. Simpson's motion was denied.

Now, on the trial's twenty-fifth and final day, following the testimony of 178 witnesses, Simpson made an appeal to the jury's collective conscience. One juror, he pointed out, moving in close enough that he could have stepped on the toes of those in the front row, was a friend of Clarence Case's. Another juror's son, according to Simpson, worked for an "intimate friend" of Case's. "But that should not sway him," he said. "I do not know whether it will or not." Addressing the full body, Simpson continued, "It doesn't make any difference what county you are in. You are human beings with a human being's sense of justice." At ten minutes past noon, Simpson brought his summation to a solemn denouement: "The voice of justice—see if it can get you into a frame of mind to clean the administration of justice in this state. As I talk to you, I have faith not necessarily in you, but in the human institution of faith in justice and the spirit of justice."

Earlier in his closing, Simpson took a moment to applaud the man who had handed him the most famous trial of his career. "I say we owe a great debt to the New York *Mirror*," he said, to the immense satisfaction of Phil Payne, "which had the courage to begin publication of evidence in this case."

At 1:45 P.M., after Justice Parker issued his instructions to the jury, the defendants were taken back to the jail, where they reunited with their cousin, Henry Carpender. His fate depended on theirs—if a guilty verdict was returned, the state would try Carpender next.

Back at the courthouse, the jurors began their deliberations. The crowd, expecting a speedy resolution, at first remained glued to their seats. But as the hours ticked by, many of them grew restless, stepping outside to chat in the hallways or smoke. Inside the jury room, unanimity was proving elusive. There were several things about which all twelve men seemed to agree. First and foremost, Jane Gibson's testimony was unbelievable, in the literal sense. Her story not only defied logic, the jurors concurred, but certain details had shifted so many times as to render it preposterous. Conversely, the testimonies of Henry, Willie, and Frances had impressed the jurors. Despite Simpson's suspicions of bias within the jury, the jurors felt that his handling of the case was admirable. As one of them put it, the prosecutor had "done the best he could with the evidence he had." The sticking point was Edward's calling card. Two jurors found the fingerprint evidence compelling enough to issue a conviction. The other ten were determined to change the minority's minds, and so the debate unfolded.

As the hands of the clock neared seven, the courtroom remained mostly empty, except for a couple of lawyers and a smattering of journalists munching on sandwiches for dinner. Suddenly, like a flood rushing in, word began to spread that the jury had reached a verdict. Reporters snapped to attention. Townspeople hurried back to their seats. The courtroom erupted in a din of excitement as the defendants were escorted back to their attorneys. The siblings immediately found themselves swarmed by relatives, who arrayed themselves in a half circle around the defense table.

The judges took their seats behind the bench, and the bailiff, calling the courtroom to order, blared out his last "Hear ye!" of the trial. Moments later, the jury box welcomed back the twelve men who had kept its seats warm for more than a month. The room pulsed with nervous anticipation, in contrast to the placid flurries of snow drifting down outside. Frances sat with a faint smile. Henry leaned forward anxiously in his chair. Willie fastened his large brown eyes on the jurors, whose decision was summoned by the court clerk. The moment of truth had arrived.

"Gentleman of the jury," the clerk began, "have you agreed?"

"We have," came the choruslike reply.

"Foreman, what do you find as to Henry Stevens?"

"Not guilty."

"Foreman, what do you find as to William Stevens?"

"Not guilty."

"Foreman, what do you find as to Frances N. Hall?"

"Not guilty."

Frances smiled as she looked upon the jury with gratitude. Willie beamed with joy. Henry burst into tears, and as his wife's hand touched his shoulder, he grasped it. After four long years, two grand juries, fifty-five hundred pages of trial transcripts, countless newspaper articles, and an immeasurable amount of opprobrium, the nightmare was finally over. Simpson must have suspected the verdict would not be in his favor—he had already returned to Jersey

City and didn't bother dragging himself back to court. As the verdicts were proclaimed, a great melee ensued among the assembled reporters. Without a second to waste in phoning their newsrooms, they fell over one another racing for the exit. Justice Parker had ordered that the doors were to remain shut until he declared otherwise, and guards sprang forward to hold back the stampede. When one journalist was knocked to the floor and pinned down by guards, Leo Casey of the *Evening Graphic* shouted, "You can't do that!" The next thing Casey knew, he too was being shoved around by an officer of the court. The *Graphic*'s other reporter, Jack Miley, rushed to Casey's aid, leading to "as dramatic a tug-of-war as was ever staged." Other reporters turned their attention to the front of the room, where they were able to capture the defendants' reactions. Grace Robinson watched Frances as she swayed triumphantly in the embrace of a cousin and gave the newspapers a brusque parting remark: "I am through being a public character."

Arriving home shortly thereafter, Frances was greeted by a swarm of photographers. They closed in around her, snapping away as she climbed the steps to her front porch. She posed for the cameras and, with a ripple of laughter, declared of the all-too-familiar exercise, "I hate it! I hate it!" But that didn't matter now. "I am so happy, so happy. I cannot tell you how happy I am." Sally Peters, who had just arrived from New York, appeared at the door and whisked her friend inside, where congratulatory flowers and telegrams awaited. A few blocks away, the mood was less festive at 49 Carman Street, where Jim Mills cracked open the door and told a group of reporters to get lost: "I ain't talking to nobody!" Charlotte was less circumspect. "Money can buy anything," she said.

Phil Payne agreed. "Senator Simpson has said that 'Jersey Justice' should be embalmed and sent to the British Museum," he ranted. "I echo what the senator has said, with the exception that I would rather not insult the British Museum." Still, Payne was undeniably giddy about his starring role in the trial, which had resulted in newspapers telegraphing more than eleven million words from the courthouse basement, many of those words in the *Daily Mirror* itself. The *Mirror* was now a household name all over the country, and its numbers were on the rise. By the end of September, when the latest biannual circulation figures came out, the *Mirror*'s average daily circulation had risen to 380,000 from 250,000 a year earlier. (Still a far cry from the *Daily News'* 1.08 million.) The *Evening Graphic*'s circulation had climbed as well, to around 243,000 from 97,000 the previous year. The *Graphic* had effectively positioned itself as the anti-*Mirror*, carrying water for the defense—"the 'front office' angle," as one staffer put it. The zaniest of the tabloids may have been seen as an also-ran, but at least it had put its money on the winning team. "The most sensational murder trial of the age ended last evening just as the *Graphic* said it would months ago," Leo Casey wrote. He went on to suggest that the *Mirror*, "for the purposes of circulation," had "caused an innocent woman and three of her menfolk to be arrested." The criticism enraged Payne. "Bernarr Macfadden's *Graphic* has criminally and civilly libeled me many times since the Hall case started," he wrote to Hearst. "I am very sore about it and if you have no objection, will bring a personal action against him. I can bring the action in Hudson County, N.J., where I live, and I feel certain he will be indicted." Payne had access to prestigious counsel: "Senator Simpson will represent me in that action." But Payne also had other legal matters to worry about: as soon as the trial was over, Frances Hall's attorneys announced that they planned to sue the *Mirror* for libel.

None of that dampened Payne's enthusiasm. In an interview with *Editor & Publisher*, he said, "It was a grand fight. . . . There is nothing for me to defend. Please make that plain. I would do it all over again. . . . I still believe that whenever there is evidence of corruption of justice, it is the duty of a newspaper to expose it." Payne also insisted that his Hall-Mills crusade hadn't helped the *Mirror*'s circulation. "There was too much sameness to the daily pictures. We couldn't give the space to it that the standard size papers could."

Payne wasn't being entirely disingenuous. In a November 14 telegram, Hearst had advised, "Don't think your hopes of gaining much individual circulation from Hall case can be realized because all papers appreciate value of case and it is no longer exclusive for you. You better depend on various features we discussed and on vivid fiction and plenty of it and on improvement in comics." Payne heeded these instructions, but he also boasted to Hearst's chief of staff, Joseph Willicombe, about the "hundreds of letters" and "scores of commendatory messages" praising the *Mirror*'s coverage.

"One thing is sure," Payne declared. "The Hall case put the Mirror on the map."

"He thinks you did wonderful newspaper work and agrees with you about [the] failure to convict," Willicombe concurred, adding, gently, that Hearst thought the *Mirror* had done "a little too much" about the case, and that it was time to move on to new topics that would yield the "most circulation."

"I quite agree with you," Payne replied. "We are going ahead to make a real drive for more circulation."

His biggest stunt was yet to come.

OLD GLORY

The verdict in Somerville greatly disappointed Payne, who was loath to abandon his cause célèbre. "For the time being, the story is ended," he said. "I won't admit that the case is closed." But for Payne, who had sparked the nationwide fervor surrounding the trial, other priorities beckoned. The first of these was personal.

At thirty-three, Payne was flying high, deputy to one of the most powerful men in America. Hearst's influence stretched from Hollywood to the White House to New York, where the *Daily Mirror* was the mogul's newest weapon in the circulation wars, and Payne his trusted general. Even so, something was missing from Payne's life. The grief of Payne's first marriage, cut tragically short with the death of his beloved Helena, haunted him still. For a time, romance proved elusive. Payne's liaisons with Peggy Joyce were a fleeting dalliance, although the two remained friends. His closest colleague and wingman, Francis Farley, encouraged the affections of Payne's secretary, who doted on Payne, ensuring his clothes were always neat and his office free of clutter, and that he never wanted for a home-cooked meal. But Farley turned out to be an ineffectual Cupid—Payne never so much as asked the young woman to lunch.

It took a stunning showgirl from Brooklyn to eventually fill the hole in Payne's heart. Her name was Dorothy Hughes, and she embodied all the progressive flair and glamour that had come to define the age. Alternately described as a "typical American girl," "the perfect flapper" and, in the words of the great portrait artist Joseph Cummings Chase, "the most beautiful girl in America," Hughes was recognizable to habitués of the musical comedy circuit, and she'd recently been cast in a D. W. Griffith film, *The Sorrows of Satan*. With wavy brown hair, pearly skin, and delicate lips, Hughes was a pageant queen who had represented New York in the 1922 Miss America competition in Atlantic City. That same year, at the age of fifteen, Hughes won a beauty contest sponsored by the *Daily News*, where Payne, then happily married, worked as city editor at the time. A few years later, after Helena had died and Hughes had come of age, their paths crossed again, and a romance blossomed. Payne would never stop loving his first spouse, but the young widower was ready to share his life anew.

Days after the acquittal in Somerville, Payne telegrammed Hearst to inform him of the imminent nuptials. He requested two weeks off after Christmas for a honeymoon to Florida. His widowed father had relocated to St. Petersburg, and the newlyweds planned to visit. For Payne, it was a much-needed sabbatical—with all the demands of the Hall-Mills investigation, he hadn't gotten around to taking a vacation.

Shortly after one o'clock on the afternoon of Monday, December 13, Payne's thirty-fourth birthday, Payne and Hughes exchanged vows at St. John the Martyr on East Seventy-second Street. Back at the *Mirror* offices, a paper scroll emblazoned with warm wishes stretched to twenty-seven feet. Hearst messaged the groom directly: "Hearty congratulations to you and the bride."

After his honeymoon, Payne jumped back into the circulation race, coming under pressure to grow the *Mirror*'s readership as quickly as possible. His immediate goal, per Hearst's orders, was for the *Mirror* to reach an average of five hundred thousand weekday readers. To achieve this, Payne pulled out every trick in the book. A rain-slicker giveaway garnered more than five thousand letters a day. A special typeface for the sensational divorce of Peaches and Daddy Browning resulted in what Payne described as "tremendous circulation growth." No stunt was too big—a twenty-five-thousand-dollar swimming derby between Long Beach and Asbury Park, for instance. "You give your OK and I'll put it over and will guarantee you the single biggest promotion stunt ever done by a newspaper," Payne promised Hearst. Nor was any stunt too absurd—or controversial. "I believe Mussolini could be talked into doing a daily signed editorial for all Hearst newspapers," Payne proposed. "To secure him for start would put proposed Mirror syndicate over with smash. Believe a Mussolini signed editorial exclusively in Mirror would mean hundred thousand extra daily circulation for us in New York." Hearst thought it was a "great" idea (though it never came to fruition).

One day in February, the *Mirror* edged past half a million copies for the first time. "Congratulations on circulation. It is wonderful," Hearst telegrammed Payne. "Important thing for newspaper to do in making circulation is to get excited when public excited. People will buy any paper which seems to express their feelings in addition to printing the facts."

Like Joe Patterson, Hearst was a demanding boss with high expectations. But whereas Patterson could be curt and condescending, Hearst's interactions with Payne were much friendlier, and their correspondence betrayed a sense of mutual warmth and affection. This close rapport worked to Payne's advantage when, on March 16, Hearst and the *Mirror* were hit with a $1.5 million libel suit initiated by Frances Hall, Willie Stevens, and Henry de la Bruyere Carpender.

"I realize that libel suits are expensive and am going to be very very careful in future," Payne wrote in a nervous telegram after the complaint was filed. "But certainly we were justified in publishing what we did, and everything we charged was proved at the trial. Their motive in bringing action is purely out of revenge."

"I am not worrying about libel case," Hearst replied. "I am only thinking about that five hundred thousand circulation that I hope we are going to get."

"Your wire relieved me," Payne wrote back. "Your [*sic*] a darn good sport and we are going to get that five hundred thousand soon. We are getting closer to it all the time."

As Payne dreamed up new ways to attract readers, an obscure aviator from St. Louis was preparing to achieve a milestone of his own, one that would inspire the greatest stunt of Payne's career. His name was Charles Lindbergh.

AVIATION, ALONG WITH BOXING, ENDURANCE swimming, and mah-jongg, was one in a gaggle of competitive sensations forged in the clamor of the Roaring Twenties. The First World War, for all its death and destruction, brought significant advances in aerial technology, spawning a generation of pilots eager to burnish their aeronautical skills in a civilian capacity. No one had ever traveled from one side of the ocean to the other unless in a boat. The prospect of making this journey thousands of feet in the air—chancing tempests, pushing one's stamina to the limits of human possibility—seemed, to the average person, both profoundly terrifying and utterly fanciful. But that was all about to change.

The first non-stop transatlantic flight, inspired by a hefty cash prize from Britain's *Daily Mail*, crossed the skies from Newfoundland to Ireland in 1919. The fervor took off from there, as a growing number of daredevils lifted off on dangerous, and sometimes fatal, missions over the seas. In 1927, three teams of American aviators set their sights on a twenty-five-thousand-dollar trophy offered by a Manhattan hotel impresario for the first nonstop flight from New

York to Paris. Lindbergh, at the time a little-known army veteran and airmail pilot, aged twenty-five, decided to join the fray. He was a latecomer and a dark horse, but he added an audacious ripple to the foolhardy tournament: Lindbergh planned to attempt the flight by himself, in a single-engine monoplane, which many thought was suicidal.

On Friday, May 20, Lindbergh's *Spirit of St. Louis* got a jump on the other pilots planning to leave that day. Shortly before 8:00 A.M., as a light rain dampened the coast, the plane bounced down the runway of Roosevelt Field and climbed into the gloomy skies over Long Island Sound. Thirty-three and a half hours later, when Lindbergh touched down in Paris at 10:22 P.M., it was as if Jesus himself emerged from the cockpit. Lindbergh became an instant celebrity, feted by adoring throngs from Le Bourget Airport to Times Square. The millions of dollars he would reap in promotional revenues was enough to set the young pilot up for life, never mind the twenty-five-thousand-dollar prize money. But Lindbergh wasn't the only beneficiary of his success. The press now had an epic story to exploit—not some squalid murder saga, but the coronation of a new American hero. Lindbergh, to the delight of publishers like Hearst, lifted circulation by the tens of thousands. "Every record for mass excitement and mass enthusiasm in the age of ballyhoo was smashed," the author Frederick Lewis Allen observed. "Nothing seemed to matter, either to the newspapers or to the people who read them, but Lindbergh and his story." As Allen also noted, "The profits of heroism were so apparent that a horde of seekers after cash and glory appeared." One such glory-seeker was Phil Payne.

Within days of Lindbergh's triumph, Payne busily worked on plans for a transatlantic crossing of his own design. At Payne's urging, Hearst agreed to sponsor a flight from New York to Rome, a route yet to be attempted. Announced on July 6, the flight was touted as "part of the campaign for advancing aeronautics [Hearst] has waged for years in his publications." Payne of course harbored a more cynical motive: promoting the *Daily Mirror* and selling lots of newspapers in his blood quest to overtake the *Daily News*.

To kick off the adventure, Hearst purchased a single-engine monoplane from the Atlantic Aircraft Corporation of Hasbrouck Heights, New Jersey, an American subsidiary of Anthony Fokker's Dutch aircraft manufacturer. She was a beauty of a plane, with a sixty-foot wingspan and a 450-horsepower engine that could cruise through the clouds at 110 miles an hour. They named her *Old Glory* and paired her with two accomplished pilots: James DeWitt Hill and Lloyd Bertaud. Bertaud was one of the pilots Lindbergh had defeated in the race to Paris, and Payne offered him another chance at stardom—for two hundred dollars a week (the equivalent of his airmail salary) and a cut of the syndication proceeds. As Hill and Bertaud began preparations for the flight, Payne embarked on a publicity campaign, ensuring that *Old Glory* made headlines not only in the States, but on the Continent as well. "I do not think the CHIEF could have bought the prestige he is gaining through this trip for a million dollars expended in ordinary manner, do you?" Payne wrote to Hearst's right-hand man, Joe Willicombe. "The papers in Europe are printing many columns and of course the big rush is yet to come."

Energized by the endeavor, Payne pitched other ideas to Hearst, like an aviation magazine that would capitalize on the "millions of young men and women interested in flying now." He also pushed to increase the *Mirror*'s print schedule from six days a week to seven. "Hope you will give me Sunday paper," he told Hearst, promising to "stop the News growth when you do."

On the rain-drenched afternoon of Sunday, July 31, thousands of people trudged into the mud of Curtiss Airfield in Hempstead, Long Island, to celebrate the baptism of *Old Glory*. With dark skies rolling in from the coast, various dignitaries stood atop a small wooden platform and lauded Hearst for supporting the mission.

Speakers included the New York congressman (and future New York City mayor) Fiorello La Guardia, and Baron Giacomo de Martino, the Italian ambassador, who predicted *Old Glory* would unite the U.S. and Italy. A young woman from the Bronx stepped forward holding a bottle of mineral water, which she smashed across the plane's exhaust pipe, declaring, "I christen thee *Old Glory!*" Bertaud and Hill took the plane up and dazzled the crowd with a demonstration, disappearing behind dark clouds and taunting bolts of lightning that flashed in the distance. Payne described the fanfare in an effusive telegram to Hearst, in which he also made a request: "Will you please send letter to Mussolini and Pope to go on plane, and also autographed photo of yourself?"

After the event, Hill and Bertaud moved *Old Glory* to Roosevelt Field, where Lindbergh had taken off for Paris months earlier. In the coming weeks, they tinkered with propellers and radio transmitters, calculated fuel and load distribution, monitored weather reports, and resolved problems with the undercarriage. They also carried out a series of test flights, including one in which the noted physician C. Ward Crampton went up in the air to instruct Payne on techniques for reducing motion sickness (Payne's boss didn't know it yet, but he had every intention of accompanying the pilots.) On August 19, Hearst's semi-estranged wife, Millicent Hearst, visited the airfield. She "wanted to ride so of course I took her up, rode with her myself," Payne telegrammed Willicombe. "She had wonderful time was very nervy and a great sport. Hope Chief won't be offended but I couldn't refuse to take her up when she asked to go. Said it was thrill of her lifetime. . . . It made great hit with two pilots when she rode with them as it showed confidence Mr. Hearst has in them."

Hearst did have confidence in the pilots, but he was nonetheless shaken by an unfolding air disaster over the Pacific. Two planes had just gone missing in a race from Oakland to Honolulu, and one of the planes, the *Golden Eagle*, had been sponsored by Hearst's son, George Hearst, publisher of the *San Francisco Examiner*. The day after Mrs. Hearst's impromptu test flight—during which she took the controls at two thousand feet ("The most marvelous thrill in the world!")—Hearst conveyed his anxieties in an exchange with Payne.

"Am very much distressed over apparent loss of Golden Eagle and unwilling for our plane [to] leave on the Rome flight unless it's safest possible kind [of] plane provided with all floatation improvements and radio broadcasting and everything to insure safety."

"Our plane built by Fokker, world's greatest airplane builder," Payne replied. "It was the ten thousandth machine he has completed and he says it is his best. It is fully equipped with every modern life-saving device. . . . Both of our pilots are crack flyers of the United States air mail and they are thoroughly satisfied with their equipment. . . . They are ready to start and are merely waiting for best possible weather conditions. All experts agree Old Glory is built best. It would break hearts of our pilots should anything stop them from flying now"

"Don't want to stop Old Glory from flying," Hearst went on. "Just want to make sure its right."

Despite Payne's guarantees, Hearst's nerves continued to fray.

"I would rather give the pilots the compensation in full and not have them go at all on account of Hawaiian disaster," he told Payne on August 27.

"Rest assured they will succeed," Payne wrote back. "They have enough gasoline for fifteen hours margin of safety, which is far more than any other trans-Atlantic fliers have had and they are determined to succeed for the honor of the U.S. air mail and you."

Hearst was none too pleased when word got out that Payne, in addition to managing the flight, also planned to participate in it, assuming the winds at takeoff were strong enough for *Old Glory* to get off the ground with an extra passenger. Bertaud and Hill weren't thrilled with the idea, either. The plane's full weight, including the fuel and equipment required for a transatlantic crossing, was already up to 12,500 pounds. Payne would add another 200 once suited up in his flight gear. Every ounce would count. But Payne was in command of the operation, and the pilots had no choice but to indulge him. Payne's father tried to dissuade his son from flying, but the younger Payne insisted, "I cannot send the men where I would not go myself."

In the meantime, weather conditions hindered the group's departure. Days of heavy rain had turned Roosevelt Field into a swamp, and fickle winds kept *Old Glory* locked away in her hangar. Then, on September 1, came news of another tragedy. The *Saint Raphael*—attempting the first flight from England to Canada, carrying the sixty-three-year-old British socialite Princess Anne of Löwenstein-Wertheim-Freudenberg—had gone missing over the Atlantic. Between lousy weather and planes literally falling out of the sky, portents filled the air. But *Old Glory*'s crew was undeterred. If Long Island wouldn't permit them a safe takeoff, they'd have to find somewhere that would, and so they did.

AT 5:46 P.M. ON SATURDAY, September 3, *Old Glory* lifted off from Roosevelt Field and flew north to Old Orchard Beach, Maine, a seaside resort thirteen miles south of Portland. One thousand fifty gallons of fuel had been drained out of her tank and loaded onto two large trucks, giving the plane a suitable weight for takeoff in Long Island's heady crosswinds. At Old Orchard Beach, there was a mild forecast and, more important, a two-and-a-half-mile strip of hard-packed sand that was said to be the best natural runway in the United States. Nevertheless, Hearst's anxiety grew by the day. In a pair of telegrams from his oceanfront castle at San Simeon, he tried to convince Payne of the mission's folly:

I DO NOT THINK OLD GLORY SHOULD START EXCEPT UNDER THE AUSPICES AND WITH THE FULL APPROVAL OF THE GOVERNMENT. IN VIEW OF THE RECENT DISASTERS, I WILL NOT ASSUME RESPONSIBILITY

BUT WILL PROCEED IF THE GOVERNMENT WILL ASSUME AUTHORITY AND
RESPONSIBILITY. THE FLIGHT IS NOT TAKEN FOR PROMOTION PURPOSES BUT
TO ADVANCE AVIATION, AND IT IS DOUBTFUL WHETHER IN LIGHT OF RECENT
EVENTS THESE FLIGHTS DO ADVANCE AVIATION. THESE NUMEROUS DISASTERS
MAY RETARD IT. . . .

I NOTE BY THE PAPERS THAT ENGLAND AND THE UNITED STATES AND SOME
OTHER GOVERNMENTS ARE PROPOSING TO BAR THESE HAZARDOUS FLIGHTS
AS SUICIDAL. . . . I WILL NOT BE DIRECTLY OR INDIRECTLY RESPONSIBLE
FOR ANY MORE DEATHS, NOR WILL I LEAVE MYSELF OPEN TO CRITICISM
FOR ALLOWING THESE COURAGEOUS PILOTS TO RISK THEIR LIVES AND
POSSIBLY LOSE THEM. I, AND YOU TOO, HAVE BEEN TRYING TO DO WHAT
WAS BENEFICIAL TO AVIATION, BUT AS I WIRED YOU YESTERDAY, I AM
AFRAID THESE NUMEROUS DISASTERS HAVE DONE MORE TO HINDER THE
DEVELOPMENT OF AVIATION THAN DEVELOP IT.

Payne argued that *Old Glory* had been rigorously tested and that
its flight to Maine went off without a hitch. The fatal flights that
were all over the newspapers were manned by "men of reckless daring," he said, and had failed "due in most cases to gross carelessness." Bertaud and Hill, on the other hand, were "recommended as
[the] two best in air mail." These pilots, according to Payne, "would
rather give up all the money in the world than forgo their flight.
Most assured they will succeed."

On September 5, Hearst made one last desperate plea for
Payne to call the whole thing off: "Please think of my situation.
Have had one airplane lost and two fine men drowned. If another
such disaster occurred effect would be terrible not only on my
peace of mind but on public opinion." He implored Payne to convince Hill and Bertaud to "accept prize and give up dangerous
adventure."

Payne composed a response as *Old Glory* was undergoing her
eleventh-hour preparations to cross the ocean. There was something

final about his message, fatalistic even. For all of Payne's bravado and assurances, he wrote to Hearst as if doing so for the last time.

DEAR CHIEF,

THE PILOTS APPRECIATE YOUR MAGNANIMOUS OFFER, BUT INSIST THEY BE ALLOWED TO FULFILL THEIR CONTRACTS TO FLY. WEATHER IDEAL TODAY AND FURTHER DELAY RUINOUS TO MORALE OF PILOTS. EVERY POSSIBLE PRECAUTION TAKEN. ARMY AND STATE INSPECTORS WENT OVER OLD GLORY THIS MORNING AND GAVE WRITTEN APPROVAL TO FLIGHT. YOU HAVE BEEN A GREAT CHIEF TO WORK FOR. I HONOR AND LOVE YOU, AND I KNOW YOU WILL FORGIVE ME ANY MISTAKES I HAVE MADE.

AFFECTIONATELY,
PHIL PAYNE

Payne handed the message to a friend to see that it was wired to Hearst. After weeks of delays, the time had come at last. All of Payne's lifelong ambition had built up to this moment. The sporty teenager from small-town New Jersey had grown into a man of consequence, with an ability to capture the attention of the world. He'd served his country at war, ascended to the heights of his profession, penetrated the corridors of power, and created one of the biggest media spectacles America had ever seen. Now he was about to make history with a groundbreaking flight to the Eternal City, advancing the fame and fortunes of his tabloid along the way.

The morning of September 6 was crystal clear, with sunlight glistening on Saco Bay. The coastline, as one local put it, jutted out "like a purpled pencil line against the blue water." Crowds gathered near the plane, waiting for the tide to recede. After a special mass at St. Margaret's Church, atop Old Orchard's main drag, Payne walked to the spot where *Old Glory* awaited her forty-five-hundred-mile journey across the sea. As mechanics and radio experts put the finishing touches on the plane's equipment, Hill turned to Payne with a smile.

"Well, all we have to do is name the hour," the pilot said.

"How would twelve o'clock suit you?" Payne replied.

"Fine. Let's make it that."

A short while later, Bertaud joined them on the beach with thermoses of coffee and soup. The previous evening, Mrs. Dorothy Payne and Mrs. Helen Bertaud had packed the crew a veritable feast: chicken and ham sandwiches; stuffed eggs; several loaves of bread; a huge slab of cheese; and several gallons of water. They would not go hungry before reaching Rome, nor would they lack reading material to pass the time: Dorothy and Helen had scribbled out long letters to their husbands. They also wrote one for Hill, who was single: "You are a great fellow. We all love you."

As the appointed hour drew near, a priest splashed holy water on the nose of the plane while National Guardsmen held back the crowd, all abuzz with newspapermen. A mechanic cranked the engine starter and *Old Glory*'s motor roared to life. Payne and Bertaud embraced their wives. Then Payne stood beside the plane and flipped a coin to decide whether Hill or Bertaud would get the controls at takeoff. He dropped the coin on his first attempt, eliciting chuckles from the pilots, but the second toss was successful.

"The ship is yours," Bertaud said.

"Just like another airmail flight," Hill replied with a smile.

The three men climbed into the fuselage and sealed the hatch. Payne strapped himself into a chair beside the chart table and radio set. He gazed out the window at the adoring spectators, his round glasses suggesting "an owl-like appearance," in the words of someone who was there. In just another moment, he would be Rome bound.

The assembled onlookers watched nervously as *Old Glory* began to speed down the beach, kicking up sand in her wake. "She'll never get off," said one. "I hear they didn't want to go," another gossiped. "Someone told me Bertaud said they don't have a chance!" proclaimed a third. An awestruck young boy stared at the plane and prayed: *"Please get up."*

With half a mile left between the sand and the pier, *Old Glory's* wheels remained on the ground. In the distance, the crowd grew silent and tense. Hearts raced. Visions of a deadly crash flashed across people's minds. Suddenly, at the last possible moment—*liftoff*.

Old Glory was airborne, but just barely. Hill swung out over the ocean, struggling to gain altitude. At first, the plane hovered perilously close to the churning waves of the Atlantic. But the holy water did its job: a burst of air came up from the southeast and carried *Old Glory* into the sky along her northeasterly course, a magnificent sight for all to behold. Back on the beach, the spellbound crowd squinted into the distance for a good fifteen minutes, until the tiny speck containing two courageous pilots and one madcap newspaper editor finally disappeared.

Back at the hotel, Dorothy Payne wired Hearst with the wonderful news. "Phil and Old Glory hopped off for Rome one eighteen this afternoon. Takeoff was splendid and all three expect to dine with Mussolini Thursday evening. Bertaud and Hill are best pilots in the world and I have no doubt that they will arrive on schedule. I am so terribly proud of Phil and so confident that he will arrive safely. He is most grateful to you for all your kindness and joins me in sending our best regards."

IT WAS AROUND FOUR IN the morning when a startling message crackled across the radio transmitters of two ocean liners bobbing in the choppy North Atlantic.

"OLD GLORY! SOS! SOS!"

The radio operators shot up, frantically responding with requests for *Old Glory's* position. Six minutes passed before another chilling distress signal arrived.

"OLD GLORY SOS! SOS! FIVE HOURS OUT FROM NEWFOUNDLAND BOUND EAST!"

That horrifying message was the last anyone ever heard from Philip Alan Payne, presumed to have operated the radio, because a seasoned navigator like Bertaud or Hill could have provided the exact coordinates in a pinch. Ships in the vicinity of the estimated crash site immediately began scouring the sixty-two-degree waters, battered by rough waves and squalls of rain. But the rescue mission was futile. At 8:00 P.M. on September 7, the captain of the S.S. *Transylvania* sent out the following message: "Have searched the area without result. Think little hope [of] survival."

In death, Payne had pulled off one last blockbuster story, perhaps his biggest yet. The search for *Old Glory* became worldwide news, leaving readers in suspense with each passing day. Pope Pius prayed for a miracle, and Mussolini asked to be kept abreast of any developments.

On the evening of September 12, nearly a week after *Old Glory's* departure, a steamship chartered by Hearst and the *Daily Mirror* retrieved the wing of a Fokker plane, still attached to portions of the landing gear with the left wheel intact. The wreckage was discovered about a hundred miles from the spot where *Old Glory's* fatal SOS had been transmitted. Dorothy Payne and Helen Bertaud held out hope, telling themselves the crew must have deployed their inflatable rescue boat, equipped with flares, emergency rations, and a transmitter. Perhaps they had been picked up by a small vessel lacking a radio. But this was magical thinking. As the *New York Times* noted in a front-page story the following day, "It may never be known whether those in the plane had a fighting chance for life."

In a final letter before the plane took off, Payne had told his father, "If I don't return, dad dear, don't grieve. I shall have stepped on to meet mother and my darling Helena with a smile, knowing I have done a few things to make life better for some people." Payne's father wrote to Hearst: "He thought so highly of you, and we know you thought so much of him. We do not regret the venture. There is reproach for no one." Hearst replied, "Phil was my very close friend. I admired his brilliance, his ambition, his devotion to his objects and ideals. I am overcome with sorrow at his death."

In addition to his family, friends, admirers, and the small army of journalists who'd benefited from his mentorship, including pioneering tabloid women like Julia Harpman and Bernardine Szold, Payne left behind $11,600 in specific bequests: $5,000 each to his wife and sister, and $1,500 to his trusted secretary, Kathryn Coyle. Stock holdings were left to his father and a lifelong friend named Joseph Moran. Now reunited with Helena, Payne willed his residuary estate to his late wife's mother, Margaret Bechtold.

On September 17, the Newspaper Club of New York adopted a resolution in tribute to Payne, declaring that he "embodied in his brilliant career all of those qualities that we of the craft hold admirable. . . . The Newspaper Club of New York sees, and feels, in the loss of Philip A. Payne and his brave companions . . . triumph rather than defeat, a legacy of honor and courage to our profession, which will further enrich our traditions."

One month later, thousands of mourners, from Peggy Hopkins Joyce to former New York Mayor John F. Hylan, congregated in front of city hall in West New York, New Jersey. Payne's American Legion post organized the service, and a temporary monument was placed in front of the municipal building, draped in black for the solemn occasion. The American Legion promised a permanent memorial exhibit to be established in West New York's public library, which was later renamed in Payne's honor. (One of *Old Glory*'s wheels remains encased in glass at the library to this day.) New York City's current mayor, James Walker, addressed the crowd, and a eulogy was delivered by Haddon Ivins, editor of the *Hudson Dispatch*, where Payne's meteoric rise had begun years earlier. From California, Hearst sent a message to be read aloud during the ceremony: "I am extremely sorry that I am unable to reach New York in time to attend the memorial to Phil Payne. I am glad there is to be a Phil Payne memorial to maintain his memory to all those who admire competent and conscientious and heroic devotion to higher ideals."

More than a year later, in December 1928, Hearst resolved the libel suit initiated by Frances Hall, Willie Stevens, and Henry de la Bruyere Carpender, settling with the family for an undisclosed sum, rumored to be the "largest ever made by any newspaper." Payne's refusal to "admit that the case is closed" turned out to be prescient: the Hall-Mills mystery had one more twist left.

AND THEN THERE WERE NONE

In the years after the trial, the main characters of the Hall-Mills drama disappeared from the headlines, although every now and again, an article about the case would pop up. The most notable of these came in 1937, when James Thurber revisited the case for *The New Yorker*, checking in on the occupants of 23 Nichol Avenue. "Willie Stevens, at sixty-four, no longer visits the firehouse of No. 3 Engine Company every day," he wrote. "For a while, after the trial, he resumed his old routine, but now weeks, even months, elapse between his calls on old friends. They say he has aged rapidly in the last two or three years and complains of headaches and has lost weight. Several years ago he spent a month or two in bed because of a heart condition. After that his trips to the downtown section of New Brunswick became less frequent. One reason was that boys in their teens who loafed about the street corners took to taunting him with shouts of, 'Look out, Willie [Stevens] is after you!'"

Frances, for her part, never remarried, nor did she reenter New Brunswick's social orbit, preferring peaceful seclusion to the cold scrutiny of community life. She could sometimes be seen driving around town, but mostly she kept out of sight, passing the days within the confines of her grand property. Frances did, however, remain active in charity work, whether at St. John's, Daughters of the American Revolution, or other organizations close to her heart. She took long trips, although she never accompanied Willie on his summer vacations to the Jersey shore or his seasonal escapes to warmer climes. One winter, Willie booked a tour of Hawaii, where he indulged his fascination with volcanoes. After someone recognized him as the famous Willie Stevens of the Hall-Mills saga, he canceled the remainder of his monthlong hotel reservation and booked passage on the next ship home.

Henry returned to his quiet life down the shore, joining the volunteer fire department and serving several terms on the borough council, to which he was reelected despite the infamy of the trial. In the spring of 1939, Henry recovered from a heart attack. Later that year, as he and Ethel prepared for their annual winter in Florida, Henry died suddenly at their oceanfront home in Lavallette, aged seventy. The cause was heart disease, and the date was December 4, 1939, thirteen years to the day since he was declared not guilty of murder.

Heart problems ran in the family. In 1934, the same affliction killed Henry de la Bruyere Carpender at the age of fifty-two. Frances suffered several heart attacks before dying at home on the morning of December 19, 1942, aged sixty-eight, a frail woman worn down by the burdens of her past. The loss was too much for Willie to bear. Eleven days later, at the age of seventy, he too succumbed to a heart condition. Like Frances, Willie took his final breath inside the stately mansion at 23 Nichol Avenue, where, on December 30, 1942, their family line came to an end. Willie was the last of the four defendants from the Hall-Mills case, outliving the woman who had accused them by thirteen years: Jane Gibson died of cancer on February 7, 1930, taking the truth of what she witnessed on De Russey's Lane to the grave.

Pearl Bahmer, with whom this story began, appears to have

lived into old age. After Pearl recanted the allegations against Nick Bahmer, she and her father reconciled. When Nick died of tuberculosis in November 1926, Pearl was devastated, collapsing in grief at his funeral. By then, Pearl had found that special "single fellow" she'd daydreamed about to Julia Harpman four years earlier, a taxi driver named Joseph Silvia (or John Salava, depending on whether the *Daily News* or the *Daily Mirror* got the name right), to whom she was engaged. The public record on Pearl gets fuzzy from there. But when one of her brothers, Raymond Bahmer, died in New Brunswick in 1998, his obituary listed a sister named Pearl DeSantis, of Fultonville, New York, as a surviving relative. She would have been ninety years old.

As for Julia Pegler, née Harpman, her exclusive coverage of Gertrude Ederle's historic swim across the English Channel ended up being the swan song of a short but storied newspaper career, from which she receded to focus on her health. Julia and Westbrook Pegler didn't have children, but they lived a happy and fulfilling life, traveling the world and eventually settling down in Tucson, Arizona. In November 1955, while vacationing in Rome, Julia died of a heart attack at the age of sixty. Westbrook arranged for her body to be sent to New York so the funeral could be held at Church of the Blessed Sacrament, where they'd gotten married several weeks before the Hall-Mills murders.

Charlotte Mills might have achieved the type of bright future her mother wanted for her. Her newspaper columns about the trial, though composed with the assistance of a ghostwriter, were good exposure, and in the summer of 1927, the syndicated columnist Burton Rascoe reported that Charlotte was working for the *Daily Mirror*, responsible for a feature called the "Dog Exchange," in which snappy captions were paired with photos of orphaned pups. It didn't last long, but Charlotte ended up publishing a piece called "Why Make Me Pay?" in one of Hearst's more esteemed publications. "Is there no place in this world where I can lead a normal life and earn my own way?" she opined in a news-making sob story for *Cosmopolitan*. "It is said that time heals all wounds. Time hasn't healed mine."

This is where the story of Charlotte Mills takes a strange turn. According to the published record, she relocated to Philadelphia in the early 1930s, living under an assumed name and working as a caregiver to the elderly before meeting a thirty-three-year-old roofer named Harry Joseph O'Neill. They married in 1933 and had several children. Ten years later, when a reporter for the *Philadelphia Inquirer* caught up with Charlotte, she found the former flapper in a "crumbling old house" lacking natural light and sufficient furnishings, three children huddled around a tiny iron stove, a baby boy of sixteen months crying in his mother's arms. Charlotte told the reporter Harry had died, which wasn't true—his 1956 death certificate lists him as "separated" from Charlotte O'Neill. "Don't tell where I work and don't tell where I live," she instructed the reporter, who wrote, "No one would recognize Charlotte now."

The reporter was correct: no one would have recognized Charlotte because the woman in that downtrodden Philadelphia apartment was not, as she had led her family to believe, Charlotte Mills. The truth didn't come out until 1986, when the woman's children submitted their mother's obituary to the *Philadelphia Daily News*, indicating her involvement in the Hall-Mills case. A reporter for the newspaper discovered that the real Charlotte Mills had lived out her days in self-imposed anonymity in New York City, before dying of cancer at a central New Jersey nursing home in 1952. She was forty-five, eleven years older than Eleanor had been when she died. The real name of the impostor, who lived in New Brunswick at the time of the murders, was Marie Thompson, which her adult children learned for the first time. As New Brunswick's *Home News* reported in an article about the bizarre revelation, "no information has come to light that explains the motive for the puzzling ruse." A living relative told me, "This is a very twisted story in my family tree."

Jim Mills's life after the saga resembled his life before it all started: dull, monotonous, and hardworking. Jim resigned his sexton duties at St. John's but took on a custodian post at a Methodist church in neighboring Milltown, where he spent his final years living with his surviving child, Daniel Mills.

In 1964, the prominent lawyer and civil rights activist William Kunstler published a book about the Hall-Mills case. Jim spoke to Kunstler for the project. In their conversations, Jim recalled Phil Payne's séance "with a certain degree of fondness," Kunstler later told Bernardine Szold, who had portrayed Madame Astra. By the time the book came out, Jim was borderline deaf and suffering from a heart ailment. His heart stopped beating on November 8, 1965, after an extended hospital stay. He was eighty-seven.

Jim's funeral was held at St. John the Evangelist, amid the ghosts of a scandal that had forever altered the small Episcopal parish. Four years later, to everyone's surprise, the scandal would be reignited once again.

A ROOM WITH A VIEW

Julius Bolyog feared he was dying. The sixty-seven-year-old lay in bed at St. Peter's Hospital in New Brunswick, exactly forty-seven years to the day from when Edward Hall and Eleanor Mills were found murdered in what was then a desolate field within walking distance of Bolyog's hospital room. Bolyog had been admitted to St. Peter's with a case of congestive heart failure, but while doctors examined him, they discovered another serious ailment. Weeks earlier, a customer at the gas station Bolyog owned had accidentally run over his right foot. Bolyog shrugged off the injury, but it turned out to be quite severe. "Almost complete dissolution of the bone of the distal phalanx," the radiology report concluded. "Marked swelling around the osseous structures." The diagnosis was osteomyelitis, a serious complication. Bolyog spent the next two weeks convalescing, but there was little change in his condition. When he thought he heard a hospital attendant expressing doubts about his chances for survival, he reflected on his life's regrets, contemplating an episode from his past.

St. Peter's sat across the street from Buccleuch Park, a site of considerable intrigue during the murder mystery five decades earlier. Bolyog's room, No. 585, had a view of the park. As he gazed out the window, a dark secret he'd kept locked away all those years gnawed at his conscience.

Bolyog knew it was now or never, that he needed to relieve himself of the burden of the secret before it was too late. At 10:43 A.M. on September 30, 1969, he picked up the phone and called the police.

THE POLICE REPORT READ AS follows: "A Mr. Bolyog called hdqtrs. and told me, Sgt. Cipolla, that he could solve a murder case that happened over forty years ago. . . . I questioned Mr. Bolyog on the phone and he told me that a man by the name of Willie Stevens who belonged to the Hall family planned the murder for a long time. Mr. Bolyog told me that Willie Stevens who was a good friend of his spoke to him every day about his plans."

Detective George Saloom stared at these sentences, utterly intrigued. It was four months later, and Saloom felt like he'd just lucked into the most riveting assignment of his career. Born and raised in New Brunswick, Saloom was thirty-nine years old—fourteen of those years spent on the force—and he'd long been fascinated by the unsolved double homicide embedded in the lore of his city. He'd devoured everything that was written about the Hall-Mills case over the years. Now he had a chance to solve it—a slim chance, Saloom figured, but a chance all the same.

The police report had been gathering dust since the morning it was filed. Bolyog had picked a bad time to contact the understaffed New Brunswick Police Department, whose entire detective division had been dispatched to the local high school amid an eruption of racial violence. By day's end, the detectives were still out of the office, and a secretary filed away the report in a folder full of other reports. There it sat until the chilly afternoon of March 27, 1970, when a detective captain asked Saloom if he was interested. Saloom wasn't just interested—he pounced.

Saloom quickly tracked down Bolyog, who had survived his

bone infection. Not only was he still alive, but he happened to live in an apartment complex on a four-lane thoroughfare that, fifty years earlier, had been a dirt road called De Russey's Lane. On the morning of March 31, Saloom pulled out of police headquarters in New Brunswick and drove to 429 Franklin Boulevard, less than a mile from where the bodies were found, now a suburban community.

When the door opened, Saloom was greeted by a balding sexagenarian, five and a half feet tall, who walked with the assistance of a cane. Saloom stepped inside and the two men got to talking, Bolyog in a thick accent that betrayed his Hungarian roots. His family had immigrated to New Jersey prior to the First World War—in which Bolyog served in the U.S. Army—settling down in Edison, a town adjacent to New Brunswick. Earlier in life, before opening his gas station, Bolyog had been a chemist until retiring in 1946. Saloom could tell he was smart and well read, and he thought Bolyog had a rich sense of humor. After dispensing with the small talk, Saloom turned on his tape recorder and asked Bolyog to tell him everything he knew about the murders.

Bolyog said he first encountered Willie Stevens in New Brunswick around 1921. Willie was known to socialize with members of New Brunswick's Hungarian community, and Bolyog met him at the home of a widowed Hungarian woman whose last name was Lengyel. Willie was friendly with Mrs. Lengyel, helping her out with money as much as he could. She had a daughter named Elizabeth, whom Bolyog was courting, which is how he and Willie ended up crossing paths. Despite their age difference—Bolyog was in his early twenties, Willie in his late forties—they became fast friends, and Willie confided about his troubles at home.

"His problem in life," Bolyog told Saloom, "is that he's so rich, and the preacher is his guardian and don't want give him no money. Twenty-five dollars a week and very seldom fifty dollars. He says, 'I ain't gonna put up with that. That's part of my money, too. One of these days, I'm going to get enough money and I'm going to take care of him.'"

Willie, according to Bolyog, was no fool about what his brother-in-law had been getting up to with Eleanor Mills. "He knew about what's loving going on," Bolyog said, adding—in an X-rated and perhaps embellished description—that Reverend Hall "was sucking her ass, and she had to piss in his mouth and everything. . . . Mrs. Hall decided that this gotta be stopped." Bolyog told Saloom that the family offered Edward money "to make a settlement and divorce," but Edward refused. Willie's enmity toward the reverend was such that "he was shaking, almost spitting blood, he was so mad, aggravated, every time he mentioned Mr. Hall's name."

Back in those days, Bolyog frequented a Hungarian restaurant named Kalman's in downtown New Brunswick, next door to a speakeasy. The proprietor of the speakeasy was a man named Ike, and Ike had a sidekick named Freddie. Bolyog tended to keep his distance from the small-time gangsters, but Willie seemed eager for an introduction. "Them people is bad," Bolyog warned. "Them people will cut your throat for twenty-five dollars."

One day, when Bolyog ran into Freddie on the street, Freddie accused him of negatively influencing Willie's opinion of the duo. "What you getting so smart for?" Freddie snapped. "We wanna get that job!"

It wasn't clear what job Freddie was referring to. But not long after, on a warm and sunny afternoon in September 1922, as Bolyog rested on a bench after lunch at Kalman's, Willie appeared as if out of thin air, standing over him.

"Julius, Julius," Willie whispered. "I'm in trouble."

"What do you want?" Bolyog replied.

"Do me a favor and come help me. Come and see Mrs. Hall."

They walked a few blocks and Willie pointed to a Model T Ford with a man and a woman inside. "Go see Mrs. Hall," Willie instructed.

Bolyog crossed the street and approached the car. A "big tall woman, very high-classy dressed," exited the vehicle and asked what he wanted.

"Willie says to see you," Bolyog replied, gesturing to his friend on the other side of the road. "I don't know. He's over there."

The woman, visibly annoyed, looked at the man in the driver's seat and said, "Wolf, come here."

When the man called Wolf stepped out, Bolyog saw "a little short guy," maybe fifty or older, with a mustache. Wolf and the woman conferred between themselves before the woman handed Bolyog two envelopes. "Go see Willie," she said.

Bolyog walked back over to Willie, who led Bolyog into a nearby alley where he saw Ike and Freddie. "Go see your friends," Willie ordered. Bolyog did as he was told, handing the two envelopes to Ike, who handed one to Freddie. Ike examined the parcels.

"There's three thousand dollars in each," Ike observed.

"We'll let them know," said Freddie, adding, "You keep your mouth shut, if you know what's good for you."

After the handoff, Willie told Bolyog to let the woman in the car know that the envelopes had been placed in the hands of their intended recipients. Bolyog delivered the message, but the woman said nothing in return, and Bolyog walked away, trying to pretend as if the whole thing had never happened. Later that night, Bolyog ran into Willie again.

"Well," said Willie, "they're finished!"

"What are you talking about?"

"They didn't want to hit the woman, but they got Mr. Hall by the Catholic church on John Street," Willie replied, referring to a street near the river. "The woman put up such a fight that they just cut her to pieces too."

"Holy God!" Bolyog exclaimed. "Willie, what's the matter with you? I don't want no part of it."

Saloom hung on every word of Bolyog's story. He had so many questions he didn't know where to start.

"Why do you think Willie got you to take the envelopes off her and take them down to Ike and Freddie?"

"I figured that he was so nervous, that I could remember more [than Willie could] what they gonna tell me to tell Mrs. Hall. Because I know he was so nervous, he just couldn't talk."

"You think he was madder at the fact that Mr. Hall was his guardian, or that he was going out with Mrs. Mills?"

"He was mad because Mr. Hall didn't allocate him enough money. He said, 'Julius, if he gave me a hundred dollars a week it wouldn't even budge the interest on our money.'"

"She offered Mr. Hall money to leave town?"

"Leave town, for divorce—I don't remember. Well, he demanded forty thousand dollars. They was going to pay him off for divorce, get out of town. . . . But he won't take it. He was ready to leave, one of these days, but figured he might get more money out of it."

"You say you thought Ike and Freddie were only intending to hit Mr. Hall?"

"That I don't know, what they was intend to do. Only thing is that Willie said, 'Well, he's had it. He's got what's coming to him.'"

SALOOM'S MIND RACED ON THE drive back to police headquarters. Like any good detective, he had been skeptical going in, keeping his expectations low. To Saloom's surprise, Bolyog's tale was not only highly provocative, but included a level of detail that he found to be convincing. The problem was it also seemed unprovable. It's hopeless, Saloom thought in the car that day, "trying to find people who lived here almost fifty years ago. Some of the people mentioned by Bolyog were young women then, who had married. Others must have moved away and some have to be dead." Still, when Saloom got back to the station and played the interview for his boss, both men agreed: Bolyog's allegations were strong enough to reopen a decades-old cold case—there was no statute of limitations on murder.

Saloom first sought to identify Ike. Bolyog had mentioned a rumor that Ike was found dead in the trunk of a car in the 1930s. Saloom found records from an incident in 1934, in which the bodies of three New Brunswick hoodlums turned up bound and gagged in an abandoned car. One of the men was Isadore Gutman, nick-named Ike, a twenty-nine-year-old whose rap sheet included crap-shooting, gambling, kidnapping, robbery, receipt of stolen goods, sale of liquor, and disorderly conduct. In an eerie coincidence, there had been a fresh development in Ike's unsolved triple homicide just a couple of months earlier. A story about the case had appeared on the front page of New Brunswick's *Home News*, including mug shots of the victims. Two days after his first visit, Saloom went back to Bolyog's apartment and showed him the article, concealing the headline and photo captions. Without hesitation, Bolyog pointed to the photo in the center, depicting a round-faced fellow with beady eyes and a flat cap. It was Isadore Gutman, the same man Bolyog had handed the envelopes to. The positive identification strength-ened Saloom's confidence that Bolyog hadn't made the whole thing up. Now all he had to do was corroborate as many other aspects of Boylog's story as possible.

By now, Saloom wasn't the only sleuth on the trail. Bolyog, un-burdened by the deadly secret he'd harbored for forty-seven years, repeated his story to an acquaintance, which is how a tip-off landed in the ears of Reginald Kavanaugh, a bespectacled reporter in his early forties who wrote about crime for the *Home News*, the same pa-per that published Albert Cardinal's very first scoop about the Hall-Mills murders in 1922. Kavanaugh also happened to be the reporter who'd written the recent article revisiting Isadore Gutman's 1934 gang slaying. Sensing a scoop, he visited Bolyog for an interview before calling Saloom, who made Kavanaugh an irresistible offer:

if he agreed to hold the story, they could work in tandem trying to prove or disprove Bolyog's claims. Kavanaugh happily agreed.

Kavanaugh dove into the police files from the original investigations in 1922 and 1926, an archive consisting of thousands of pages of documents housed in a steamer trunk in the Somerset County prosecutor's office. Poring over the vast trove of statements, depositions, and transcripts, Kavanaugh found bits and pieces of corroborating information, including several references to Willie's charitable friendship with a down-on-her-luck Hungarian woman. Willie's cousin Sydney Carpender had told detectives in 1922 that he'd given Willie fifty dollars to help "a Hungarian family . . . in poor circumstances," whom Willie was "friendly with." Asked about this family during one of his interrogations, Willie hesitated to discuss them, but he did provide their surname (Lengyel), their address (25 Washington Street) and their employer (Johnson & Johnson). In this same interview, Willie confirmed he received an allowance of eight to ten dollars a week—even less than the twenty-five dollars that Bolyog recalled—from a trust officer at the family's bank. Willie had expressed no aggrievement about this arrangement to detectives. But gossip in newspaper reports at the time suggested otherwise, mirroring Bolyog's assertion that Willie's stipend was a sore subject. Additionally, Bolyog's claim that the reverend had been offered a payout jibed with the prosecution's claim, during the 1926 investigation, that family members had confronted Hall about the affair.

While Kavanaugh combed through old investigative files and newspaper clippings, Saloom began the arduous task of searching for witnesses to corroborate Bolyog's story. He interviewed a Hungarian woman named Elizabeth Spinelli, née Lengyel, who confirmed she knew Willie Stevens and that she "knew he had money." Saloom also found several former associates of Ike's, including his brother-in-law, sister-in-law, and former partner in the speakeasy. These interviews yielded little useful information, other than confirming that Ike, a "hi-jacker," as one person described him, had been involved in "shady dealings." Saloom also learned that Ike had a son, Gerald Gutman, whose whereabouts evaded him. In all, Saloom contacted more than two hundred potential witnesses, from old-time residents of the Hungarian quarter to local business owners from the olden days. But there was no smoking gun, and no trace of Freddie. Saloom looked for a paper trail documenting a large withdrawal from Frances Hall's bank account in September 1922, only to discover the bank's records had been destroyed in a fire.

Saloom and Kavanaugh acknowledged that parts of Bolyog's narrative didn't add up. For instance, he said he'd seen Frances and Wolf in a Model T Ford, but neither Frances nor her brothers owned such a car. Bolyog alleged that Willie told him Edward and Eleanor were killed on a street in New Brunswick, but the soil analysis from 1922 suggested the victims were killed on the Phillips farm, in the same spot where their bodies were found. The one thing that troubled Saloom more than any other was Bolyog's recollection of the day on which he'd acted as a go-between. Bolyog swore he'd delivered the cash-filled envelopes on a Saturday, learning from Willie later that same evening that Edward and Eleanor had been killed. This didn't line up with the established timeline of the murders, which began on the evening of Thursday, September 14, when Eleanor and Edward disappeared, and culminated on the afternoon of Saturday, September 16, when news about the bodies became widespread. Was Bolyog's memory flawed? Was he lying? Saloom decided to put him to the test.

SALOOM MET AGAIN WITH BOLYOG and showed him a picture of a middle-aged man with brown hair, glasses, and a mustache. Bolyog identified the man as Wolf, whom he'd seen in the car when taking the envelopes. The photograph was, in fact, a picture of Henry Stevens.

That same day, Detective Sergeant Philip Calitre from the New

Jersey State Police administered a polygraph examination. "Everything I ask him, he's OK," said Calitre, a veteran lie detector operator. In Calitre's report, he wrote, "It is the opinion of this examiner that he has told the truth." But there was a caveat: "It should be taken into consideration the length of time that has passed (approximately forty-eight years) since the murder." In other words, Bolyog might not have been lying, but that didn't mean his memory was infallible.

Two weeks later, on the morning of April 21, Bolyog underwent a second polygraph exam. This time, Calitre asked him thirty-two carefully selected questions, including:

"Do you have any doubts that the Ike to whom you gave the envelope is the same man . . . you identified for Detective Saloom?"

"Did Willie tell you where they were killed?"

"Are you sure that Mrs. Hall and Wolf were in a Model T Ford?"

"Mr. Hall and Mrs. Mills were killed on a Thursday night. Could you have made the payoff on Friday, the next day, and not Saturday, as you seem to recall?"

"Do you expect to gain anything for yourself because you have told your story?"

Once again, despite Calitre's attempts to trip him up, Bolyog passed with flying colors. "It is the opinion of this examiner," Calitre wrote, "that Julius Bolyog has told the truth regarding the subsequent issues: 1. He did in fact give an envelope with the amount of $3,000 to a man named 'Ike' and also [an] envelope with the amount of $3,000 written on it to a man named 'Freddy.' (These envelopes came from Mrs. Hall.) 2. Willie Stevens did make a statement to him stating, 'We got them on John Street.' 3. Julius Bolyog is not making up the story about the murder for his own personal gain."

In a follow-up interview, Bolyog swore to Saloom that he hadn't recently read anything about the Hall-Mills case before contacting the police, and that he hadn't seen the January newspaper article revisiting Isadore Gutman's murder. Until now, Bolyog had never told a soul about his brush with Ike and Freddie, not even his wife and two grown children. In his own words, he feared that if he talked, he would be "rubbed out."

Despite Bolyog's passing the lie detector tests, Saloom still worried something could be off. What if Bolyog suffered from a mental illness? To answer this question, Saloom took Bolyog to the offices of Dr. James B. Spradley, an eminent Trenton psychiatrist who'd served as superintendent of the New Jersey State Hospital for the Insane. Spradley could not say with certainty that Bolyog was telling the truth. But after interviewing him for an hour, the doctor concluded, "Mr. Bolyog is not suffering from any sort of psychiatric disorder. . . . He is normally intelligent and understands that he was involved in what transpired before the murder. . . . I offer no opinion on the correctness and veracity of the information he has given about his participation with the above-named people, but I have a very definite opinion that he is mentally capable of recalling accurately what transpired and, if the statements made by him were corroborated by information on record or additional facts that have developed, it would be presumptive that the information which he has given to you is largely factual."

BY EARLY MAY, REGINALD KAVANAUGH was ready to publish his bombshell about the revived investigation. Saloom gave Bolyog a heads-up so he could tell his family that a big newspaper feature was imminent. The story broke on Tuesday, May 12, 1970, on the front page of the *Home News*. "Bolyog's story," wrote Kavanaugh, "certainly does not provide the solution sought for close to half a century. It does, however, throw a bright shaft of light on a side of the bizarre case that before was never illuminated."

Despite his thorough legwork, Saloom was far from being able to prove Bolyog's allegations. But Kavanaugh's article helped shake the trees, leading to a fresh batch of leads. Two of these involved the ever-mysterious Freddie, who, if he was still alive—and if he could be located—potentially held the key to the mystery. A woman named Mary Jackson told Saloom the man he was looking for was one Fred King, a redhead who lived in New Brunswick at the time of the murders and would now be around seventy years old. Similarly, none other than Daniel Mills invited Saloom to his home in Milltown, recalling that Ike Gutman had been friends with "a big strapping red-headed Hungarian," whose name might have been Freddie. Though intriguing, these vague revelations didn't give Saloom much to go on, and they conflicted with Bolyog's description of Freddie as "five foot six inches tall, thin built, straight light hair, clear skin." On another matter, Daniel claimed Henry Stevens's nickname was Bunk, not Wolf, while the father of one of Saloom's colleagues claimed there was in fact someone in the Hall-Stevens orbit nicknamed Wolf, but that it wasn't Henry—it was Peter Tumulty, the family's trusted gardener and chauffeur, who owned an old Ford at the time. (If Saloom pursued this, there's no indication of it in the historical record.)

The most intriguing tip came two weeks after Kavanaugh's story ran, when Saloom received an anonymous letter at police headquarters. The writer claimed that on Saturday, September 16, 1922, he'd given a lift to Catherine Rastall, who'd been in Ralph Gorsline's car on De Russey's Lane the night of the murders. "If anybody asks where you were Thursday night," the mystery man claimed Rastall said to him, "you were with me." The letter, which Saloom sent to the FBI to be checked for fingerprints, was signed, "NOT ON TRIAL."

On June 23, Kavanaugh published an item in the *Home News* advertising Saloom's "plea" for the man who wrote the letter to come forward. A few days later, another anonymous letter arrived. The man described himself as a former New Brunswick businessman, well known to many residents, who now lived in Jersey City. He asked Saloom to arrange for another story to be published in the *Home News*, this time claiming the letter writer had come forward, identifying himself as a resident of South Brunswick. "Many local people know that I have taken up residence in Jersey City, and this will throw them off," he said. "After this is done, I will write to you and give you my name and address and make plans for an interview."

Saloom and Kavanaugh played along, and as promised, the man wrote to Saloom again on July 1. His name was Carl Ruppert, and he began by saying he wanted "no compensation or publicity for the information I am about to give." Sixty-seven years old and suffering from Parkinson's disease, Ruppert now lived in a Jersey City nursing home. He told Saloom that at the time of the murders, he worked at the New Brunswick Fire Insurance Company with Catherine Rastall. (A *New York Times* article from October 1922 indicated Rastall worked as a stenographer for a lumber company.) Around 8:30 P.M. on the day the bodies were discovered, while stopped at a traffic light on George Street, he saw Rastall walking on the sidewalk. She "ran from the curb and got into the car," Rupert wrote in his letter to Saloom. "All she said was, 'if anybody asks if I was with you on Thursday night you say "yes."' I did not know then about the Hall-Mills murder. When we got in front of Clapp's jewelry store . . . I stopped the car and Miss Rastall got out. On Monday when I got to work . . . the place was buzzing about how Miss Rastall was out with Ralph Gorsline and they knew something about the murder." Like Bolyog, Ruppert had carried around this burning secret for nearly fifty years. "I decided right then that I would say nothing about the case and what I knew, and I have said nothing until this time. At present the only people who know about this incident are my sister, the head nurse at this institution, you and myself."

On a Thursday evening in July, Saloom drove to Jersey City to visit Ruppert at his nursing home. He had a list of questions, which Ruppert answered, to the best of his ability, in a follow-up letter on July 19. Ruppert told Saloom he had worked with Rastall for "about two years." She told him "nothing" about the murder. He knew Willie Stevens through a close friend, Willie's driver. He didn't know Ike Gutman, or anybody named Freddie, or anybody nicknamed Wolf. "I do not know anybody who would know about the murder," Ruppert wrote, "unless it was Miss Rastall." He provided a list of current and former law enforcement officials who could vouch for his credibility, and he reiterated that Saloom should keep his identity out of the public domain. "If I think of anything further on this case that I have not told you, I will write," concluded Ruppert, who died two years later. "Hope I have been of some help to you."

That's where Saloom's file on the case comes to an end. It's unclear if he ever attempted to speak with Rastall, who was very much alive and still active within St. John the Evangelist. Or if he kept looking for Freddie, or Gutman's son, or anyone else who might have had some ancient secret to reveal. By the end of the summer, Saloom got back to chasing present-day crimes: convenience store robberies, LSD smuggling, financial grifts, etc. It was nothing like his brief but memorable adventure with Julius Bolyog, who went on to live another six years, dying on October 4, 1976, at the age of seventy-four.

Before moving on, Saloom asked two highly qualified experts to review his investigation. One was a former Somerset County prosecutor named Arthur Meredith, who now served as a judge in the very same courtroom where the Hall-Mills trial took place. During his time as prosecutor, Meredith had studied the case extensively, and he strongly believed that Frances and members of her family were involved in the killings. Saloom's detective work, he said, "bears out suspicions I have held all along," and "certainly seems consistent with the facts and makes sense."

The other person Saloom consulted was Edward Dolan, then the prosecutor of Middlesex County. Dolan wasn't as certain about who'd done it, but he *was* certain of this: "There is no question in my mind," he told Saloom, "that had Mr. Bolyog told his story in 1922, there would have been a far different result."

Of all the law enforcement officials who investigated the case before him, George Saloom may have come closest to discovering what really happened to Edward Hall and Eleanor Mills of St. John the Evangelist. The 156-year-old church still stands, down the road from the former Hall mansion, around the corner from the old Mills residence, looking today much like it did back then, its historic features still intact, its secrets floating in the air like ghosts. There's an old legend at St. John's, passed down over the years from one generation to the next. If you look hard enough, they say, you'll find the names of the killers on an old piece of paper, hidden away inside the walls.

EPILOGUE

◈

When you start researching a cold case nearly a century after the fact, you hope to talk to any and all living descendants of the victims and the accused. With the Hall-Mills case, there is no such legacy—no long-lost diaries sitting at the bottom of a trunk in some great-grandchild's attic; no hidden knowledge or juicy secrets passed down from one generation to the next. Every person at the center of this story took his or her truth to the grave. Frances and her brothers had no children. Nor did Henry Carpender. Nor did Charlotte or Daniel Mills, who died in 1992 at the age of eighty-one. There's no one alive today whose family line leads back to the main characters, at least not directly.

Peter Tumulty comes close. He's the great-great-grandson of the Hall family's gardener and chauffeur, with whom he shares a name. He learned about his notorious ancestor from talking to his own grandfather, Frank Tumulty, the elder Peter Tumulty's grandson. The younger Peter, who began researching his family history as a teenager, told me that Frank, who died in February 2021, lived in the same house as the original Peter Tumulty during his childhood.

(Frank was ten when Tumulty died of a stroke in 1941, aged sixty-five, nearly twenty years after the murders.) In Frank's conversations with Peter, he described Tumulty as a good and honest man—a God-fearing Catholic who could always be counted upon to buy him ice cream after mass. Frank didn't believe the allegations claiming Tumulty had driven the murderers to the crime scene, and that he had been paid for his silence. Peter doesn't believe them either. "It was a rumor that went through the neighborhood, and a handful of people believed it," Peter told me. "It's very much my belief that it's all conjecture." (He said there's another branch of the extended family that believes otherwise.)

Peter's certainty in the innocence of his forebear was reinforced by an article he came across from New Brunswick's *Sunday Times*, published on July 18, 1926, two days after Phil Payne reignited the Hall-Mills case in the *Daily Mirror*. It quoted a prominent local judge, and future New Jersey Supreme Court justice, named Peter F. Daly. "If Peter Tumulty knew anything about a murder being committed," Daly said, "he would consider it his obligation to his church and humanity to publish the fact to the world. Peter Tumulty is just one of the old Irish type who go to church, confession and communion regularly, and who feels that a murder is not only a crime against man, but a crime against God." I told Peter about the tip George Saloom had received, claiming that Peter's great-great-grandfather was nicknamed Wolf. I asked him if he had ever come across a reference to this nickname in his exploration of the Tumulty family lore. If he had, it would mean that Tumulty, and not Henry, could have been the man Julius Bolyog claimed to have seen in the car with Frances when he took the envelopes to Ike and Freddie. Alas, this was the first that Peter had ever heard of it.

There are various other people alive today with ties to characters from the saga's supporting cast. I located a relative of Pearl Bahmer, whose family photo album, visible on ancestry.com, includes an image of a middle-aged Pearl strumming an electric guitar in a sparkly purple dress. (Attempts to contact this member of the Bahmer clan were unsuccessful.) When I was rummaging through prosecution transcripts in the basement of the New Brunswick Public Library one day, I met a man named Thomas Maugham, whose mother was among the curiosity seekers at the crime scene, seeing the bodies up close. Maugham's grandfather, Joseph Baier, was a justice of the peace who knew Jane Gibson and was interviewed by prosecution officials. "He could never believe they would put her on a witness stand," Maugham told me.

I visited the home of Frank Deiner Jr., a feisty nonagenarian whose father, Frank Deiner, was the reporter who identified the body of Eleanor Mills. Back in the day, the Deiners lived around the block from the Hall home. "As a kid, we always thought of it as a haunted mansion," Deiner said. He reminisced about Willie Stevens shooing him away when he and his friends would partake in a bit of mischief that involved running up to the rear entrance of 23 Nichol Avenue, touching the stoop, and running back. "It was the greatest dare," he said. Deiner told me that his father, who died of a heart attack in 1971, was convinced that Frances and her brothers were guilty. His father was among those who suspected that Azariah Beekman and Wilbur Mott had been paid to tank the case in 1922. "There was too much money," the younger Deiner said.

If I had begun working on this book several months earlier than I did, I might have been able to ask Detective George Saloom if he'd ever discovered anything that didn't make it into his investigative files. Saloom died in April 2018 at the age of eighty-seven. Nine months earlier, he gave a talk at the New Brunswick Public Library. There's no recording of the event, at least not that I could track down. But I did speak with a woman who was there, Susan Mollica, who recalled that someone in the audience asked Saloom about one of the biggest riddles of the case: *Where was the gun?* "It's in the ocean in Lavallette," Saloom replied, seeming to indicate that his suspicions had shifted from the paid-for-hire gangsters to Henry

Stevens himself. Mollica also told me that Saloom had recorded dozens of the interviews he'd conducted over the course of his investigation. She said he gave the tapes to Stephen Longstreet, a prolific screenwriter, author, and New Brunswick native who wrote a 1959 mystery novel, *The Crime*, based on the Hall-Mills murders. Longstreet apparently took the tapes to Beverly Hills, where he had settled down, with the intention of working on a Hollywood script. He died in 2002 and, according to Mollica, "no one knows what happened to those very valuable recordings."

Mollica's late uncle, Ralph Petrone, was New Brunswick's police chief when Saloom reopened the case. At the time, Petrone had praised Saloom, telling the *Daily Home News* that he "went out and did a heck of a lot of work." Privately, however, Petrone found Saloom's detective work to be "one dimensional," according to Mollica, who said her uncle thought Saloom should have pursued other possibilities beyond Julius Bolyog's story. Specifically, Petrone thought Saloom should have taken a closer look at Ralph Gorsline. "My uncle was very certain that Eleanor Mills had several affairs, and one was with Gorsline," she said. "My uncle was an outspoken man, and I'm sure he told Saloom what his feelings and theories were, but it seemed that not all theories were considered or addressed."

By 1970, Ralph Gorsline was a ghost—he died in 1945, "after a short illness," at the age of sixty-six. It's possible that Saloom interrogated Gorsline's paramour, Catherine Rastall, in light of the information he'd received from Carl Ruppert, the man who claimed Rastall had asked him to give her an alibi. During the 1926 investigation, Rastall admitted that she'd been in Gorsline's car near the Phillips farm on the night of the murders, and that they'd heard gunshots. Whether Rastall knew more than that remains the stuff of speculation to this day.

"I think Catherine knew what happened," a woman named Susan Huslage told me one afternoon in the fall of 2019. We were sitting in the assembly hall of St. John the Evangelist, where Huslage, a psychologist, became the church organist in the mid-2000s. Huslage first heard about the Hall-Mill saga shortly after joining St. John's in 1979. She quickly realized the murders were a forbidden topic. "We do not talk about that," a fellow parishioner warned her. Huslage handed me a photograph that was taken in front of St. John's in the 1980s. In the picture, Huslage is standing next to an elderly woman with bright white hair, large oval eyeglasses, and a wide smile. The woman was none other than Catherine Rastall, who sang soprano in the choir until the very end, when she died in a car accident in February 1992, aged ninety-one. "She was a feisty lady, but she was very dedicated to the church," Huslage recalled.

Sometime before Rastall died, according to Huslage, the rector of St. John's at the time worked up the nerve to ask Rastall if Frances was guilty. Even all those years later, Rastall kept her cards close to the vest. "I'm not saying yes," she replied, "and I'm not saying no."

ON OCTOBER 16, 1963, THIRTY-SIX years after Phil Payne plunged into the cold waters of the North Atlantic, the tabloid war that Payne fomented during the Hall-Mills case came to an end. A little before 5:00 A.M. that morning, in a printing plant on East Forty-fifth Street, the New York *Daily Mirror* rolled off the presses for the last time, ending its nearly forty-year hostilities with the New York *Daily News*. The men who'd brought these papers to life decades earlier were long gone. William Randolph Hearst died of a brain hemorrhage in 1951, aged eighty-eight. He was remembered on the front page of the *New York Times* as "one of the most controversial figures in American journalism and politics." Joseph Medill Patterson perished in 1946, aged sixty-seven. His death, following years of hard drinking that wreaked havoc on his liver, was announced on the front page of the *Daily News*. Hearst and Patterson's onetime competitor, the flamboyant publisher and fitness fanatic Bernarr Macfadden, outlived them both. Macfadden died in 1955, aged eighty-seven, following a bout of jaundice that his doctor said was aggravated by a three-day fast. Macfadden's tabloid, the New York *Evening Graphic*, did not enjoy the same longevity as its competitors. It ceased publication in 1932, saddled with $3.1 million in liabilities and the legal costs associated with $7 million worth of libel suits. Despite its ill repute, the *Graphic* was a breeding ground for marquee talent. In addition to hiring a young Walter Winchell, who was later poached by the *Mirror* and went on to become America's most legendary gossip columnist, it also launched the career of Ed Sullivan, who got his start as a junior staffer in the sports department. Still, the paper's circulation consistently trailed its tabloid rivals: by the time of the *Graphic*'s demise, readership had plummeted to a paltry 180,000.

Both the *Graphic* and the *Mirror* were conceived as challengers to Patterson's *Daily News*, but the *Mirror* proved to be a more formidable and long-lasting opponent. It easily eclipsed the five hundred thousand milestone that Payne was chasing at the time of his death, topping out at nearly nine hundred thousand weekday copies and more than a million on Sundays. But that was never enough: the *News* sailed past two million on weekdays and three million on Sundays. Being the second most widely read newspaper in America was not, in fact, a profitable position. By 1963, the *Mirror*'s annual losses were said to be $2.5 million. That year's 114-day newspaper strike sealed its fate. Explaining why the *Mirror*'s October 16 edition would be its last, an executive lamented, "In the metropolitan area, the *News* is the predominant tabloid paper in terms of ads. There was just not enough advertising left for the *Mirror*." In one final indignity, the *Mirror*'s name, circulation lists, feature rights, and library were sold off to the parent company of the *News*. Patterson smiled down from heaven. Hearst and Payne rolled over in their graves.

While the *Daily Mirror* has been consigned to the depths of obscurity, the *Daily News* holds the distinction of being the bestselling newspaper in U.S. history, reaching a circulation of more than

2.4 million weekday copies and 4.7 million Sunday editions at its 1947 peak. It's an American icon—an eleven-time Pulitzer Prize winner that inspired Superman's *Daily Planet*, erected a landmark skyscraper in midtown Manhattan, gave rise to legends like Jimmy Breslin and Pete Hamill, and weathered a second tabloid war with Rupert Murdoch's *New York Post*. Sadly, the *Daily News* of 2022 is a shell of its former self, beaten down by the same economic headwinds that have befallen so many newspapers in the digital era. In the 2010s, there was a seemingly never-ending series of layoffs, buyouts, downsizings, defections, and strategy pivots. During the pandemic, the *Daily News*'s latter-day headquarters at 4 New York Plaza was permanently closed, making it "a newspaper without a newsroom," as the *Times* put it.

The birth of tabloid journalism was an inexorable, unprecedented cultural force that not only changed the course of justice in the Hall-Mills investigation but shaped the modern world. Newspapers have been dishing out murder and mayhem since the early Victorian era. But the tabloids of the Roaring Twenties took that obsession to new heights, packaging it into cheap handheld entertainment for the masses that delivered an irresistible mix of news and frivolity. Phil Payne and the other pioneering tabloid editors of the day hooked their readers with a photographic focus on sex, scandal, and crime, but also, as the journalism historian Andie Tucher told me, "an emphasis on big personalities"—whether that was Rudolph Valentino or Charles Lindbergh or the Pig Woman. Today's celebrity culture, Tucher proposed, "was essentially born in this era." Martin Weyrauch, a former *Graphic* editor, similarly suggested of the original tabloids in a 1927 essay, "They introduced a style of journalism that concerns itself primarily with the drama of life."

The tabloid sensibility is everywhere we turn, from the low-rent clickbait that clutters our social media feeds, to the reality television we binge as a guilty pleasure, to the society murders that echo the Hall-Mills caper of a century ago. If Phil Payne were alive and working today, he surely would have plumbed the strange vanishing of Jennifer Dulos in New Canaan, Connecticut, say, or the Murdaugh family saga that rippled across South Carolina's Lowcountry.

True crime, of course, has been captivating readers for at least two hundred years. But the early New York tabloids arguably laid the groundwork for the genre as we know it, by transforming true crime into something more vivid and compelling than a dense wilderness of small-font newsprint. The Hall-Mills mystery and other tabloid crimes of Jazz Age New York were the zeitgeist-setting murder podcasts and Netflix documentaries of their day. With the Hall-Mills case, it was the tabloid press, not the police, that ultimately drove the case to its apex, hooking the nation on courtroom drama and helping to secure tabloidism as a fixture of American culture.

But the tabloids, despite their best efforts, couldn't solve the mystery. Even now, a whole century later, the million-dollar question remains: *Whodunnit?*

THE DECADES SINCE THE MURDERS have spawned numerous competing theories, some more compelling than others. In 1964, William Kunstler published *The Minister and the Choir Singer*, a nonfiction book about the case. In the final chapter, Kunstler argues that none of the canonical suspects were likely to have killed Edward Hall and Eleanor Mills. As a typical Victorian matriarch, Frances "must have known that her husband's violent death would inevitably subject her and her relationship with him to the glare of sensational publicity. It is indeed improbable that she would have deliberately chosen the greater of two evils." Kunstler describes the testimony claiming that Willie sought directions to the farm at a stranger's home on the night of the murders as literally "incredible." On the other hand, he concludes that the witnesses who placed Henry Stevens on the beach in Lavalette were quite credible, even if their memories were fuzzy. He describes Henry Carpender's alibi—dining with friends in the town next door—as "airtight." As for Jane Gibson's testimony, Kunstler found it to be as fantastical as the jury had in 1926. He likewise felt confident in the innocence of Jim Mills, who was seen on his porch around nine o'clock on the murder night. "[A]lmost nobody believed that he was capable of violence," Kunstler writes. "It is highly likely that not only was he completely unconcerned by his wife's romance with Hall, but that he welcomed the limited economic benefits that it brought."

In Kunstler's view, the only possibility to be considered "with any claim to logic and reason" was that Edward and Eleanor were the victims of vigilante justice. The only vigilantes who would have "murdered the pair for their flagrant violation of . . . standards of sexual morality," Kunstler argued, were members of the Ku Klux Klan.

This theory wasn't novel. Authorities had considered it in the earliest days of their investigation, and it even circulated in newspaper reports at the time. One such article, in the *New York Herald*, alleged that "a New Brunswick businessman socially and politically respected is a high official of the Ku Klux Klan. Also, it was hinted, a young man who was known to have been friendly to Miss Mattie Long, the girl who was jilted by the Rev. Mr. Hall . . . is a klansman." Florence North, the young attorney who briefly represented Charlotte Mills, said she had received anonymous letters suggesting that the Klan was active within St. John's. ("Find out who belongs to the order in the church," one letter said.) And then there was Arthur Riehl's explosive annulment petition, which included an allegation that Louise Geist was a member of the Klan's women's auxiliary.

Kunstler runs through a list of floggings, tarring and featherings, kidnappings, and other vigilante actions perpetrated by Klansmen around the country (and a few in New Jersey) against men and women accused of varying degrees of moral transgression, including adultery. "The elaborate positioning of the bodies was wholly in keeping with Klan practices," writes Kunstler. But he acknowledges that the Klan's playbook did not typically include murder. "It is possible, of course, that the Klansmen concerned did not intend to kill the couple." As Kunstler also acknowledges, "It is conceded that the case against the Klan is a wholly circumstantial one."

The Klan theory is widely disregarded among students of the Hall-Mills case. In his 2011 book, *Popular Crime*, the historian and statistician Bill James takes a chain saw to Kunstler's argument. "The 'pattern crimes' that Kunstler cites have almost nothing in common with the murders of Hall and Mills. The crimes were mostly committed against black people living hundreds or thousands of miles from New Jersey. Kunstler's theory has *nothing* going for it."

As James sees it, the most likely suspect was Jim Mills. What evidence is there for this? For starters, there was the disproportionate violence committed on Eleanor, "a sign of anger toward one victim." There was the possibility, or perhaps even probability, that Jim may have discovered the love letters and "boiled into a rage." There was also Eleanor's taunting remark as she stormed out of the apartment en route to her fatal rendezvous ("Follow me and find out"). Bill James thinks little of the witness statements (two of which came from the Mills children) placing Jim at 49 Carman Street, first at 9:00 P.M. and again shortly before 10:30. (He could have theoretically huffed it to the farm and back in the space of an hour and twenty minutes.) "Is there some sort of law that mousy, ineffectual people don't commit murder in New Jersey?" the author writes. "Mrs. Hall called the police the morning after the murders to ask if there had been any reported 'casualties.' The state tried to use this fact against her at her trial. But James Mills didn't contact the police. He said that it was common for his wife to disappear for a couple of days at a time—a remarkable claim for which there is no corroboration."

When I got ahold of a Hall-Mills buff named Kim Raymond

Kowalczyk to chat about the case, he was unfamiliar with Bill
James, but he shares the author's theory. A retired former U.S.
Army investigator who's researched the murders as a hobby for
years, Kowalczyk's interest is as ardent as they come. He has an
impressive collection of Hall-Mills memorabilia—from vintage
press photos to his own copy of an obscure black magic book that
Eleanor was said to have owned—and he's given presentations about
the crime with fellow Hall-Mills obsessives. He also moderates a
private Facebook group where enthusiasts trade knowledge and
theories, including various members with familial ties to the saga: a
grandchild of the original owner of the Phillips farm, descendants
of a witness who testified at the trial, and so on. Theories on the
Facebook group are all over the map, but Kowalczyk gave me his
theory over the phone one day while packing up for a move from
Central Jersey to Florida. "Everything for me keeps coming back
to James Mills," he said. "He doesn't strike me as the squeaky little
guy they portray him as."

Kowalczyk noted that Edward and Eleanor were known to visit
the Parker Home on Thursday nights in an official church capacity.
(There are references to this in the historical record.) He told me
he's contacted the still-active assisted living facility, now known as
Parker at Landing Lane, in search of archival visitor logs to confirm
if they visited on the night of the murders, but no dice. Jim wouldn't
necessarily had to have suspected that Eleanor and Edward were
in the vicinity the Parker Home in order to find them. "When she
told him to follow her," Kowalczyk said, "I think he did follow her.
I think he followed them up to the Phillips farm, and I think he did
them in. There was more than enough time. I've walked all over
Buccleuch Park. I think it could have been done. All the other theories, I'm not discounting any of 'em. I just find a lot of holes. The part
I get stuck on every time is the staging of the scene. I can't think
of any case I've ever read about where people"—meaning Frances
and her brothers—"would stage the scene to implicate themselves. I

don't see three people in Hall's family standing around in the dark trying to stage the bodies."

Yet another intriguing theory concerns a figure who hovered on the periphery of the central cast. In her 2018 e-book, *Moonlight Murder on Lovers' Lane*, the forensic psychology professor Katherine Ramsland takes a crack at Ralph Gorsline. A big part of her case rests on the gold tie clip that Edward Hall wore when he was murdered, inscribed with the letter *G*. Ramsland was alerted to it by an amateur researcher named Wayne Guinn. (He's friends with Kowalczyk, who believes the clasp looks like it was meant for a woman's scarf, not a tie.) Ramsland wonders whether the clasp was a calling card planted by the killer. "Why would Hall be wearing a tie clasp having a letter other than his first or last name? Why was this never noticed over a period of 89 years? Did it belong to Ralph V. Gorsline?" The tie clip, of course, *had* been noticed back in 1922, as I note in chapter 10. Frances claimed that Edward "found it in the Sunday school room of the church and had tried unsuccessfully to find the owner." Alternatively, an unnamed source "in Mrs. Mills' confidence" told the *New York Tribune* that the clasp had been a gift from Eleanor, the *G* signifying one of Edward's pet names for her: Gypsy. Whichever version is true (after all, could Eleanor have squirreled away enough money to afford such a gift?), the tie clip was not some deep mystery. Even so, the Gorsline theory doesn't entirely fall apart. He lied about being with Catherine Rastall near the farm that night. Throughout the investigation, rumors percolated that Gorsline had been involved. There were also rumors that Gorsline and Eleanor had once had a fling of their own, although Gorsline responded to these rumors by dubiously claiming it was Eleanor who had put the moves on him, only to be rejected. Assessing the case through the lens of her criminology background, Ramsland writes, "It's quite possible that Ralph Gorsline was a stalker. Gorsline was seen spying on the two. It seems an unlikely coincidence that he would have been at De Russey's Lane on the very night that Edward and Eleanor were meeting there without knowing it. He was alert to their movements. Could this jealous stalker have taken things too far? Just how cold-blooded might he have been?" Intriguing? Yes. Likely? Unclear.

On Thursday, October 17, 2019, I paid a visit to the Douglass campus of Rutgers University, a picturesque enclave in the southeast corner of New Brunswick. Back in the 1920s, this same leafy district was inhabited by Frances Hall and her extended family, whose domiciles were later converted into administrative buildings for the university. Carpender Hall, which blends the Queen Anne and Shingle styles of Victorian architecture, was once the home of Edwin and Elovine Carpender, two of Frances's closest relations. The majestic Lindenwood estate, developed by Frances's grandfather around the dawn of the First World War, is now the Rutgers University Inn and Conference Center. The nearby Douglass Writing Center, with its inviting front porch and concave Mansard roof—where, coincidentally, I worked as a writing tutor while attending Rutgers—was also likely a Carpender residence in its day.

As a Rutgers graduate, I knew the area well, but I'd never experienced it as the characters in my story had. That's what brought me to New Brunswick on this crisp autumn afternoon, foliage blazing, the same atmosphere that served as a backdrop for the investigation in 1922. Joined by my literary agent, who had become similarly engrossed in the case, I met up with a man named Richard Sears Walling, a retired history teacher who has researched the case extensively. At the time, Walling had been hosting a series of seasonally appropriate Hall-Mills walking tours, and he offered to give us a private one. We started on Nichol Avenue at the former Hall mansion, now a faculty residence, which has retained its regal countenance. We turned left onto George Street and walked down the hill to St. John the Evangelist, still handsome and well maintained despite the waning of its membership over the years. Across the street was Lord Stirling Community School, home of the LSCS

Knights, where Jim Mills once roamed the halls as a custodian. Finally, around the corner, we came to the erstwhile Mills residence at 49 Carman Street, now clad in shabby white vinyl siding. There were two satellite dishes poking out of the roof, providing the home with a form of entertainment that Charlotte could only have imagined in her wildest dreams.

As we walked the same route that Frances and Willie had taken when they ventured out in search of Edward, Walling's suspicions came into focus. He's of the belief that Frances and her brothers had to have been involved in the killings, and that their money must have helped to cover them up. A few weeks after the walking tour, Walling emailed me about a lead that may or may not support this theory. He'd stumbled upon a fascinating tidbit concerning George Totten, the lead detective from 1922 and a key figure in the subsequent events of 1926. According to newspaper reports following Totten's death in 1942, his estate was valued at a whopping $91,825, including $85,673 in cash—the equivalent of $1.5 million today. How had this working-class retired detective come to possess such a fortune? It isn't too "far-fetched," Walling suggested, that Totten may have been "bribed to clear the primary suspect." Then again, it was Totten who first brought Jane Gibson into the mix, who cleared Clifford Hayes after he was wrongly arrested for the murders, and who helped Phil Payne reignite the case against Frances and her brothers—not exactly the actions you'd expect of a man in the pockets of the defense.

And yet I tend to agree that the most plausible solution to the mystery is probably the most obvious one. There was too much smoke around Frances and her brothers for there not to have been any fire. Maybe Jane Gibson was a preternatural fabulist. Maybe Arthur Riehl concocted those allegations to get revenge on his estranged wife. Maybe the state trooper Henry Dickman lied about being bribed into leaving town. Maybe the people who claimed Willie showed up on their doorstep asking for directions to De Russey's

Lane were simply mistaken. Maybe Willie's fingerprint actually wasn't on the calling card. Maybe Marie Demarest only thought she saw Henry Stevens in New Brunswick on the morning of September 15. Maybe Henry really was fishing on the beach that night. Maybe Frances truly didn't have a hand in the killings.

But what are the odds that none of it was true? That Frances was genuinely ignorant of the affair? That Willie and Henry didn't have any hard feelings toward the man who'd married their sister, leeched off her fortune, and sullied their family honor? That Ralph Gorsline and Catherine Rastall just happened to be on De Russey's Lane at the very moment their church mates were executed? That Felix De Martini was simply trying to get to the bottom of Edward's murder? That every single person who furnished evidence against the defendants was either lying, crazy, or so swept up in the fervor and publicity surrounding the case that they were willing to do or say anything for a moment in the spotlight?

That's to say nothing of Julius Bolyog. Is it possible he was lying, too? Indeed. But what motivation could this quiet little man have harbored to make the whole thing up, out of nowhere, forty-seven years after the murders? Not to mention the tiny shards of evidence that seem to support his claims. George Saloom didn't find a smoking gun, but he corroborated key details, including the identity of one of the accused hit men. And Bolyog withstood the scrutiny not only of a psychological evaluation, but two lie detector tests—hardly ironclad, but not nothing. That said, memory is fallible, especially after the passing of decades, and perhaps more so in someone who is elderly and infirm. Do I find it hard to believe that Frances, Henry, and Willie would have met up with a stranger in broad daylight and handed him six thousand dollars to be delivered to a pair of gangsters a few blocks away? I do. Do I find it hard to believe that a member of the family may have hired a pair of thugs to put an end to Edward's indiscretions? That things might have gotten out of hand? That the family would have gone to great lengths to conceal their involvement? No, I don't find any of that hard to believe. Which is to say I do believe there is at least some kernel of truth to Bolyog's tale. Gun to my head, I'd say one or more of Frances's male relatives orchestrated the murders, and if Frances didn't know about them ahead of time, she had no choice but to join the conspiracy after the fact.

It's tragic that the killer or killers were never brought to justice, and that the victims were only able to achieve in death the everlasting union they longed for in life. But as with so many famous mysteries, it is the allure of the unknowable that draws us in. Would we be endlessly fascinated with Jack the Ripper if we knew who he was, or with Amelia Earhart if we knew how she disappeared?

And so it is with the Hall-Mills case, one of the most extraordinary stories in the annals of American crime. There's no neat and tidy ending here. It is, admittedly, a story without a satisfying conclusion. But sometimes, those are the greatest stories of all.

ACKNOWLEDGMENTS

◈

Thanks to my editor at William Morrow, Mauro DiPreta, whose guidance, sharp sense of story, and surgical line-editing made this book what it is. Associate editor Vedika Khanna helped shepherd my manuscript at every stage of the journey, and eagle-eyed copyeditor Greg Villepique rescued me from grammatical and stylistic degradation. Thanks also to my irreplaceable literary agent, Jen Marshall at Aevitas Creative Management, who believed in this project from the start and shaped it artfully, becoming a Hall-Mills buff along the way. On that note, many thanks to Marisa Meltzer for the introduction, and to Jane von Mehren at Aevitas for her crucial feedback on the proposal.

Back in 2007 and 2008, as a graduate student at the Columbia Journalism School, I devoured the history lectures of Professor Andie Tucher, who hooked me on newspaper sensations of old. It was a conversation with Professor Tucher ten years later—about crime, scandal, and the 1920s tabloids—that provided the spark for *Blood & Ink*. I'm grateful that she shared her knowledge, vetted sections of my manuscript, and introduced me to Joanna Arcieri, a fellow tabloid scholar who fact-checked this book, assisted with research, and helped format the first bibliography I've done since I was a lowly undergrad. Yet another brilliant academic, Adam Morris, put his archival muscle to work when I asked him to sort and scan hundreds of pages of correspondence at U.C. Berkeley's Bancroft Library, saving me the cost of a plane ticket.

I owe thanks to numerous archivists and librarians, especially those who digitized files during a pandemic that precluded in-person research for more than a year. Among them: Kim Adams and Bob Belvin at the New Brunswick Free Public Library; Christine Lutz at Special Collections and University Archives, Rutgers University Libraries; Don Cornelius at the New Jersey State Archives; Anne Thomason of the Donnelley and Lee Library at Lake Forest College; Maurice Klapwald at New York Public Library Research Services; Patrick Cullen at the West New York Public Library; Judy Humphries and Barry Brock of the Gravenhurst Archives; and the staff of the Beinecke Rare Book & Manuscript Library at Yale University. Others who were helpful to my research include: Ken Pryor, Mike Wilder, and Jeanne Trillhause of the Somerset County Prosecutor's Office; Johnny Meyer of Thinkery & Verse; Susan Huslage of St. John the Evangelist; Peter Tumulty; Susan Mollica; Richard Sears Walling; Kim Raymond Kowalczyk; Frank Deiner Jr.; Patterson Smith; Jacqueline Litt; George Wilson; Thomas Maugham; and Rick Stattler.

Thanks to my editors, past and present, at *Vanity Fair*. In 2018, Jon Kelly and John Homans gave me their blessing to pursue this project in my free time—essentially a second full-time job. (We lost John Homans in July 2020, but I carry his mentorship with me.) Radhika Jones, Miriam Elder, Michael Calderone, and Caryn Prime were supportive throughout.

Special thanks to my friends Brian Smith and Jill Hetman, whose beautiful old colonial on the outskirts of New Brunswick happens to be a short walk from the spot where the murders took place. I couldn't have asked for a better home base during research trips—or for a better amateur photographer than Brian to run out and take snaps of St. John the Evangelist and the former Hall home when I needed them in a pinch for the photo insert. For wisdom, feedback, and encouragement, I alphabetically thank: Bryan Burrough, William D. Cohan, Pamela Colloff, Kate Winkler Dawson, Emily Jane Fox, George Gibson, David Grann, Skip Hollandsworth, Alexandra Jacobs, Katherine Sharp Landdeck, Matthew Lynch, David Nasaw, Brad Ricca, Andrew Rice, Constance Rosenblum, Maria Russo, and Charlie Spicer.

Love and thanks to my wife, Jessanne Collins, for proofreading the manuscript and putting up with my sometimes all-consuming immersion in this project over the past four years. To my children, whose curiosity about *Blood & Ink* I promise to indulge when they are a bit older. To my parents for instilling in me a love of reading, and to my in-laws for letting me talk their ears off about this story during visits to their house in the country. I'm terrified that I've forgotten someone. If that person is you, please accept my deepest mortification and insufficient apologies.

A NOTE ON RESEARCH AND SOURCES

❖

This book begins with my visit, on February 1, 2019, to the evidence unit of the Somerset County Prosecutor's Office, where I sifted through several totes full of chilling physical evidence—those shriveled black stockings!—as well as all manner of documents from the original 1922 investigation. I had, in fact, already encountered many of these documents—or, rather, photocopies neatly cataloged in the fantastic Hall-Mills archive at Rutgers University's Alexander Library (where a much younger me spent many an evening researching English-lit papers). Conspicuously absent from the prosecutor's archive were the original witness statements and depositions, which the evidence unit supervisor, Ken Pryor, told me must have been either lost or destroyed long ago. I resigned myself to this likelihood, and then something miraculous happened.

A few weeks after my visit to the prosecutor's office, two archivists, one from Rutgers and one from New Brunswick's public library, visited the home of an elderly New Brunswick resident named George Wilson. Downsizing after the death of his wife, Wilson had invited the archivists to rummage through the couple's possessions. Most of it, paintings and porcelain and such, wasn't of interest. But something caught their eye. "Way down in the basement, there was a large, sad-looking box that had papers in it," recalls Kim Adams, archivist of the New Brunswick Public Library. "It was the Hall Mills records"—which Adams accepted, sorted through, and organized into a new Hall-Mills Murder Case Collection.

Upon learning of the long-lost archive's existence a few months later, I felt like I'd won the lottery. But it wasn't until first viewing the documents in July 2019 that I grasped the size of the jackpot. The archive, now housed in the library's charmingly cluttered basement office, was divided into three main components: statements and depositions from 1922; transcripts of the 1922 grand jury proceedings; and statements and depositions from 1926. There were several thousand pages in all, containing firsthand recollections and dialogue from dozens and dozens of witnesses, including my main characters. Pure gold.

I called Wilson one day not only to thank him, but to satisfy my curiosity about how he had come to possess such treasure. A jovial Australian, Wilson told me he had settled in New Brunswick in the 1950s after traveling the world with his British wife, Avice Wilson, whose career as a laboratory technician landed her a job with a local dairy lab. Back then, the Wilsons lived in an apartment near Rutgers University's College Avenue campus, where their next-door neighbor was a secretary for a lawyer involved in the 1926 trial. This attorney, Wilson recalled, was in the process of cleaning out his office ahead of a relocation. The secretary, knowing her neighbors to be history buffs, asked the Wilsons if they were interested in the Hall-Mills files. They were indeed, and so she handed them over rather than tossing them in the trash. By the time I spoke with Wilson decades later, he reckoned the files had been sitting in the cellar of his latter-day New Brunswick home, in a leafy suburban neighborhood on the far end of town, for at least fifteen or twenty years. "This house is a time capsule," he told me.

Throughout the summer and fall of 2019, I returned to the New

Brunswick Public Library again and again, often on Friday afternoons, scanning every last page of the Hall-Mills archive with
an iPhone app that converts photos to PDFs. These sessions were
followed by repeated visits to the copy center of my local Staples,
where I printed the pages and transferred them into black binders.
The collection was utterly invaluable in researching and writing this
book, which I now believe would not have come together without it.

Several other libraries and archives made this book possible.
I spent an afternoon pouring over ancient ledgers at St. John the
Evangelist, where I found birth records, baptismal records, meeting minutes of the vestry and church council, and more. Another
afternoon was spent gathering documents in the West New York
Public Library, where I held a baseball once owned by Phil Payne
and gazed upon a wheel from the plane that ended his life. The
Donnelley and Lee Library at Lake Forest College supplied voluminous correspondence between Payne and Joseph Medill Patterson;
the Bancroft Library at U.C. Berkeley provided the same between
Payne and William Randolph Hearst. Additional Payne material
was obtained from the volunteer-run Gravenhurst Archives in
Payne's childhood hometown of Gravenhurst, Ontario, Canada. My
knowledge of Payne and the 1920s tabloids was further enriched
by the archives of *Editor & Publisher* and the *Fourth Estate*, as well
as numerous books, articles, and master's theses documenting the
journalism of the era.

Three books that chronicled the Hall-Mills case prior to mine
served as helpful blueprints: *The Girl in Lover's Lane* (1953), *The Minister and the Choir Singer* (1964), and *Fatal Tryst* (1999). But my reconstruction of the case primarily draws on the Hall-Mills Murder Case
Collection, as well as hundreds of newspaper articles. For the 1922
investigation, I leaned heavily on the *New York Times*, *Daily News*, *New
York Tribune*, *New York Herald*, *Evening World*, and *Daily Home News*,
all of them digitized on newspapers.com. (Sister website ancestry
.com was a goldmine for census records, city directories, birth and

death certificates, passport applications, draft registration cards, etc.) Of these publications, only the *Daily News* and *Daily Home News* are digitized for 1926. I accessed the *New York Times'* coverage from that year through the *Times'* web-based digital replica service, TimesMachine, and I obtained months of *Daily Mirror* scans from the New York Public Library, whose collection also includes the New York *Evening Graphic*. Unfortunately, the microfilm for the *Graphic* between 1924 and 1928 is missing, so I had to rely on secondary sources in describing the *Graphic*'s Hall-Mills coverage. Many other newspapers spanning some five decades are likewise reflected in the narrative.

Various magazine archives, especially *The New Yorker*'s, filled out my research. And I'd be remiss not to acknowledge another small miracle that occurred as this book was coming together. I had been corresponding with Brad Ricca, author of *Mrs. Sherlock Holmes*, who pointed me in the direction of Patterson Smith, an antiquarian bookseller with a massive collection of vintage detective magazines. Not only did Smith's collection include essential issues of *True Detective Mysteries* and *Inside Detective*, but it turned out he lived in the same town as me. (What are the odds?) I got in my car, drove eight minutes down the road, and happily forked over a check for the originals.

Two events deserve a mention. In the fall of 2019, I joined dozens of lawyers at the New Jersey Law Center, on the outskirts of New Brunswick, for a four-hour seminar about the Hall-Mills trial, presented by the New Jersey Institute for Continuing Legal Education. Around the same time, I enjoyed a memorable evening at St. John the Evangelist, where a local theater company called Thinkery & Verse staged *Thou Shalt Not*, a dark, funny, well researched, and altogether dazzling play about the Hall-Mills saga. This immersive theatrical performance helped bring the drama to life in the very surroundings where it unfolded. Additionally, Jacquelyn Litt, the dean of Rutgers University's Douglass Residential College and current occupant of the former Hall mansion, allowed me into her home to experience it as Frances, Edward, and Willie would have a century earlier. I somehow never encountered the Hall-Mills case during my time as a Rutgers undergraduate more than two decades ago. But the four years I lived in New Brunswick went a long way when it came time to tell this story.

Blood & Ink is the most comprehensive and exhaustively researched book about the Hall-Mills case. It includes numerous scenes, storylines, and revelations that do not appear in any of the other major works—mostly notably the story of how New York's warring tabloids, and in particular the *Daily Mirror*, endeavored to solve the murders. I took pains to make my contribution to the Hall-Mills canon as accurate as possible. Any dialogue that appears in quotation marks comes directly from a source. Some quotes, such as those from depositions and courtroom testimony, are direct transcripts of what a character said. Others, such as from books and magazines, may instead reflect a character's recollection of certain dialogue. In several sections, particularly courtroom scenes, dialogue has been lightly condensed for narrative flow and readability. But I did not alter or invent any quotes. The same goes for physical action, gestures, and thoughts.

Chapter I—The Crabapple Tree

Pearl Bahmer and Ray Schneider's discovery of the bodies comes from their statements, depositions, and grand jury testimonies from 1922 and 1926, the Hall-Mills Murder Case Collection, New Brunswick Public Library; the *New York Tribune*, September 17, 1922; the *New York Herald*, September 17, 1922; the *New York Times*, September 26, 1922; and *True Detective Mysteries* magazine, September 1931. Weather details are from the New Brunswick *Daily Home News* and the *Asbury Park Press*, September 15, 1922.

Pearl's age was confirmed by the 1920 U.S. Census, and her siblings are listed in a family tree on ancestry.com. Pearl and Ray's physical descriptions come from photographs in *the New York Times* and the *Daily News*. Ray's background comes from his 1922 grand jury testimony and the *Daily Home News*, July 1, 1920.

The George Washington anecdote comes from a history of Franklin Township on the township's official website.

The physical description of the area around the farm is from *The Girl in Lover's Lane*, p. 9, and *True Detective Mysteries*, July 1931.

Grace Edwards's 1922 grand jury testimony describes Ray's call to the police. Ray describes the same in his grand jury testimony and depositions from 1922 and 1926.

Edward Garrigan and James Curran's arrival at the crime scene and inspection of the bodies comes from their 1922 grand jury testimonies and 1926 depositions; Garrigan's 1926 trial testimony; the 1922 grand jury testimony of Samuel Sutphen; the *Daily Home News*, November 4, 1926; the *Bridgeport Telegram*, November 4, 1926; and *The Girl in Lover's Lane*, p. 10.

Details about crime in and around New Brunswick in the early 1920s come from a variety of articles in the *Daily Home News*.

The Albert Cardinal scene comes from his 1922 grand jury testimony and 1926 deposition; and the *Hartford Courant*, August 17, 1926.

The Elton Loblein scene comes from his 1922 grand jury testimony and 1926 statement.

The Daniel Wray scene comes from his 1922 grand jury testimony and 1926 deposition; and the *Daily Home News*, September 16, 1922.

Chapter 2—The Heiress

The opening section comes from Louise Geist's 1922 and 1926 depositions and her 1922 grand jury testimony; Barbara Tough's 1922 grand jury testimony; and the *New York Tribune*, September 20, 1922.

The details about Willie Stevens's employment come from his 1926 trial testimony. The details about Willie's bedroom come from "A Sort of Genius," *The New Yorker*, January 15, 1927.

"a face to look twice at . . .": the *New York Times*, November 2, 1922.

"the head and features of a man": the *New York Herald*, November 2, 1922.

Description of the Hall mansion interior comes from *The Girl in Lover's Lane*.

Frances's call to the police comes from the *New York Times*, September 24, 1922, and *True Detective Mysteries* magazine, June 1931.

The Stevens family history comes from *Erasmus Stevens and His Descendants*; the Ebenezer Stevens Papers, Rutgers University Libraries; and Edith Wharton, *A Backward Glance*.

The Carpender family history comes from *Genealogical and Memorial History of the State of New Jersey*; Scannell's *New Jersey's First Citizens and State*

Guide; the *New York Times*, June 25, 1920; the *Indiana Evening Gazette*, August 26, 1926; "A Look Inside Our Original Building," July 12, 2010, kilmerhouse.com; "The Story of How Johnson & Johnson Was Born," September 2, 2015, jnj.com; "Historic Lindenwood Carpender House" and "The Arbor Trail," website of the Rutgers University Inn and Conference Center.

Frances Hall's history and biographical details come from her 1926 trial testimony; the *Poughkeepsie Journal*, March 1, 1874; numerous articles from the New Brunswick *Daily Times* and *Daily Home News* between 1895 and 1910; the *Daily Mirror*, November 2, 1926; and U.S. Census records. The closing section comes from Frances's 1922 deposition, Edwin Carpender's 1922 deposition, and Albert Cardinal's 1926 deposition; as well as the *New York Times*, August 17 and November 25, 1926.

Chapter 3—The Tabloid Editor

Phil Payne's promotion comes from Leo McGivena, *The News*, p. 96; the *Fourth Estate*, October 21, 1922; and *Editor & Publisher*, October 21, 1922.

The newsroom description comes from a historical photo published in the *Tribeca Trib*, June 3, 2013.

Payne's physical characteristics are from his World War I draft registration card, found on ancestry.com; *Editor & Publisher*, January 19, 1924; and various photographs from the historical record.

The Julia Harpman details are from her testimony in *Julia Harpman vs. Eighth Avenue Railroad Company*, 1921; her death report in the U.S. State Department Decimal File; the *Daily News*, January 30, 1920, April 7, 1921, and August 29, 1922; *Ladies of the Press*, pp. 264–68; and *Pegler: Angry Man of the Press*, pp. 86–90.

"the moment it broke . . .": *Tell It to Sweeney*, p. 225.

"Tabloids were just as inevitable . . .": "Are Tabloid Newspapers a Menace?", *The Forum*, March 1927.

The details on crime are from "Prohibition and the Rise of the American Gangster," published on the website of the National Archives; "The FBI and the American Gangster, 1924–1938," fbi.gov; and "Historical Data," from the Justice Research and Statistics Association.

"(1) Love or Sex, (2) Money, (3) Murder . . .": *Supreme City*, p. 349.

The section on the origin story of the *Daily News* draws on *Tell It to Sweeney*; McGivena, *The News*; *The Magnificent Medills*; *Chicago Tribune*; *Poor Little Rich Boy*; and "The Picture Papers Win," *The Nation*, October 21, 1925.

The salaries and other details about the start of the *News*, as well as details on the New York newspaper market, are from *Tell It to Sweeney*.

The figures charting early circulation growth are from McGivena, *The News*, p. 78, and the *Daily News*, March 7, 1999.

"a whale of a newspaper editor . . .": *Editor & Publisher*, January 19, 1924

Payne's physical impairments are described in numerous sources, including an article one of his doctors wrote for *Boys' Life* magazine in August 1940.

"He had a quirky imagination . . ." and "did not believe in doing anything conventionally . . .": McGivena, *The News*, pp. 40 and 277.

The details about Payne's birth, parents, and siblings are from the 1910 U.S. Census. The section on his adolescence, early adulthood, and career origins comes from the 1915 New Jersey State Census; an entry on Payne's father in *History of Florida*; various editions of the *Perth Amboy Evening News*, 1906 to 1915; the *Fourth Estate*, March 8, 1913; *Editor & Publisher*, January 19, 1924; and the *Toronto Star*, September 15, 1927.

The paragraph on Payne's marriage and honeymoon comes from the New Jersey Marriage Index, 1915–1919; Phil Payne's 1918 U.S. passport application; the 1920 U.S. Census; *Editor & Publisher*, July 3, 1915; the *Daily News*, April 20, 1923; and the *Toronto Star*, September 15, 1927.

The section on Payne's World War 1 service comes from an article Payne wrote for "Welcome Home Our Heroes," a special publication published by the town of West New York, July 4, 1919; Payne's 1918 U.S. passport application; the *Fourth Estate*, July 13, August 24, and November 16, 1918; the *Perth Amboy Evening News*, September 28, 1918; the *Jersey Journal*, November 4 and December 14, 1918, and January 7, 1919; and *Sauce for the Gander*, p. 263.

The details on Payne's postwar employment with Hearst are from the *Fourth Estate*, August 30, 1919, as well as various articles carrying his byline.

The details on Payne's hiring at the *Daily News* and subsequent promotion come from *Editor & Publisher*, April 10, 1920, and the *Fourth Estate*, April 10, 1920.

"quick to spot a good story . . .": *Ladies of the Press*, p. 263.

The paragraph describing coverage overseen by Payne comes from the *Daily News*, November 26, 1920, and January 4 and 10, 1921; *Tell It to Sweeney*, p. 97; and McGivena, *The News*, p. 85.

The details on Julia Harpman's crime reporting come from Payne's testimony in *Julia Harpman vs. Eighth Avenue Railroad Company* and *Ladies of the Press*, p. 261.

The Elwell murder is covered at length in "Who Killed Joe Elwell," *Esquire*, October 1, 1950.

Chapter 4—The Reverend

The opening scenes of Edward Hall at the church are from New Brunswick's *Daily Home News*, June 7 and June 18, 1909; and *Daily Times*, July 19, 1909.

Hall's eye color is listed on his World War 1 draft registration card; his height comes from a copy of the morgue report, September 16, 1922.

Hall's personal history and biographical details come from various documents in St. John the Evangelist's church archive, including meeting minutes of the vestry and church council; Hall's draft registration card; "My Story" by Charlotte Mills, syndicated in the *Windsor Star*, September 3, 1926; the Rochester *Democrat and Chronicle*, June 19, 1902; the *New York Times*, June 19, 1905, and October 15, 1922; the *Daily Home News*, June 18, September 15, and October 4, 1909, and October 23, 1922; the *New Brunswick Times*, November 27, 1909; the *New York Herald*, September 19 and 25, 1922; the *Buffalo Times*, November 2, 1922; and numerous articles in the *Brooklyn Daily Eagle*, the Brooklyn *Standard Union*, and the *Brooklyn Citizen* between 1897 and 1905.

Details about the Christmas fair come from the *Daily Times*, December 1, 1909, and the *Daily Home News*, December 2, 1909.

Frances teaching Sunday school is from the *New York Times*, December 20, 1942.

The Mattie Long details come from the 1905 New Jersey State Census; the 1903 New Brunswick city directory; the *Daily News*, November 1, 1926; the *Tampa Tribune*, November 1, 1926; and the *Dayton Daily News*, November 4, 1926.

Edward Hall's salary is from meeting minutes contained in the St. John's archive; Frances Hall's rumored net worth is from the *New York Times*, September 17, 1922.

The wedding scene comes from the *Daily Home News*, July 20, 1911, and *The Girl in Lover's Lane*, p. 15.

Maggots in Edward's nostrils and under his eyelids were described by George Totten in his 1922 grand jury testimony.

Totten's physical description comes from a photo in the *Daily News*, October 28, 1922; his biographical details are from the *Daily Home News*, September 4, 1941.

Totten's crime scene inspection comes from the grand jury testimonies of Totten, Joseph Navatto, and Samuel Sutphen; Totten's 1926 trial testimony; and *The Girl in Lover's Lane*, p. 14.

The William Long details are from Long's 1922 grand jury testimony and 1926 deposition.

The Bogart Conkling details are from Conkling's 1922 grand jury testimony and 1926 deposition.

"Everything points to murder . . .": the *Daily Home News*, September 16, 1922.

The description of the mob at the crime scene comes from Frank Deiner's 1922 grand jury testimony and 1926 deposition; William Long's 1926 deposition; and *The Girl in Lover's Lane*, p. 13.

Frank Deiner's identification of Eleanor Mills is from his 1922 grand jury testimony.

The Edwin Carpender details are from his 1922 deposition; John Hubbard's 1926 deposition; Deiner's 1922 grand jury testimony; and the *New York Herald*, October 22, 1922.

The closing scene is from Frances's 1922 deposition and Elovine's 1926 trial testimony.

Chapter 5—The Choir Singer

Details of Jim and Eleanor's marital strife are from Jim's 1922 deposition and the *New York Times*, September 27, 1922.

Jim's duties as church sexton are from his 1922 deposition and grand jury testimony, and his 1926 trial testimony.

Eleanor leaving the house is from Jim's 1922 deposition and grand jury testimony, and his 1926 statement.

Jim and Charlotte learning of Eleanor's death comes from Jim's 1926 statement and 1926 trial testimony.

The backstory of Jim and Eleanor's relationship comes from the *Daily Home News*, December 17, 1904, and December 20, 1905; and "My Story" by Charlotte Mills, syndicated in the *Windsor Star*, September 2, 1926.

Charlotte Mills's birth is confirmed by the U.S. Find a Grave Index; Daniel Mills's birth is confirmed by the U.S. Social Security Death Index.

The details of 49 Carman Street are from "My Story" by Charlotte Mills, syndicated in the *Windsor Star*, September 1, 1926.

Eleanor's family details are from "My Story" by Charlotte Mills, syndicated in the *Windsor Star*, September 2, 1926; and *The Girl in Lover's Lane*, p. 19.

Eleanor's physical appearance, habits, and personality come from various installments of "My Story" by Charlotte Mills; as well as copies of Eleanor's love letters to Edward Hall; the *New York Tribune*, September 17, 1922; the *Evening World*, September 23, 1922; and the *New York Times*, September 23, 1922.

"sing like a nightingale . . .": *The Girl in Lover's Lane*, p. 20.

"make a speech or a sermon . . ." and "had a better education . . .": the *Daily Home News*, October 26, 1922.

Jim's birth is confirmed by U.S. Census records; his parents' birthplace is confirmed by the New Jersey Births and Christenings Index, 1660–1931.

Jim's physical characteristics, habits, and personality come from his World War 1 draft registration card; his 1922 deposition; *The Girl in Lover's Lane*, p. 19; and various newspaper articles and photographs.

"We called him Simple Jim . . .": the *New York Tribune*, October 29, 1922.

"You could always study . . .": "My Story" by Charlotte Mills, the *Windsor Star*, September 4, 1926.

"Those were the days . . .": the *Daily Home News*, October 26, 1922.

Jim's career details come from the *Daily Home News*, October 26, 1922; his salary comes from his 1926 trial testimony.

"Be something, kid . . .": "My Story" by Charlotte Mills, the *Windsor Star*, September 4, 1926. The Daniel Mills details also come from "My Story."

"she felt tied down . . ."; "he is your father . . ."; and "Have some kind of life . . ." all come from "My Story," which also describes Jim's relationship with Charlotte.

Details about Eleanor's wishes for Charlotte are supplemented by Charlotte's article "Why Make Me Pay?", *Cosmopolitan*, May 1929.

The paragraph describing Eleanor's side jobs is based on the *New York Times*, October 24, 1922, and "My Story."

The section describing the relationship between the Hall and Mills families draws on the 1922 depositions of Jim Mills and Dr. A. L. Smith; various installments of "My Story" by Charlotte Mills; and *The Girl in Lover's Lane*, p. 22.

Details about the Lake Hopatcong trip come from Minnie Clark's 1922 deposition, and the *New York Times*, September 24, 1922.

Only five people: Jim Mills's 1926 trial testimony.

Details of Edward Hall's interactions with the Mills family are from various installments of "My Story."

Eleanor's activities at St. John's are described in the 1922 grand jury testimonies of Jim Mills and Millie Opie; Charlotte Mills's 1926 trial testimony; and "My Story."

"she didn't want to leave the church . . .": "My Story," the *Windsor Star*, September 4, 1926.

The origins and development of Edward and Eleanor's relationship come from various installments of "My Story"; the *Daily Home News*, October 6, 1922; the *New York Herald*, October 23, 1922; *The Girl in Lover's Lane*, pp. 20–21; and *Edward & Eleanor and the Wages of Sin*, p. 68.

"There isn't another married woman . . .": Elsie Barnhardt's 1922 grand
jury testimony.

"You would do more for the church . . .": Millie Opie's 1922 statement.

Church gossip about Edward and Eleanor is described in Millie Opie and
Russell Gildersleeve's 1922 statements; as well as the *Evening World*, September 25, 1922.

Copies of Edward and Eleanor's love letters and Edward's diary from
Maine were obtained from the Hall-Mills collection at Rutgers University Libraries. This section was supplemented by the *Daily Home News*,
September 25, 1922; the *New York Herald* and *New York Tribune*, October 17, 1922; and the *Evening World*, October 19, 1922.

The chapter's closing section comes from Jim's 1926 statement and the
New York Times, September 17, 1922.

Chapter 6—"Hark! Hark, My Soul!"

Frances Hall's interrogation is reconstructed from the *New York Times* and
New York Herald, September 17, 1922; the *New York Times*, *New York Herald*,
New York Tribune, and *Daily Home News*, September 18, 1922; and *True
Detective Mysteries*, June 1931.

The details about Jim Mills searching the church come from his 1922
deposition; the *New York Times*, September 18, 1922; and the *New York
Herald*, September 20, 1922.

The details of Frances and Jim's interactions come from Jim's 1922 deposition and grand jury testimony; the *New York Times*, September 18, 23,
and 26, October 6, and November 4, 1922; the *New York Tribune*, September 26 and October 1, 1922; and the *Daily Home News*, November 3, 1922.

"I take no stock . . ." and "She was fond . . .": the *New York Times*, September 18, 1922.

Frances at the courthouse comes from her 1922 deposition; as well as the
New York Times, *New York Tribune*, *New York Herald*, and *Daily News*, September 24, 1922.

Sally Peters's biographical details come from the *New York Tribune*, February 16 and November 3, 1920; the *Daily News*, October 5, 1920; and
a finding aid to the Diary of Thomas McClure Peters, the North Jersey
History and Genealogy Center, Morristown, New Jersey.

The reporter interviewing Frances at her house comes from the *New York
Times*, *New York Tribune*, and *New York Herald*, September 24, 1922.

The section chronicling rumors and gossip about the affair comes from the
1922 and 1926 statements and depositions of Russell Gildersleeve, Millie
Opie, Elsie Barnhardt, and Joseph Baier; Charlotte Mills's 1926 trial

testimony; the *New York Times*, September 17, 22, 24, 25, and 27, and October 4, 1922; the *Daily Home News*, September 23 and October 5, 1922; the *New York Tribune*, September 25, 1922; the *Evening World*, September 26 and October 5, 18, and 31, 1922; the *New York Herald*, September 27 and October 4 and 7, 1922; and the *Daily News*, October 6 and 7, 1922.

Edward's funeral comes from the *Daily Home News*, September 18, 1922; and the *New York Times* and *New York Tribune*, September 19, 1922.

Eleanor's funeral comes from the *New York Times* and *New York Tribune*, September 20, 1922.

Chapter 7—"Billy Goat! Billy Goat!"

Eleanor and Edward's timeline comes from the *New York Times*, September 17, 20, 24, 27, and 28, 1922; the *Daily News*, September 17, 1922; the *New York Herald* and *New York Tribune*, September 24, 1922; the *New York Herald* and *Evening World*, September 27, 1922; Charlotte Mills's 1926 trial testimony; and the 1926 deposition of Mrs. Leo Harkins.

Details about people hearing screams and gunshots come from depositions and statements from Norman Tingle, Anna Hoag, Anna Fraley, and John Lathrop, 1922 and 1926; the *New York Times*, September 19 and October 27, 1922; and the *Daily Home News*, September 21 and October 5, 1922.

Details concerning the early theories of the crime come from the *New York Times*, September 17, 18, 19, 20, 22, 25, and 30, and October 5, 1922; the *New York Herald*, September 17, 1922; the *New York Tribune*, September 22 and 23, 1922; a copy of the soil analysis conducted by E. R. Squibb & Sons; and Henry Stevens's 1922 deposition.

Sources for the paragraph with alibis and evidence for Frances Hall and Jim Mills include the 1922 depositions of Jim Mills, Charlotte Mills, and Charles Collins; Jim Mills's 1926 trial testimony; the *Daily Home News*, September 18, 1922; and the *New York Times*, September 21 and October 3, 1922.

Henry Stevens's biographical details are from Henry's 1922 deposition and 1926 trial testimony; and the *New York Herald*, September 21 and October 25, 1922. The alibi details come from his 1922 deposition; the *New York Herald*, September 21, 1922; and the *New York Times*, September 25, 1922.

The details on Willie's revolver come from the *New York Times*, September 19 and October 7, 1922; the *Evening World*, September 21, 1922; and the *New York Herald*, September 22, 1922.

Willie's biographical details are from the *New York Times*, September 18 and 19, 1922; the *New York Herald*, September 19 and 22, 1922; the *Evening*

World, September 20 and 23, 1922; the *Daily News*, September 22, 1922; *The New Yorker*, January 23, 1937; and *The Girl in Lover's Lane*, pp. 17–18.

The paragraph on autism and early-twentieth-century psychology comes from "A Historical Timeline of Modern Psychology," verywellmind.com, April 30, 2020; "Developmental Psychology in the 1920s: A Period of Major Transition," *The Journal of Genetic Psychology*, November–December 2016; "How Autism Became Autism," *History of the Human Sciences*, July 2013; "Leo Kanner, Hans Asperger, and the Discovery of Autism," *The Lancet*, October 2015.

Willie at the courthouse is from the *New York Times*, *New York Herald*, and *New York Tribune*, September 29, 1922.

Details on Willie's finances are from the *New York Times*, September 18 and 19, 1922; and the *New York Herald*, September 19, 1922.

Willie's suspicious remarks are from George Kuhn's 1922 deposition; the *Daily News*, September 17, 1922; and the *New York Times*, *New York Herald*, and *New York Tribune*, September 18, 1922.

"We haven't eliminated anybody . . .": the *New York Tribune*, September 22, 1922.

Chapter 8—The Flapper

The opening scene comes from Charlotte Mills's 1922 deposition; and the *New York Times*, *New York Tribune*, *New York Herald*, and *Daily News*, September 19, 1922.

Charlotte turning on Frances Hall comes from the *New York Times*, *New York Herald*, and *Daily News*, September 23, 1922. The coffee details are from Charlotte's 1922 deposition; the *Daily Home News*, September 22, 1922; and the *New York Times*, September 23, 1922.

"I think more than one person . . .": the *Evening World*, September 23, 1922.

Charlotte's portrayal in the press comes from the *New York Herald*, September 20, 1922. Her physical appearance comes from various photographs in the historical record.

"We are the younger generation . . .": "A Flapper's Appeal to Parents," *The Outlook* magazine, December 6, 1922.

Details on early-twentieth-century forensics are from *American Sherlock* and *Encyclopedia Britannica*. The prosecution's early forensic missteps are from the *New York Herald*, September 18 and October 1, 1922; the *New York Tribune*, September 30 and October 16, 1922; the *New York Times*, September 30, 1922; and William Long's morgue report, contained in the Hall-Mills collection at Rutgers University Libraries.

Eleanor's exhumation comes from the *Daily Home News*, September 29, 1922; and the *New York Tribune* and *New York Herald*, September 30, 1922. Edward's exhumation comes from the *New York Times*, October 6, 1922. Their autopsy reports were obtained from the Hall-Mills collection at Rutgers University Libraries. Additional details from the *Evening World*, September 29, 1922.

The paragraph on jurisdictional tensions comes from the *Daily Home News* and *New York Tribune*, September 18 and 28, 1922; and the *New York Herald*, September 20, 1922.

"I think the Hall family know . . .": Charlotte Mills's 1922 deposition.

The passage with Charlotte Mills and Governor Edwards comes from Charlotte's 1922 deposition; the *New York Times* and *Daily News*, September 28, 1922; and the *New York Times* and *New York Tribune*, September 30, 1922. Edwards summoning the prosecutors to Trenton is from the *New York Times*, September 29, 1922.

The details about mounting pressure to solve the murders and the entrance of the state troopers are from the *Daily Home News*, September 28, 1922; the *New York Times*, September 29 and 30, and October 1 and 4, 1922; and the *Evening World*, October 6, 1922.

Willie's midnight interrogation comes from the *New York Times*, *New York Herald*, and *New York Tribune*, October 8, 1922.

"This murder must be cleared up . . .": the *New York Times*, October 8, 1922.

Chapter 9—The Sideshow

The courthouse color comes from the *New York Times* and *New York Tribune*, October 9, 1922; the *Plainfield Courier-News*, August 23, 1960; and *Middlesex County Court House, New Brunswick, N. J. 1900–1950*, New Brunswick Free Public Library, via RUcore: https://doi.org/doi:10.7282/T3MG7NCZ.

The details on Ray Schneider and Pearl Bahmer reentering the investigation come from Ray's 1922 deposition; the *New York Times*, September 25 and 26, 1922; and the *New York Herald*, September 25, 1926. The *Times* reported that Hall baptized Pearl at St. John's in 1921 and the *Tribune* that he confirmed her, but there is no record of either in St. John's church service ledger. (Neither is there a record of Charlotte Mills's baptism, although her brother Daniel's was recorded.)

Leon Kaufman's recollection comes from his 1922 statement and the *New York Times*, October 9, 1922.

owner of a poolroom and speakeasy: the *New York Times*, October 13, 1922.

who vigorously objected: the *New York Tribune*, September 25, 1922.

"Upon information in the prosecutor's office . . .": the *New York Times*, October 10, 1922.

Details on Hayes and Schneider's interrogations and Schneider's confession are from the *New York Times* and *New York Tribune*, October 10, 1922, as are Hayes's physical features, biographical details, and statement to the press.

John Toolan and Azariah Beekman's dialogue with reporters is from the *New York Times*, October 10, 1922.

"Someone had to be made a goat . . ." and "Isn't it wonderful . . .": the *Daily News*, October 10, 1922.

Jim and Charlotte Mills, who didn't believe: the *New York Times*, October 10, 1922.

"We are all mystified by the arrest . . .": the *New York Times*, October 12, 1922.

"He was very jealous of me . . .": Pearl Bahmer, 1922 statement.

"Ray seemed to take me . . .": the *Daily News*, October 10, 1922.

"I want to see Clifford . . .": the *New York Times*, October 19, 1922.

Pearl and Ray's biographical details are from the *Evening World*, October 10, 1922; the *New York Times*, October 11, 1922; the *Daily News*, October 11 and 12, 1922; *True Detective Mysteries*, August 1931; and ancestry.com.

"About six months ago . . .": Pearl Bahmer, 1922 statement.

Nick Bahmer's biographical details are from the *New York Times* and *Daily News*, October 12, 1922. His arrest and jailhouse interview are from the *New York Times*, *Daily News*, and *New York Tribune*, October 11, 1922.

The *Daily News'* coverage of the Schneider-Bahmer fiasco is from the issues of October 11, 12, and 13, 1922.

The unraveling of the case against Hayes, as well as Beekman's "Truth?" quote, comes from the *New York Times*, October 11 and 12, 1922. Local support for Hayes comes from the same, as well as the *Evening World*, October 11, 1922.

George Totten breaking Ray's false allegation comes from the *Evening World*, October 10, 1922; the *Daily News*, October 11 and 13, 1922; the *New York Herald*, October 12, 1922; the *New York Times*, October 12 and 13, 1922; and *True Detective Mysteries*, October 1931.

Hayes's jailhouse hearing and homecoming scenes are from the *New York Times*, *New York Tribune*, *New York Herald*, and *Daily News*, October 13, 1922.

"In baseball parlance . . .": the *New York Herald*, October 13, 1922.

Chapter 10—"House of Mystery"

Payne's promotion is from the *Fourth Estate*, October 21, 1922.

"What do you think . . .": Telegram from Phil Payne to Joe Patterson, October 29, 1922, Joseph Medill Patterson Papers, Lake Forest College Archives and Special Collections.

The *Daily News* circulation and advertising growth is from *Editor & Publisher*, October 7, 1922, and *Tell It to Sweeney*, p. 124.

"As new evidence . . .": the *Daily News*, October 21, 1922.

The description of crowds at the Phillips farm comes from the *New York Times*, October 16 and 23, 1922; and the *Daily Home News*, October 23, 1922. The rumors about the farm are from the *New York Tribune* and *New York Herald*, September 17, 1922; and the *New York Times* and *Evening World*, September 21, 1922. The farmhouse details are from the *New York Times*, *New York Herald*, *New York Tribune*, and *Evening World*, September 20, 1922; and the *Daily News*, September 21, 1922. The pillaging of the farmhouse is from the *New York Times* and *Daily Home News*, October 23, 1922; the *Daily News*, October 30, 1922; and the *New York Herald*, October 31, 1922.

Details about journalists in New Brunswick are from the *Daily Home News*, September 22, 1922.

"When the *Daily News* prints it . . .": *The Kingdom and the Power*, p. 342.

The developments in the investigation are from the *Evening World* and *Daily Home News*, October 16, 1922; the *New York Times*, *New York Herald*, and *New York Tribune*, October 17, 1922; and the *New York Times*, October 24, 1922.

The Edwin Carpender details are from the *New York Times*, October 20 and 21, 1922.

Henry Stevens missing the wedding comes from the *Evening World*, October 21, 1922, and the *New York Times*, October 22, 1922.

The paragraphs on Ralph Gorsline and Catherine Rastall come from the *Daily Home News*, September 23 and October 24, 1922; the *New York Herald*, October 9, 1922; the *Daily News*, October 12, 1922; the *New York Times*, October 9, 12, 13, 22, and 25, 1922; and the 1920 U.S. Census.

The Florence North material comes from the *New York Times*, October 17 and 19, 1922; the *Enquirer and Evening News*, October 19, 1922; and the 1920 U.S. Census.

Details on the letters are from Charlotte's 1922 grand jury testimony; the *New York Times*, October 17 and 18, 1922; the Wilmington *News Journal*, October 18, 1922; the *El Paso Times*, October 19, 1922; and the *St. Louis Star*, October 24, 1922.

"They certainly made a sucker . . .": the *New York Times*, October 20, 1922.

"Mrs. Hall had better . . .": the *New York Times*, October 18, 1922.

The courthouse scene comes from the *New York Times*, *New York Tribune*, and *Daily News*, October 18, 1922.

Chapter 11—The Pig Woman

The Julia Harpman material in the opener comes from *Pegler: Angry Man of the Press*, pp. 86–91; *Julia Harpman vs. Eighth Avenue Railroad Company*, 1921; and the *Daily News*, April 7, 1921, and June 24 and August 29, 1922.

Harpman's pursuit of Jane Gibson comes from the *Daily News*, October 21 and 22, 1922; and *Tell It to Sweeney*, p. 225.

"EYEWITNESS VERSION . . .": the *Evening World*, October 24, 1922.

Newspaper descriptions of Gibson are from the *New York Times*, *New York Herald*, *New York Tribune*, and *Daily News*, October 25, 1922.

The material on Gibson and Totten comes from *True Detective Mysteries*, September and October 1931; and Gibson's 1922 deposition.

Journalists swarming Gibson's farm is from the *New York Times* and *Daily News*, October 25, 1922. The barnyard interview is from the *New York Times*, *New York Tribune*, *Daily News*, and *Evening World*, October 26, 1922. The daylight saving detail is from *True Detective Mysteries*, October 1931. The photo of Edward is from the New York *News*, October 26, 1922.

The subsequent versions of Gibson's account come from the *New York Times*, October 27 and 28, 1922.

"She hints at a life . . .": the *New York Tribune*, October 28, 1922.

"one of the oddest characters . . .": the *Evening World*, October 25, 1922.

The Marguerite Mooers Marshall scene is from the *Evening World*, October 27, 1922. The minister detail is from the *New York Herald*, October 28, 1922. The barn-fire detail is from the *Daily News*, October 25, 1922.

The paragraphs detailing Gibson's backstory come from the *New York Herald*, October 28, 1922; the *New York Times*, October 31, and November 1 and 2, 1922; the *New York Tribune*, October 31, 1922; the *Daily News*, October 31 and November 2, 1922; and the U.S. Census for 1910 and 1920.

The paragraph on Gibson's reputation comes from the *New York Herald*, October 28 and 29, 1922; the *New York Tribune*, October 29, 1922; and the *Daily Home News*, October 30, 1922.

Timothy Pfeiffer's comments to reporters are from the *New York Times*, October 27, 1922.

watched the girl say her prayers: the *New York Times*, October 31, 1922.

The details on Henry's alibi are from the *New York Times*, October 28, 1922.

Governor Edwards appointing a special prosecutor comes from the *New York Times*, October 14, 1922.

Wilbur Mott's biographical details come from the *New York Times*, October 24, 1922.

The reconstruction of the mule ride comes from *True Detective Mysteries*, October 1931.

"Do not think of this case . . .": the *Evening World*, October 27, 1922.

George Totten posed with Gibson's mule on the front page of the *Daily News*, October 28, 1922.

"Mrs. Gibson, the pig lady . . .": *Careless People*, p. 183.

Gibson shooting at the photographers comes from the *Daily Home News*, October 31, 1922; and *the New York Times*, *New York Herald*, and *Daily News*, November 1, 1922.

Gibson's poem was printed in the *Daily News* on November 1, 1922.

Chapter 12—Meet the Press

The photo shoot comes from the *New York Times*, *New York Tribune*, and *Daily News*, November 2, 1922.

Frances's home confinement is from Louise Geist's 1922 grand jury testimony; the *Evening World*, October 14, 1922; the *New York Times*, October 15, 29, and 31, and November 2, 1922; the *New York Tribune*, October 29, 1922; and the *New York Herald*, October 31, 1922.

The press conference scene comes from the *New York Times*, *New York Herald*, *New York Tribune*, and *Daily News*, November 2, 1922. Mott's inspection of the transcript comes from the *New York Times* and *Daily News*, November 3, 1922.

"That is a lie . . .": the *Daily News*, November 3, 1922.

In the latest version: the *Evening World*, November 5, 1922.

"The story I told . . .": the *New York Times*, November 5, 1922.

The Paul Hamborzsky material comes from the *New York Times* and *Daily Home News*, November 18, 1922.

The paragraph detailing Mott's theory of the crime comes from the *New York Times*, November 8 and 12, 1922; and the *New York Tribune*, November 9 and 12, 1922.

The Felix De Martini details are from Louise Geist's 1922 grand jury testimony; the *Evening World* and *Daily Home News*, November 6, 1922; *True Detective Mysteries*, February 1930; and the *New York Times*, October 15, 1962.

The final paragraphs on Gibson and Nellie Lo Russell come from Russell's sworn statement in the Hall-Mills collection at Rutgers University

Libraries; the *New York Times*, November 13, 14, and 15, 1922; the *Daily News*, November 14, 1922; and the *Evening World*, November 14, 1922.

Chapter 13—The Grand Jury

The newspaper reunion comes from the *Perth Amboy Evening News*, November 18 and 20, 1922.

Through 1922, Julia Harpman used the pen name "Investigator." Any *Daily News* articles about the Hall-Mills case under this byline are presumed to be Harpman's. The Harpman excerpt at the beginning of this chapter is from the issue of November 20, 1922.

The letter of support was published in the *Daily Home News*, November 21, 1922. Emily Post's biographical details are from the *New York Times*, October 24, 2008, and emilypost.com.

Details on the grand jury members are from the *Daily Home News*, November 20, 1922; and the *New York Times* and *New York Tribune*, November 21, 1922.

Beekman's skepticism is from the *Daily Home News*, November 10, 1922, and *New York Tribune*, November 12, 1922.

The description of the grand jury room comes from the *New York Times*, *New York Tribune*, and *Daily News*, November 21, 1922. The scene outside the jury room comes from the *Evening World*, *Daily News*, and *New York Tribune*, November 21, 1922; and the *New York Times*, November 29, 1922.

All quotations and paraphrasing of the grand jury proceedings come from transcripts housed in the New Brunswick Public Library's Hall-Mills Murder Case Collection.

Pearl and Ray's arrivals are from the *New York Times*, November 21, 1922.

Charlotte's wardrobe is from the *New York Times*, October 27 and November 23, 1922; the *Daily News*, October 27, 1922; and the *New York Tribune*, November 23, 1922.

Louise Geist's clothing is from the *New York Times*, November 28, 1922.

Barbara Tough's background is from her grand jury testimony.

"less than five minutes . . ." and "Yesterday's proceedings . . .": the *Daily News*, November 28, 1922.

"a collective gasp . . .": the *New York Tribune*, November 28, 1922.

Henry Carpender's alibi is from the *New York Times*, November 12, 1922.

The scenes of Gibson entering and exiting the grand jury room come from the *New York Times*, *New York Herald*, *New York Tribune*, and *Daily News*, November 29, 1922.

"Here comes the dramatic moment . . .": the *New York Tribune*, November 29, 1922.

The descriptions of locals anticipating the decision are from the *New York Times* and *New York Tribune*, November 29, 1922.

The scene where the decision is announced comes from the *New York Times*, *New York Herald*, and *New York Tribune*, November 29, 1922.

Reactions to the decision are from the *New York Times*, November 29, 1922, and the *Daily Home News*, November 28, 1922.

Jim Mills in his kitchen comes from the *New York Herald*, November 29, 1922.

"one of the most dramatic days . . .": the *Daily News*, November 29, 1922.

Chapter 14—Madame Astra

The opening paragraphs of Frances leaving for Italy come from the *Daily News* and *Daily Home News*, February 7, 1923; and the *New York Times*, February 8, 1923.

Ellis Parker's biographical details are from the Camden *Courier-Post*, May 1, 1922, and the *Daily Home News*, October 21, 1922. I also consulted *Master Detective: The Life and Crimes of Ellis Parker, America's Real-Life Sherlock Holmes*.

"would be no reflection . . .": the *Daily Home News*, October 3, 1922.

Charlotte's letter to Parker is from the *Evening World* and *Daily Home News*, October 3, 1922.

"They're following blind trails . . .": the *Daily Home News*, October 21, 1922.

"The name Ellis Parker . . .": the *Daily News*, December 31, 1922.

Jim Mills confronting the governor comes from the *Daily News*, *Daily Home News*, and *Long Branch Daily Record*, January 17, 1923.

Parker's visit to the Mills residence comes from Jim's 1926 trial testimony.

"exploitable peculiarities . . .": Westbrook Pegler's newspaper column, syndicated in the *Nashville Tennessean*, September 29, 1954.

The background on 1920s spiritualism comes from the *Sun and the New York Herald* Magazine Section, February 15, 1920; and the *Daily News*, February 20, 1922.

The Arthur Conan Doyle material comes from the *New York Times Book Review*, June 9, 1918, and November 27, 1921; the *New York Tribune*, December 20, 1919; the *New York Times*, April 10 and 13, 1922; and the *San Francisco Examiner*, April 10, 1922.

Charlotte Mills's spiritualist conversion comes from the *New York Times* and *New York Herald*, December 2, 1922.

Eleanor's correspondence with the spiritualist comes from the *Evening World*, October 3 and 5, 1922; the *Daily Home News*, October 3, 1922; the *New York Herald*, October 4 and 5, 1922; and the *Daily News*, October 5, 1922.

"Let's pitch to this guy's weakness . . .": *Ladies of the Press*, p. 265.

I re-created the séance from Westbrook Pegler's newspaper columns, syndicated in the *Nashville Tennessean*, September 29 and 30, 1954; *Ladies of the Press*, p. 265; the *Daily News*, November 2, 1924; and the *Daily Mirror*, November 2, 1926.

Bernardine Szold's biographical details are from the *Los Angeles Times*, June 12, 1977.

Jim's visit to Ellis Parker is described in a letter from Parker to George Totten in the Hall-Mills collection at Rutgers University Libraries.

Otto Liveright and Julia Harpman's visit to Jim Mills comes from Westbrook Pegler's column, syndicated in the *Cincinnati Enquirer*, September 30, 1954.

Chapter 15—"A New, Mongrel Fourth Estate"

Helena Payne's death comes from the *Daily News*, April 20, 23, and 24, 1923; the *Perth Amboy Evening News*, April 21, 1923; the *Jersey Journal*, April 24, 1923; *Sauce for the Gander*, pp. 237–38; and the *Toronto Star*, September 15, 1927. Payne's board of education trusteeship is documented in multiple articles in the *Jersey Journal*, 1923, as well as *History of West New York, New Jersey*. The Paynes' membership in the Cusick American Legion Post is documented in *History of West New York, New Jersey*.

The *Daily News'* development under Payne comes from numerous articles in the paper from 1923; Phil Payne's correspondence with Joseph Medill Patterson, December 6, 1922, and February 8 and March 9, 1923; and Leo McGivena, *The News*, p. 99.

Background on Hearst's media empire in the early 1920s comes from *Editor & Publisher*, October 6, 1923, and June 14, 1924; *The Chief*, p. 379; and the video short *History of Hearst*.

The expansion of America's tabloid press was chronicled in *Editor & Publisher*, July 26, 1924.

Material on the *Daily Mirror*'s debut comes from a scan of its first issue, June 24, 1924; *Editor & Publisher*, June 28, 1924; and "The Picture Papers Win," *The Nation*, October 21, 1925.

The section on Bernarr Macfadden and the *Evening Graphic* comes from *Editor & Publisher*, September 20, 1924; Phil Payne's correspondence with Joe Patterson, July 17 and September 15, 1924; "The Picture Papers Win," *The Nation*, October 21, 1925; Arthur Sarell Rudd, "The Development of Illustrated Tabloid Journalism in the United States," master's thesis, Columbia Journalism School, 1925; "Physical Culture," *The New Yorker*, October 15, 21, and 28, 1950; *My Last Million Readers*, p. 102; *Jazz*

Journalism, chapter 10; Lester Cohen, *The New York Graphic*, pp. 1–6; and a gallery of the *Graphic*'s composite illustrations in *Sauce for the Gander*.

The paragraph on Payne's personal and social development comes from *Sauce for the Gander*, pp. 236–38; *Brooklyn Life*, January 17, 1925; *The New Yorker*, March 14, 1925; and the *Daily News*, March 29, 1925.

The Peggy Hopkins Joyce section comes from Payne's correspondence with Joe Patterson, October 27, 1923, and October 17, 1925; *Sauce for the Gander*, p. 238; the *Daily News*, June 8 and July 30, 1924; the *Davenport Democrat and Leader*, September 18, 1927; the *Paterson Evening News*, June 29, 1954; the *Fort Lauderdale News*, January 15, 1956; and the *Bergen Record*, June 29, 1957.

The paragraphs on Payne leaving the *News* for the *Mirror* come from *Editor & Publisher*, April 11, May 9, 16, and 20, and June 13, 1925; "The Picture Papers Win," *The Nation*, October 21, 1925; and Patterson's correspondence with William H. Field.

"The tabloid picture paper . . .": "The Picture Papers Win," *The Nation*, October 21, 1925.

"youthful crusading spirit . . .": "Are Tabloid Newspapers a Menace?", *The Forum*, March 1927.

"With unction and spurious gravity . . .": "These Tabloids," *The New Yorker*, October 3, 1925.

The paragraphs detailing Payne's efforts at the *Mirror* come from *Editor & Publisher*, June 20 and October 31, 1925, and March 6, 1926; the *New York Times*, March 6, 1947, and January 16, 1989; and *Ladies of the Press*, pp. 303–4.

The Harry Thaw section comes from the *Daily News*, April 15, July 12, and September 16, 1925; the *Daily Mirror*, September 18, 1925; *Editor & Publisher*, October 31, 1925; and *Time*, September 28, 1925.

The closing section on the Earl Carroll scandal comes from the *New York Times*, February 10, 25, and 27, and May 22 and 26, 1926, and March 16, 1932; the *Daily Mirror*, February 24, 1926; the *St. Petersburg Times* and *Scranton Times*, February 24, 1926; the *Baltimore Sun*, May 21, 1926; the *Daily News*, May 26, 1926; "Orgy: American Style," *The New Yorker*, June 5, 1926; and Cohen, *The New York Graphic*, p. 103.

Chapter 16—"Investigation A"

Payne's meeting with Totten is described at length, from Totten's perspective, in the December 1931 issue of *True Detective Mysteries*. Additional details come from *Editor & Publisher*, September 24, 1926, and the *New York Times*, August 14, 1926. The details on Azariah Beekman's death are from the *Daily Home News* and *Plainfield Courier-News*, March 22 and April 2, 1926. Totten's firing and appeal are from the *Plainfield Courier-News*, April 2 and 28, 1926, and the *Daily Home News*, April 28, 1926. Totten's age is confirmed by the 1920 U.S. Census. Arthur Riehl's age and occupation are from his World War I draft registration card and U.S. Census records.

The *Graphic*'s attempt to revive the case comes from *My Last Million Readers*, pp. 103 and 108; Lester Cohen, *The New York Graphic*, pp. 8–10 and 103; and the *Graphic*'s correspondence with county and state officials, from the Hall-Mills collection at Rutgers University Libraries.

My reconstruction of the *Mirror*'s revival of the case comes from *Editor & Publisher*, September 4, 1926; the *Daily Mirror*, July 17, 1926; and *Sauce for the Gander*, pp. 136–41. Herbert Mayer's biographical details are from the *New York Times*, March 16, 1957. Peter Tumulty's physical description is from the *New York Times*, August 19, 1926.

Arthur Riehl's affidavit is from the New Brunswick Public Library's Hall-Mills Murder Case Collection.

Chapter 17—"A Tissue of Disgusting Lies"

The Frances Hall material in the opening paragraph comes from the *Daily News*, April 15, June 10, and December 13, and 17, 1925; the *Kansas City Star*, December 11, 1925; and the *Daily Home News*, December 17, 1925.

Herbert Mayer recounted his conversation with Frances Hall in the *Daily Mirror*, July 16, 1926.

Totten losing his appeal and the annulment petition details both come from the *Daily Home News*, July 16, 1926.

Louise Geist's comments were reported in the *Daily Home News*, July 16, 1926, and the *Daily News*, July 18, 1926.

"I have investigated . . ." and "Despite sensational stories . . .": the *Daily News*, July 18, 1926.

Details in the paragraph beginning "Phil Payne was unfazed" are from the *Daily Mirror*, July 17, 1926.

"was said to have solved . . ." and "succession of startling neglect . . .": the *Daily Mirror*, July 24, 1926.

The Felix De Martini material comes from the *Daily Mirror*, July 23, 1926; and Peter Somers's 1926 deposition.

Jim Mills's remarks are from the *Daily Mirror*, July 26, 1926.

"High-priced lawyers . . .": the *Daily Mirror*, July 27, 1926.

"It is nothing more . . .": the Camden *Evening Courier*, July 17, 1926.

The paragraph about the case "gathering strength" comes from *Editor &*

Publisher, September 4, 1926; and the 1926 statements/depositions of Arthur Riehl, Peter Somers, and Mary and Lewis Blackwell.

The closing section about Frances Hall's arrest comes from the *Daily Mirror*, July 29, 1926; the *New York Times*, July 29 and 30, 1926; the *Daily Home News*, July 29, 1926; and *Editor & Publisher*, September 4, 1926.

Chapter 18—The Arrests

Frances Hall's release from jail and Timothy Pfeiffer hitting the photographer come from the *Daily News*, *Daily Mirror*, and *New York Times*, July 31, 1926.

Robert McCarter's biographical details are from the *New York Times*, May 31, 1941, and *Scannell's New Jersey's First Citizens and State Guide*.

Alexander Simpson's biographical details are from the *New York Times*, July 31, 1926, and July 21, 1953; the *Daily Mirror*, July 31, and November 1 and 18, 1926; the *Daily News*, August 26, 1923; and *The Girl in Lover's Lane*, p. 42.

Reporters in Somerville are described in the *Daily Mirror*, July 31, 1926.

Simpson's PR strategy is from the *New York Times*, August 5, 1926.

"I am absolutely convinced . . .": the *New York Times*, August 3, 1926.

"The facts discovered . . .": "A Mystery Revived," *The New Yorker*, August 7, 1926.

Simpson's interview with Louise Geist comes from her 1926 depositions.

The Peter Tumulty material comes from his 1926 statement and the 1922 statement of his son, Peter Francis Tumulty.

The John Hubbard and Samuel Sutphen interviews come from their 1926 depositions.

The Charlotte Mills material is from her 1926 deposition and the *New York Times*, August 5, 1926.

The arrest of Willie Stevens and Henry Carpender comes from the *Daily Mirror*, *Daily News*, and *New York Times*, August 13, 1926.

The Grace Robinson material is from *Ladies of the Press*, pp. 270–77, and the *New York Times*, August 13, 1926.

"The character of this evidence . . .": the *Daily Mirror*, August 13, 1926.

The material on the calling card is from the *Daily Mirror*, August 27 and 28, 1926; *Editor & Publisher*, September 4, 1926; and George Totten's 1926 statement.

Details from the bail and preliminary hearings are from the *New York Times*, August 27, 1926.

Details about the missing documents are from the *Daily Mirror*, August 13, 1926, and the *New York Times*, August 14, 1926.

The Robert Earling details are from the *New York Times*, August 17, 1926.

John Stillwell described seeing a scratch on Frances Hall's face in his 1926 statement.

Paul Hamborzsky recounted conversations with Edward Hall in his 1926 statement.

Simpson investigating Henry's alibi comes from the 1926 statements/depositions of Arthur Applegate and William Eger; and the *New York Times*, September 2 and 4, 1926.

The Ralph Gorsline and Catherine Rastall material comes from the *New York Times*, September 10, 11, and 12, 1926; and the *Daily News*, September 12, 1926. Gorsline's visit to the Burns Agency was described in John MacDonough's 1926 affidavit.

The grand jury details are from the *New York Times*, September 15, 1926.

Henry's arrest is from the *New York Times*, September 16, 1926.

The state's theory was described in the *New York Times*, September 20, 1926.

The Minnie Clark material is from her 1926 statement; the *New York Times*, October 21 and 23, 1926; and the *Daily Mirror*, October 21, 1926.

Felix De Martini's arrest and release is from the *New York Times*, October 3 and 5, 1926.

Henry Carpender's alibi is from his 1926 deposition.

"It is my firm conviction . . .": the *New York Times*, October 8, 1926.

Eleanor's second exhumation is from the *New York Times*, October 28, 1926, and the *Daily Mirror*, October 29, 1926.

The Henry Dickman material comes from Dickman's 1926 deposition; the *New York Times*, August 11 and October 1, 1926; and the *Daily Mirror*, August 11, 1926.

The section on Frances courting reporters comes from the *New York Times*, September 7 and 29, 1926; and the *Daily News*, October 18, 1926.

The *Daily Mirror*'s circulation was published in its issue of October 4, 1926.

"innocuous": the *Daily Mirror*, September 29, 1926.

Frances Hall's attack on the *Mirror* is from the *New York Times* and *Daily Mirror*, October 18, 1926. Phil Payne's response was published in the *Daily Home News*, October 18, 1926. Frances further responded to the *Daily Home News* on October 19, 1926.

Chapter 19—Trial of the Century

Somerville color in the opening two paragraphs comes from *Editor & Publisher*, November 4, 1926.

"Business is good . . .": the *Brooklyn Daily Times*, November 15, 1926.

"To believe that one . . .": the *New York Times*, August 20, 1926.

The correspondent roster comes from the *Daily Mirror*, November 3, 1926; *Editor & Publisher*, November 4, 1926; "Under the Apple Tree," *Time*, November 15, 1926; Lester Cohen, *The New York Graphic*, pp. 105–6; the Wallace Conover Files, Rutgers University Libraries; and "Elizabeth M. Gilmer as Dorothy Dix," The Dorothy Dix Collection at Austin Peay State University.

"taken on some of the aspects . . .": *Trials and Tribulations*, p. 12.

The courthouse setup comes from *Editor & Publisher*, November 4, 1926; *The Girl in Lover's Lane*, p. 46; and the Hall-Mills Trial Transcripts, New Jersey State Archives.

"It's got the Thaw case . . .": *Editor & Publisher*, November 4, 1926.

Willie and the two Henrys in jail comes from the *New York Times*, November 1, 1926.

Frances Hall's portrait session comes from the *New York Times*, October 31, 1926.

Frances going to the courthouse comes from the *New York Times* and *Editor & Publisher*, November 4, 1926.

The description of the courtroom comes from *Trials and Tribulations*, p. 14.

The description of the judges comes from the *Daily News*, November 3, 1926.

The defendants' outfits are described in the *New York Times*, November 4, 1926; and *Trials and Tribulations*, pp. 15–17.

Simpson's physical description is from the *Daily News*, November 7, 1926, and *Trials and Tribulations*, p. 13.

Simpson's opening argument is from the Hall-Mills Trial Transcripts, New Jersey State Archives.

Jane Gibson falling ill is from the *Daily Mirror*, November 4, 1926; and the *New York Times*, November 6 and 8, 1926.

The John and Charlotte Dickson material is from the Hall-Mills Trial Transcripts, New Jersey State Archives; and the *New York Times*, *Daily Mirror*, and *Daily News*, November 4, 1926.

Ralph Gorsline's testimony is from the Hall-Mills Trial Transcripts, New Jersey State Archives.

The William Garven material is from the *New York Times*, November 9, 1926.

The Henry Dickman material is from the *New York Times*, November 7, 1926.

The Marie Demarest material is from the *New York Times*, November 6, 1926.

Louise Geist's testimony is from the Hall-Mills Trial Transcripts, New Jersey State Archives. Additional color from Geist's 1926 deposition and the *New York Times*, November 13, 1926. Arthur Riehl dropping his annulment petition is from the *New York Times*, November 6, 1926.

The Otto Schultz material comes from the *New York Times* and *Daily News*, November 10, 1964.

"I would rather . . .": the *Daily Mirror*, November 10, 1926.

Charlotte's testimony is from the Hall-Mills Trial Transcripts, New Jersey State Archives. Additional color from the *New York Times*, November 4, 1926.

Jim's testimony is from the Hall-Mills Trial Transcripts, New Jersey State Archives. Additional color from the *New York Times*, November 6, 1926.

The material on Timothy Pfeiffer and Bernardine Szold comes from the *Daily Mirror*, November 2, 1926, and the Bernardine Szold-Fritz Correspondence, Beinecke Rare Book & Manuscript Library, Yale University.

The background on fingerprinting comes from "The Hall-Mills Murder — Takeaways from an Unsolved Murder in NJ," October 18, 2019, seminar, New Jersey Institute for Continuing Legal Education; and *The Fingerprint Sourcebook*, U.S. Department of Justice Office of Justice Programs.

Joseph Faurot and Edward Schwartz's fingerprints testimony is from the *New York Times* and the *Philadelphia Inquirer*, November 5, 1926.

Payne's testimony is from the Hall-Mills Trial Transcripts, New Jersey State Archives. Additional color from the *Brooklyn Daily Eagle*, the *Brooklyn Citizen*, and the *Daily Mirror*, November 12, 1926; the *Daily News*, November 13, 1926; *The Girl in Lover's Lane*, pp. 87–90; and *The Minister and the Choir Singer*, p. 224.

"It was amusing . . .": the *Daily Mirror*, November 12, 1926.

Chapter 20—"I Have Told Them the Truth, So Help Me God!"

The hospital scene is from the *New York Times*, November 18, 1926.

Jane Gibson's ride to the courthouse and the scene inside the courtroom come from the *New York Times*, November 19, 1926.

"Her hands . . .": *Trials and Tribulations*, p. 57.

Gibson's testimony is from the Hall-Mills Trial Transcripts, New Jersey State Archives. Additional color from the *New York Times* and *Daily Mirror*, November 19, 1926.

Clarence E. Case's biographical details are from the *New York Times*, September 4, 1961.

Gibson's exit from the courtroom comes from the *New York Times* and *Daily News*, November 19, 1926; and *Trials and Tribulations*, p. 56.

Chapter 21—"A Sort of Genius"

Henry's testimony comes from the Hall-Mills Trial Transcripts, New Jersey State Archives. Additional color from the *New York Times*, November 21, 1926; and *Trials and Tribulations*, pp. 61–64.

"Some of them couldn't remember . . .": *Trials and Tribulations*, p. 65.

"The despicable character . . .": the *New York Times*, November 22, 1926.

"Is he normal mentally . . .": the *New York Times*, November 22, 1926.

Willie's testimony comes from the Hall-Mills Trial Transcripts, New Jersey State Archives. Additional color from the *New York Times*, *Daily News*, and *Daily Mirror*, November 24, 1926; and *The Girl in Lover's Lane*, p. 129.

"The defendant, whom even . . .": the *New York Times*, November 24, 1926.

"so earnestly and with such a show . . .": the *Daily News*, November 24, 1926.

Chapter 22—The Verdict

Thanksgiving in jail is from the *New York Times*, November 26, 1926.

Details on the witnesses before Frances are from the *New York Times*, November 23, 25, 26, and 27, 1926.

Frances Hall's testimony comes from the Hall-Mills Trial Transcripts, New Jersey State Archives. Additional color from the *New York Times*, November 28 and 30, 1926; the *Daily Mirror*, November 29 and 30, 1926; the *Daily News*, November 30, 1926; *Trials and Tribulation*, pp. 78 and 90; *The Girl in Lover's Lane*, pp. 152–61; *The Minister and the Choir Singer*, p. 283.

The defense closing arguments are from the *New York Times*, December 2 and 3, 1926; and the *Daily Mirror*, December 2, 1926.

"Dear Mr. McCarter. . . .": the *Daily Mirror*, December 2, 1926.

"For the BEST account . . .": the *Daily News*, multiple dates, November 1926.

"Let them come . . .": the *Daily Mirror*, December 3, 1926.

Simpson's motion for a mistrial is from the *New York Times*, November 30, 1926.

178 witnesses: the *New York Times*, December 4, 1926.

Simpson's closing argument is from the *New York Times*, December 4, 1926; *Trials and Tribulations*, p. 93; and *The Girl in Lover's Lane*, p. 178.

The jury deliberations and verdict are from the *New York Times*, December 4, 1926. The material about reporters reacting to the verdict comes from the *Daily Mirror*, December 4, 1926; the *Daily News*, December 4, 1926, and November 23, 1936; and *The Girl in Lover's Lane*, p. 182.

The scenes at the Hall and Mill homes following the verdict come from the *New York Times*, December 4, 1926.

"Senator Simpson has said . . .": *Editor & Publisher*, December 11, 1926.

more than eleven million words: the *New York Times*, December 4, 1926.

The circulation figures are from *Editor & Publisher*, October 9, 1926.

"The 'front office' angle . . .": Lester Cohen, *The New York Graphic*, p. 110.

"The most sensational . . .": Cohen, *The New York Graphic*, p. 111

"Bernarr Macfadden's Graphic . . .": Phil Payne's correspondence with William Randolph Hearst, December 1, 1926, William Randolph Hearst Papers, Bancroft Library, U.C. Berkeley.

"Senator Simpson will . . .": Payne-Hearst correspondence, December 2, 1926.

The libel suit was reported in the *Daily Home News*, December 4, 1926.

"It was a grand fight . . .": *Editor & Publisher*, December 11, 1926.

"Don't think your hopes . . .": Payne-Hearst correspondence, November 14, 1926,

"hundreds of letters . . .": Payne's correspondence with Joseph Willicombe, December 8, 1926, Hearst Papers.

"scores of commendatory messages . . .": Payne-Willicombe correspondence, December 9, 1926.

"One thing is sure . . .": Payne-Willicombe correspondence, December 11, 1926.

"He thinks you did wonderful . . .": Payne-Willicombe correspondence, December 10, 1926.

"I quite agree with you . . ." Payne-Willicombe correspondence, December 11, 1926.

Chapter 23—*Old Glory*

"For the time being . . .": *Editor & Publisher*, December 11, 1926.

Payne's secretary comes from *Sauce for the Gander*, p. 240.

The Dorothy Hughes material comes from the *Daily News*, August 27, 1922, and December 14, 1926; the *New York Times*, September 9, 1922; "Miss New York Dorothy Hughes," original photo caption, April 22, 1926, Getty Images.

Payne's marriage to Hughes is from Payne's correspondence with Hearst, December 10, 1926, William Randolph Hearst Papers, Bancroft Library, U.C. Berkeley; the *Daily News*, December 14, 1926; the *Brooklyn Standard Union*, December 14, 1926; and the New York, New York, U.S., Marriage License Indexes, 1907–2018.

The paragraphs detailing Payne's circulation efforts are from his correspondence with Hearst between January and May 1927.

The libel suit material is from the Payne-Hearst correspondence, March 16
and 17, 1927; the *Plainfield Courier-News*, March 16, 1927; and the *Daily
News*, March 17, 1927.

For the section on 1920s aviation, I drew on Joseph Hamlen, *Flight Fever*;
Richard Montague, *Oceans, Poles, and Airmen*; and Frederick Lewis Allen,
Only Yesterday. Footage of Charles Lindbergh's historic takeoff can be
found at criticalpast.com.

"part of the campaign . . .": the *San Francisco Examiner*, July 7, 1927.

Details on the Hearst plane are from *Flight Fever*, p. 233, and *Oceans, Poles,
and Airmen*, p. 179.

two hundred dollars a week: Payne-Hearst correspondence, July 6, 1927.

"I do not think the CHIEF . . .": Payne's correspondence with Joseph
Willicombe, July 13, 1927.

"millions of young men . . .": Payne-Hearst correspondence, August 16,
1927, Hearst Papers.

"Hope you will give me . . .": Payne-Hearst correspondence, July 14, 1927.

Old Glory's baptism is from the *New York Times*, August 1, 1927.

"Will you please send letter . . .": Payne-Hearst correspondence, August 1, 1927.

The paragraph detailing flight preparations is from *Flight Fever*, pp. 238–
41; and *Boys' Life*, August 1940.

"wanted to ride . . .": Hearst-Willicombe correspondence, August 19, 1927.

"The most marvelous thrill . . .": the *San Francisco Examiner*, August 20, 1927.

Payne and Hearst discussed Hearst's concerns about recent air disasters
in their correspondence between August 20 and 27, 1927.

Payne's decision to accompany the pilots is from the Associated Press, August 25, 1927; and the *Boston Globe*, August 26, 1927. Bertaud and Hill's
concerns are from *Flight Fever*.

"I cannot send the men . . .": the *New York Times*, September 8, 1927.

Weather delays are from the *Daily News*, August 26, 1927; International
News Service, August 28, 1927; and the Associated Press, August 30,
1927.

The Old Orchard Beach details are from *Flight Fever*, p. 254; and the *Brooklyn Daily Times*, September 4, 1927.

Payne's exchanges with Hearst in the days before the flight come from
their correspondence between September 2 and September 5, 1927.

handed the message to a friend: *Oceans, Poles, and Airmen*, p. 181.

The paragraphs on Old Glory's departure come from *Flight Fever*, pp. 261–65; and the *New York Times*, September 7, 1927.

"Phil and Old Glory hopped off . . .": telegram from Dorothy Payne to Hearst, September 6, 1927, Hearst Papers.

The SOS messages are from *Flight Fever*, p. 266.

"Have searched the area . . .": radio transmission, September 7, 1927, Hearst Papers.

The reactions of Pope Pius and Mussolini are from the Associated Press, September 9, 1927.

Recovery of the wreckage is from *Flight Fever*, pp. 268–70; and the *New York Times*, September 13, 1927.

"If I don't return . . .": the *Toronto Star*, September 15, 1927.

Tom Payne and Hearst exchanged telegrams on September 9, 1927, Hearst Papers.

Payne's will is from a newswire report on October 13, 1927.

The Newspaper Club of New York resolution was published in the *New York Times* on September 17, 1927.

Payne's funeral is from the *Daily News*, *San Francisco Examiner*, and Associated Press, October 17, 1927.

"largest ever made . . .": the *Daily Home News*, December 24, 1928.

Chapter 24—And Then There Were None

The Willie Stevens material is from "A Sort of Genius," *The New Yorker*, January 15, 1937; and the *New York Times*, December 31, 1942.

The Frances Hall material is from "A Sort of Genius," *The New Yorker*, January 15, 1937; and the *New York Times*, December 20, 1942.

The Henry Stevens material is from the *New York Times*, December 5, 1939.

Henry Carpender's death is from the *New York Times*, May 27, 1934.

Jane Gibson's death is from the *New York Times*, February 8, 1930.

The Bahmer material is from the *Daily News* and *Daily Mirror*, November 18, 1926; and the Central New Jersey *Home News Tribune*, November 4, 1998.

The Julia Harpman material is from *Ladies of the Press*, p. 269; *Angry Man of the Press*, p. 245; and United Press International, November 9, 1955.

Charlotte Mills's newspaper and magazine work comes from Burton Rascoe's syndicated newspaper column, July 11, 1927; the *Daily Home News*, April 6, 1929; and Louise Sobol's syndicated newspaper column, June 19, 1945. Charlotte's death is from the *New York Times*, February 4, 1952.

Material on the Charlotte Mills impostor, Marie Thompson, comes from the *Philadelphia Inquirer*, December 1, 1932, and December 27, 1942; the Camden *Courier-Post*, December 17, 1932; the Central New Jersey *Home News*,

March 2 and 9, 1986; the Philadelphia, Pennsylvania, U.S., Marriage Index, 1885–1951; and the death certificate of Harry Joseph O'Neill, March 7, 1956. I also corresponded with a living relative of Thompson's, who wished to remain anonymous.

The Jim Mills material is from the *New York Times*, November 9, 1965; the Bergen *Record*, November 9 and 11, 1965; and the Bernardine Szold-Fritz Correspondence, Beinecke Rare Book & Manuscript Library, Yale University. Daniel Mills's death is from the Central New Jersey *Home News*, October 15, 1992.

Chapter 25—A Room with a View

Julius Bolyog's revival of the case and George Saloom's investigation were re-created from Saloom's investigative files in the New Brunswick Public Library's Hall-Mills Murder Case Collection; and from Reginald Kavanaugh's feature in the October 1970 issue of *Inside Detective*.

Saloom's biographical details are from the Central New Jersey *Home News Tribune*, April 26, 2018.

Bolyog's biographical details are from the Saloom files.

Kavanaugh's age is from the Associated Press, August 1, 1999.

"a Hungarian family . . .": 1922 statement of Sydney Carpender, Hall-Mills Murder Case Collection, New Brunswick Public Library.

Willie hesitated to discuss: undated Willie Stevens deposition, Hall-Mills Murder Case Collection.

"rubbed out . . .": Julius Bolyog interview with WINS Radio, 1970.

"Bolyog's story . . .": the Central New Jersey *Home News*, May 12, 1970.

Carl Ruppert's death is confirmed in the New Jersey, U.S., Death Index, 1901–2017.

Saloom's cases after the Bolyog investigation are from *the Central Jersey Home News*, August 18 and 26, and September 2, 1970.

The legend referenced at the end of the chapter is from an interview with Susan Huslage, organist of St. John the Evangelist. The full legend, first relayed to Huslage by a former deacon and friend of Catherine Rastall's, is that Jim Mills knew the names of the killers, wrote them down on a piece of paper, and hid the names behind a wall in the church that he then plastered over. "It is a legend," Huslage told me, "but it is intriguing."

Epilogue

Peter Tumulty's death is from the *Plainfield Courier-News*, January 2, 1942.

"If Peter Tumulty knew . . .": the New Brunswick *Sunday Times*, July 18, 1926.

Stephen Longstreet's death is from the *Los Angeles Times*, February 22, 2002.

"went out and did . . .": the Central New Jersey *Home News*, May 12, 1970.

Ralph Gorsline's death is from the *Daily Home News*, September 28, 1945.

Catherine Rastall's death is from the *Daily Home News*, February 5, 1992.

The closure of the *Daily Mirror* is from *Editor & Publisher*, October 19, 1963.

"one of the most controversial . . .": the *New York Times*, August 15, 1951.

Patterson's death is from the *Daily News*, May 27, 1946.

Macfadden's death is from the *New York Times*, October 13, 1955.

The *Evening Graphic*'s closure and circulation is from *Editor & Publisher*, July 9, 1932.

Walter Winchell and Ed Sullivan's *Graphic* origins are from *Editor & Publisher*, October 19, 1963; *Sauce for the Gander*; and Lester Cohen, *The New York Graphic*.

The *Mirror*'s circulation figures are from the *New York Times*, October 16, 1963. Its financial losses and the sale to the *News* are from *Editor & Publisher*, October 19, 1963, and the Associated Press, October 16, 1963.

"a newspaper without a newsroom . . .": the *New York Times*, August 12, 2020.

"They introduced a style . . .": "Are Tabloid Newspapers a Menace?", *The Forum*, March 1927.

The William Kunstler material comes from *The Minister and the Choir Singer*, 1964.

Theories about a possible Ku Klux Klan link were published in the *New York Times*, September 15 and 26, and October 16 and 24, 1922; and the *New York Herald*, September 28, 1922.

The Bill James material is from *Popular Crime*, 2011.

The Katherine Ramsland material is from *Moonlight Murder on Lovers' Lane*.

"found it in the Sunday school room . . .": the *New York Times*, October 17, 1922.

"in Mrs. Mills' confidence . . .": the *New York Tribune*, October 17, 1922.

Totten's estate is from the *Daily Home News*, September 17 and 18, 1942.

SELECTED BIBLIOGRAPHY

❖

Archives

Hall-Mills Murder Case Collection, New Brunswick Free Public Library

Records relating to Hall-Mills murder case, 1922–1924, Special Collections and University Archives, Rutgers University Libraries

Stevens Family Letters, Special Collections and University Archives, Rutgers University Libraries

Wallace Conover Files, Special Collections and University Archives, Rutgers University Libraries

J. M. Paterson Papers, Donnelley and Lee Library, Lake Forest College Archives and Special Collections

William Randolph Hearst Papers, Bancroft Library, U.C. Berkeley

Bernardine Szold-Fritz Correspondence, Beinecke Rare Book & Manuscript Library, Yale University

Grace Robinson Papers, American Heritage Center, University of Wyoming

Miscellaneous documents related to Phil Payne from the Gravenhurst Archives and the West New York Public Library

Miscellaneous documents related to St. John the Evangelist from St. John's historical church records

Court Transcripts

Hall-Mills Trial Transcripts, New Jersey State Archives, 1926

Julia Harpman vs. Eighth Avenue Railroad Company, 1921

Newspapers

The New York Times
Daily News
Daily Mirror
New York Tribune
The New York Herald
The Evening World
The Daily Home News
The New Brunswick Times

Books

Allen, Frederick Lewis, *Only Yesterday: An Informal History of the 1920's*, Harper & Row, 1931.

Baatz, Simon, *The Girl on the Velvet Swing: Sex, Murder, and Madness at the Dawn of the Twentieth Century*, Mulholland Books, 2018.

Bessie, Simon Michael, *Jazz Journalism: The Story of the Tabloid Newspapers*, Dutton, 1938.

Boswell, Charles, and Thompson, Lewis, *The Girl in Lover's Lane*, Gold Medal Books/Fawcett Publications, 1953.

Chapman, John, *Tell It to Sweeney: An Informal History of the New York Daily News*, Doubleday & Company, 1961

Churchwell, Sarah, *Careless People: Murder, Mayhem, and the Invention of "The Great Gatsby,"* Penguin Books, 2013.

Cohen, Lester, *The New York Graphic: The World's Zaniest Newspaper*, Chilton Books, 1964.

Collins, Paul, *The Murder of the Century: The Gilded Age Crime That Scandalized a City & Sparked the Tabloid Wars*, Crown Publishers, 2011.

Cutler, Harry Gardner, *History of Florida: Past and Present, Historical and Biographical, Volume III*, The Lewis Publishing Company, 1923. Web. Retrieved from Google Books.

Dawson, Kate Winkler, *American Sherlock: Murder, Forensics, and the Birth of American CSI*, Putnam, 2020.

Dunton, James G., *The Murders in Lovers Lane*, Small, Maynard & Company, 1927.

Gauvreau, Emile, *My Last Million Readers*, Dutton, 1941.

Goodman, Jonathan, *The Slaying of Joseph Bowne Elwell*, Harap, 1987.

Greenburg, Michael M., *Peaches & Daddy: A Story of the Roaring 20s, The Birth of Tabloid Media, & the Corrupt Courtship That Captured the Heart and Imagination of the American Public*, The Overlook Press, 2008.

Hamlen, Joseph, *Flight Fever*, Doubleday & Company, 1971.

Hart, Frances Noyes, *The Bellamy Trial*, American Mystery Classics, Penzler Publishers, 2019.

James, Bill, *Popular Crime: Reflections on the Celebration of Violence*, Scribner, 2011.

Kunstler, William, *The Minister and the Choir Singer: The Hall-Mills Murder Case*, William Morrow & Company, 1964.

Langille, Leslie, *Men of the Rainbow*, O'Sullivan Publishing House, 1933.

Lee, Francis Bazley, *Genealogical and Memorial History of the State of New Jersey*, Lewis Historical Publishing Company. Web. Retrieved from archive.org.

Longstreet, Stephen, *The Crime*, Simon & Schuster, 1959.

Mallen, Frank, *Sauce for the Gander*, Baldwin Books, 1954.

McGivena, Leo E., *The News: The First Fifty Years of New York's Picture Newspaper*, News Syndicate Co., 1969.

McKinney, Megan, *The Magnificent Medills: America's Royal Family of Journalism During a Century of Turbulent Splendor*, HarperCollins, 2011.

Miller, Donald L., *Supreme City: How Jazz Age Manhattan Gave Birth to Modern America*, Simon & Schuster, 2014.

Montague, Richard, *Oceans, Poles and Airmen: The First Flights Over Wide Waters and Desolate Ice*, Random House, 1971.

Morgan, Gwen and Veysey, Arthur, *Poor Little Rich Boy (And How He Made Good): The Life and Times of Col. Robert R. McCormick*, Crossroads Communications, 1985.

Morris, Adam, *American Messiahs: False Prophets of a Damned Nation*, W. W. Norton, 2019.

Nasaw, David, *The Chief: The Life of William Randolph Hearst*, Houghton Mifflin Company, 2000.

New Brunswick Times, *The City of New Brunswick: Its History, Its Homes & Its Industries*, The Times Publishing Company, 1908. Web. Retrieved from archive.org.

New York Times, *The Roaring '20s*, bookazine, New York Times Company, 2020.

Pilat, Arthur, *Pegler: Angry Man of the Press*, Beacon Press, 1963.

Ramsland, Katherine, *Moonlight Murder on Lovers' Lane*, DarkHorse Multimedia, e-book, 2018.

Regan, Timothy E., *Images of America: New Brunswick*, Arcadia Publishing, 1996.

Reisinger, John, *Master Detective: The Life and Crimes of Ellis Parker, America's Real-Life Sherlock Holmes*, self-published, 2012.

Ricca, Brad, *Mrs. Sherlock Holmes*, St. Martin's Press, 2016.

Rosenblum, Constance, *Gold Digger: The Outrageous Life and Times of Peggy Hopkins Joyce*, Metropolitan Books, 2000.

Ross, Ishbell, *Ladies of the Press: The Story of Women in Journalism by an Insider*, Harper & Brothers, 1936.

Runyon, Damon, *Trials and Tribulations*, the Estate of Damon Runyon, 1946.

Scannell, John James, *Scannell's New Jersey's First Citizens and State Guide*, J.J. Scannell, 1917. Web. Retrieved from Google Books.

Stevens, Eugene R., *Erasmus Stevens and His Descendants*, 1914.

Stevens, John D., *Sensationalism and the New York Press*, Columbia University Press, 1991.

Swan, Herbert S., *The New Brunswick Plan, New Brunswick City Planning Commission*, 1925.

Talese, Gay, *The Kingdom and the Power*, Random House Trade Paperbacks, 2007.

Tomlinson, Gerald, *Fatal Tryst: Who Killed the Minister and the Choir Singer?*, Home Run Press, 1999.

Tucher, Andie, *Not Exactly Lying: Fake News and Fake Journalism in American History*, Columbia University Press, 2022.

Walling, Richard Sears, *Edward & Eleanor and the Wages of Sin: The Hall-Mills Murders of 1922*, self-published, 2019.

Wendt, Lloyd, *Chicago Tribune: The Rise of a Great American Newspaper*, Rand McNally & Company, 1979

Wharton, Edith, *A Backward Glance*, The Curtis Publishing Company, 1933.

Woolcott, Alexander, *Long, Long Ago*, The Viking Press, 1943.

Articles, Studies, Academic Papers

"A Historical Timeline of Theaters in New Brunswick," stnj.org, undated.

"Back to Back," *Time*, November 16, 1925.

"The FBI and the American Gangster, 1924–1938," fbi.gov, undated.

"Hall-Mills Murder Case," *Life*, January 2, 1950.

"How New Brunswick Was Born," cityofnewbrunswick.org, undated.

"In Interview Hearst Speaks Plainly of Policies of His Organization," *Editor & Publisher*, June 14, 1924.

"In Manhattan," *Time*, May 31, 1926.

"Mirror v. Thaw," *Time*, September 28, 1925.

"New Tabloids in New York and Montreal," *Editor & Publisher*, September 20, 1924.

"Passing of a Giant," *Time*, June 3, 1946.

"'Surprising,' Says Macfadden of New Daily," *Editor & Publisher*, August 30, 1924.

"Training Choir Boys," *The Literary Digest*, December 28, 1912.

SELECTED BIBLIOGRAPHY

"Under the Crabapple Tree," *Time*, November 15, 1926.

"What Is the Lure of the Tabloid Press?", *Editor & Publisher*, July 26, 1924.

Alexander, Jack, "Vox Populi," three-part series, *The New Yorker*, August 6, August 13, and August 20, 1938.

Barnes, Jefferey G., "History," *The Fingerprint Sourcebook*, U.S. Department of Justice Office of Justice Programs, ojp.gov, undated.

Baron-Cohen, Simon, "Kanner, Leo, Hans Asperger, and the Discovery of Autism," *The Lancet*, October 2015.

Beasley, Maurine H., "Elizabeth M. Gilmer as Dorothy Dix: A Woman Journalist Rewrites the Myth of the Southern Lady," The Dorothy Dix Collection at Austin Peay State University, library.apsu.edu, undated.

Brodeur, Jean-Paul, and Whetstone, Thomas, "Crime-Scene Investigation and Forensic Sciences, *Encyclopedia Britannica*, undated.

Brumagin, Vicki Lee, "A Study of Women in American Journalism From 1696 to 1972," master's thesis, California State University, Northridge, 1972.

Daugherty, Greg, "Talking to the Dead: How the 1918 Pandemic Spurred a Spiritualism Craze," history.com, April 21, 2020.

de Rochemont, Richard G., "The Tabloids," *The American Mercury*, October 1926.

Eickmann, Walter R., *History of West New York, New Jersey*, West New York Golden Jubilee Committee, 1948.

Episcopal Church, "Journal of the Proceedings of the Bishops, Clergy and Laity of the Protestant Episcopal Church in the United States of America, Volume 7," S. Potter & Company, 1869. Web. Retrieved from Google Books.

Evans, Bonnie, "How Autism Became Autism: The Radical Transformation of a Central Concept of Child Development in Britain," *History of the Human Sciences*, July 2013. Web. Retrieved from PubMed.

Fischer, Ezra, "Murder, Marriage, and Modernity: Understanding the Hall-Mills Case," honors thesis, Rutgers University, 2004.

Foster, A. D., "Interstate Migration of Tuberculous Persons: Its Bearing on the Public Health, with Special Reference to the States of North and South Carolina," *Public Health Reports*, March 12, 1915. Web. Retrieved from JSTOR.

Garrett, Oliver H. P., "Another True Story," *The New Yorker*, September 19, 1925.

Geffen, Pauline Felix, "Tabloid Journalism in the United States," master's thesis, Columbia University School of Journalism, 1930.

Gurowitz, Margaret, "A Look Inside Our Original Building," kilmerhouse.com, July 12, 2010.

——, "The Year Was 1886: The Story of How Johnson & Johnson Was Born," jnj.com, September 2, 2015.

Hartman, Mary S., "The Hall-Mills Murder Case: The Most Fascinating Un- solved Homicide in America," *The Journal of the Rutgers University Libraries*, 1984.

Jenkins, Jessica Kerwin, "Women of a Certain Era," *The New York Times*, February 14, 2014.

Justice Research and Statistics Association, "Historical Data," Crime and Justice Atlas 2000, U.S. Department of Justice, jrsa.org, June 2000.

Kavanaugh, Reginald, "Have the Murders of the Minister and the Choir Singer Finally Been Solved?", *Inside Detective*, October 1970.

Lippman, Walter, "Blazing Publicity," *Vanity Fair*, September 1927.

Manley, Jared L. (Thurber, James), "A Sort of Genius," *The New Yorker*, January 23, 1927.

Markey, Morris, "These Tabloids," *The New Yorker*, October 3, 1925.

——, "Orgy: American Style," *The New Yorker*, June 5, 1926.

——, "A Mystery Revived," *The New Yorker*, August 7, 1926.

——, "The Rites of Justice," *The New Yorker*, November 6, 1926.

——, "The Somerville Follies," *The New Yorker*, November 20, 1926.

——, "Who Killed Joe Elwell," *Esquire*, October 1950.

Marose, Gregory, "Prohibition and the Rise of the American Gangster," *Pieces of History*, U.S. National Archives, January 17, 2012.

McRobbie, Linda Rodriguez, "The Strange and Mysterious History of the Ouija Board," *Smithsonian*, October 27, 2013.

Mills, Charlotte, "Why Make Me Pay?", *Cosmopolitan*, May 1929.

Page, Ellen Welles, "A Flapper's Appeal to Parents," *Outlook*, December 6, 1922.

Pearson, Edmund, "Parallels of the Hall-Mills Case," *Vanity Fair*, November 1926.

—— "Trial by Tabloid," *Vanity Fair*, October 1927.

Rudd, Arthur Sarell, "The Development of Illustrated Tabloid Journalism in the United States," Columbia University School of Journalism master's thesis, 1925.

Rutgers University Inn and Conference Center, "Historic Lindenwood Carpender House," inn.rutgers.edu, undated

—— "The Arbor Trail: A History," inn.rutgers.edu, undated

Schuyler, Philip, "Newspaper Makers at Work: Philip A. Payne," *Editor & Publisher*, January 19, 1924.

—— "Into the Ring of Circus Journalism," *Editor & Publisher*, October 31, 1925.

—— "Baring America's Classic Crime Mystery," *Editor & Publisher*, September 4, 1926.

—— "Classic Vindication of Press as Safeguard Seen in New Jersey Murder Trial," *Editor & Publisher*, November 6, 1926.

—— "'I'd Do It All Over Again,' Says Payne," *Editor & Publisher*, December 11, 1926.

Shields, Kristoffer M., "Culture on Trial: Law, Morality, and the Performance Trial in the Shadow of World War 1," PhD dissertation, Rutgers University, 2015.

Stephen, Isobel, "Startling Revelations About the Hall-Mills Case," seven-part series, *True Detective*, June 1931 to December 1931.

Swerling, Jo, "The Picture Papers Win," *The Nation*, October 21, 1925.

Taylor, Robert Lewis, "Physical Culture," *The New Yorker*, three-part series, October 14, October 21, and October 28, 1950.

Thompson, Dennis, "Developmental Psychology in the 1920s: A Period of Major Transition," *The Journal of Genetic Psychology*, November–December 2016.

Villard, Garrison Oswald, and Weyrauch, Martin, "Are Tabloid Newspapers a Menace?", *The Forum*, March 1927.

Film, Audio, and Events

Burrough, Bryan, *'Til Murder Do Us Part*, Audible Originals, 2019.

"The Hall-Mills Murder—Takeaways from an Unsolved Murder in NJ," seminar, New Jersey Institute for Continuing Legal Education, October 18, 2019.

That's How the Story Goes: The Hall-Mills Murders Podcast, Thinkery & Verse, 2020.

Thou Shalt Not, theatrical performance, Thinkery & Verse, September 2019.

History of Hearst, video short, Hearst Corporation, 2019.

Interviews

Bob Belvin, Frank Deiner Jr., Susan Huslage, Kim Raymond Kowalczyk, Thomas Maugham, Susan Mollica, Andie Tucher, Peter Tumulty, Richard Sears Walling

INDEX